T0316740

# Natural Resource Endowment and the Fallacy of Development in Cameroon

Edited by

Lotsmart Fonjong

Langaa Research & Publishing CIG
Mankon, Bamenda

*Publisher:*
*Langaa* RPCIG
Langaa Research & Publishing Common Initiative Group
P.O. Box 902 Mankon
Bamenda
North West Region
Cameroon
Langaagrp@gmail.com
www.langaa-rpcig.net


Distributed in and outside N. America by African Books Collective
orders@africanbookscollective.com
www.africanbookscollective.com


*ISBN-10: 9956-551-24-4*

*ISBN-13: 978-9956-551-24-8*

# List of Contributors

**Njimanted Godfrey Forgha** is Professor of Economics and Quantitative Methods at the University of Bamenda, Cameroon. He obtained his Masters' and PhD Degrees from the University of Calabar Cross River State Nigeria in 2001 and 2004 respectively. He was recruited as Senior Instructor by the University of Buea Cameroon, where he was confirmed as Assistant Lecturer in 2005. By 2006, he was promoted to the rank of lecturer, then Associate Professor of Economics in 2011 and full Professor of Economics in 2016. Professor Njimanted has authored/co-authored 52 articles in several referred Journals and three book chapters in and out of Cameroon. He has participated in several national and international Seminars during which he presented three keynote papers. In the process, he received several International Grants, including Council for the Development of Social Science Research in Africa (CODESRIA) *Inter-Faculty* Grant in 2008, and the European American Grant on the project *'Economic Development and Sustainability'* in 2016. His research interest is in the areas of Economic Development and as a scholar, holds a lot of proficiency and scholarship towards Africa transformation via indigenous growth policies. He represented Cameroon in the 'Collaborative Think Tank Symposium' in China in 2012.Email: unicalub@yahoo.com

**Lotsmart Fonjong** is Professor of Geography at the Faculty of Social and Management Sciences, University of Buea, Cameroon. He holds a PhD in Geography from the University of Yaounde 1, Cameroon, an M.A. in Development Studies, from the University of Leeds, UK, and a Certificate in International Human Rights from the University of Cincinnati, Ohio, USA. He served as Adjunct Assistant Professor at the University of North Carolina, Greensboro in 2007, He has also been Visiting Scholar to a number of American Universities including James Madison University (2008 and 2018), the State University of New York (2008), and University of North Carolina Wilmington (2018). He is author of six books and several scientific articles on development issues in Africa. His books include Saving the Environment in Sub-Saharan Africa (2015). He has also served on the board of a number of learned societies including the Research Committees of Women and Society and currently, Environment and Society of the International Sociological Association. Email: flotsmart@gmail.com

**Balgah Sounders** is Associate Professor and the currently Vice-Dean in charge of Studies and students Affairs in the Faculty of Social and Management Sciences where he formerly served as Head of Geography Department. He holds a Bachelor of Arts and a Master of Science Degree from the University of Lagos and a PhD from the University of Buea. He is a specialist in Remote Sensing and it's applications to Urban Studies, Natural Resource Management and Land use Dynamics. His current research interest are on Population, Natural Resource Management and Development studies. Email: juniorsa2002@yahoo.co.uk

**Ernest L. Molua** is Associate Professor and the Dean of the Faculty of Agriculture and Veterinary Medicine of the University of Buea, Cameroon. He is also Director at the Centre for Independent Development Research (CIDR), Buea, Cameroon. He obtained a PhD degree in Agricultural Economics from the Georg-August University of Goettingen in Germany, as well as academic degrees from the Royal Veterinary and Agricultural University in Copenhagen, Denmark and the University of Benin, Nigeria. He is consultant to the Mathematica Policy Research Corporation, Washington DC, as well as the World Bank and the United Nations Development Programme. He is a member of the International Association of Agricultural Economists (IAAE), the African Association of Agricultural Economists (AAAE) and the Royal Economic Society (RES) of the United Kingdom.

**Fonteh Athanasius Amungwa** obtained his PhD at the University of Reading, U.K. in 2000. He had served in the Cameroon Ministry of Agriculture and Rural Development for 26 years before moving to the university sphere. He is Associate Professor of Agricultural Extension and Rural Development and Chair of Social Economy and Family Management at the Higher Technical Teacher Training College, University of Buea. He has authored 3 books on extension and rural sociology, co-authored 3 extension booklets on yams, potatoes and cassava and published several articles in scholarly journals and presented papers at national and international conferences. He is a Knight and Officer of the Cameroon Order of merit. Email: dramungwa@yahoo.com

**Charles Che Fonchingong** holds a Doctorate in Social Policy at the University of Kent, England. He has lectured at the University of Buea, Cameroon, was a sessional lecturer at the University of Kent, and currently a Senior Lecturer at Canterbury Christ Church University, United Kingdom. He has been a research fellow at the University of Oxford and served as a collaborating researcher with the United Nations Research Institute for Social Development (UNRISD) on the Project –Social and solidarity economy. He is the author of 'Growing Old in Cameroon: gender, Vulnerability and Social Capital', published by University Press of America. Email: cfonchingong@yahoo.com

**Frankline Anum Ndi** is an independent consultant and researcher on development issues in Africa. He holds a PhD in Human Geography (Melbourne University, Australia); an MSc in Rural Development (Ghent University, Belgium); an MSc in Peace and Development (Linnaeus University, Sweden) and a BSc in Sociology and Anthropology (University of Buea, Cameroon). His research interests include food security; agricultural development and transformation; rural livelihoods; conservation and development projects; and land governance and conflict in Africa. Email: ndihills@yahoo.com.

**Celestin Defo** received the MSc in water engineering from the University of Dschang in Cameroon in 2006 and a PhD in water science and technology in 2016 at the Indian Agricultural Research Institute, New Delhi, India. In 2010, he became an Assistant Lecturer at the School of Wood, Water and Natural Resources, University of Dschang. He became a Senior Lecturer in May 2017. He is the author of one book and several articles published in peer review journals and conference contributions. His research interests cover several aspects across water engineering, mainly community water supply, water pollution and remediation and computer application. Email: Celestin.defo@univ-dschang.org

**Ethel Ngere Nangia** is a Lecturer in the Department of Women and Gender Studies, University of Buea, Cameroon. She has authored and co-authored articles in international journals and has been involved in research work in both private and public institutions in Cameroon in the domains of health, violence against women, care, sports, climate change and women's rights. She is also a gender consultant and has presented a number of papers in seminars, local and international conferences. She holds a BA in English, MSc in Women and Gender Studies and a PhD in Gender and Development, all from the University of Buea, Cameroon. She is the current head of service for research in the same University. E-mail:wngere@gmail.com

**Mbu Sunday Agbor** is currently the Head of Department of the Department of Management Sciences, University of Buea, Cameroon. He studied Economics and Monetary Economics at the Graduate School of Economics, University of Port Harcourt, Nigeria. He later attended the Universities of Douala and Buea, Cameroon where he obtained a PhD specializing in Financial Economics. He teaches many courses in finance, monetary and financial economics both at the undergraduate and graduate levels at the Universities of Buea, Institut Universitaire du Golfe the Guinee (IUC), Institut Universitaire du Grande Ecole des Tropicale (IUGET), Cameroon and also an Assessor with the Cameroon General Certificate of Education Board.

**James Emmanuel Wanki** is President John Fitzgerald Kennedy Fellow and Edward S. Mason Scholar (MCMPA) at the Harvard Kennedy School of Government, University of Harvard. Prior to this, he was Commonwealth Alistair Berkeley fellow at New College, Oxford University. Until recently, he was Senior Specialist at the World Bank, where he supported the World Bank and United Nations joint efforts in the Central African Republic as the Humanitarian-Development-Peace Nexus country advisor. He has also served in various capacities in the United Nations, including as

Chief of the Political Affairs Section and Deputy Head of the United Nation's regional office in Bambari; and as Humanitarian Field Coordinator and Head of Field Offices with the United Nations Population Fund in the Central African Republic, etc. His current research interests include peace and security issues, climate change, governance and democratic deficits, gender and environmental politics in rural settings in Africa, youth and electoral processes. Email: jwanki@hks.harvard.edu | james.wanki@gmail.com

**Yungong, Theophilus Jong** is a development professional with extensive consulting experience. Some of his consulting stints include working for Africa Development Interchange Network (ADIN) and the United Nations Development Programme during the Post-2015 Development Agenda Consultations in Cameroon. He currently covers the West and Central Africa regions as Senior Policy Analyst within the Debt Management Department at the African Forum and Network for Debt and Development - a Pan African civil society organization based in Harare, Zimbabwe. He has been involved in research supervision at Euclid University, (Pôle Universitaire Euclide) - an international intergovernmental university. Theo holds a Doctorate and Master's Degrees in Development from Nelson Mandela University, South Africa and a Bachelor in Geography from the University of Buea, Cameroon. He also earned a Post-graduate Diploma in Geo-Information Production and Management (GIS specialism) from RECTAS (now AFROGIST) at Obafemi Awolowo University Campus, Nigeria. His professional and academic research interests include development financing and management, programme development and management, monitoring and evaluation, information and knowledge management for development and humanitarian work.

**Forbe Hodu Ngangnchi** is a PhD candidate in Economics at The University of Bamenda, Bamenda, Cameroon. He served as Graduate Teaching at the University of Buea, Assistant Lecturer at the Pan African Institute for Development- West Africa in 2012, Project Economist for the Cameroon Cross River Gorilla Project and the Director in charge of Technical Operations for the Environment and Rural Development Foundation. He is currently a Lecturer at the

Higher Institute of Management Studies, HIMS Buea, Buea Cameroon where he is also Registrar. He is the author and co-author of several refereed journals articles and conference contributions. And is best known for his book entitled "Masters Piece Economics"; a text book for junior secondary school and which is use in all junior secondary schools in Cameroon. His research interests cover several aspects of the society, namely, the environmental, development and socio-political issues. Email: chiefforbe@gmail.com

**Mukete Emmanuel Mbella** received his M.Sc. degree in Economics from the University of Buea in 2012. In 2014 he became an Assistant Lecturer of Economics in Catholic University Institute of Buea. He is the author and Co-author of several refereed journals articles. He became a member of the American Economic Association in 2014, and since then he has reviewed many articles in scientific journals. He became the Head of Department in Catholic University Institute of Buea and a member of the Catholic University Institute of Buea Research and Grant committee and his research interests cover several aspects of Economic Growth and Development, Environment and Food Security.
Email: mbellamukete@gmail.com.

**Fabinin Nina Akem** obtained BSc. and MSc. degrees in Agricultural Economics and Agribusiness at the University of Buea, Cameroon. She is currently at the Institute of Agricultural Economics, University of Kiel, Germany, where she is finishing a PhD and also serves as Research Associate to the Chair of Agricultural Marketing and Policy. She has co-authored scientific papers and conference contributions, delivered international talks, and received distinctions. Prior to her current position in Germany, she was a teaching assistant at the University of Buea as well as researcher at the Centre for Independent Development Research in Cameroon and worked with the European Union funded DMP at Nkong Hilltop Association for Development (NADEV). She currently specialises on agricultural market research and policy. Email: fabininakem@yahoo.com

**Nkwetta Ajong Aquilas** obtained an MSc Degree in Economics in 2015 and is currently a PhD student in Economics at the University of Buea, South West Region of Cameroon. He is an Adjunct Lecturer at the Department of Agricultural Economics and Agribusiness, Faculty of Agriculture and Veterinary Medicine of the University of Buea and Economics teacher at GHS Bonadikombo, Limbe. He has co-authored several articles in peer reviewed local and international journals and has presented a paper at an international conference. His research interest is Natural Resources and Environmental Economics.

**Ngeh Roland Nformi** received B.Sc. and M.Sc. Geography from the University of Buea of Cameroon, in 2007 and 2016 respectively. He is a Second Cycle Secondary School Teacher in Ministry of Secondary Education upon his graduation with DIPES II Geog (2011) from the University of Bamenda of Cameroon. He is an Examiner of Citizenship of Education with the Cameroon General certificate of Education Board since 2016. His research interests cover aspects such as institutions, land conflict resolution and development. Email: ngehrold@gmail.com

**Ayemeley Betrand Ayuk** is a PhD student in Natural Resources and Environmental Management, Department of Environmental Science, Faculty of Science, University of Buea, Cameroon. He received a BSc (Hons) and MSc (Hons) in Geography from the same University in 2009 and 2018 respectively. He has experience in the field of Biodiversity Conservation with previous works at the Limbe Wildlife Centre, Cameroon. His main research interest is on the management of protected areas. He is currently a course instructor at GIPS Institute Science and Technology, Douala where he teaches courses on Environmental protection and Ecotourism. Email: ayembeto@yahoo.com

**Nformi Solange Chewe** M.Ed. Psychology student received B.Ed. from the University of Buea of Cameroon, in 2017. She is a primary School Teacher upon his graduation with CAPIEMP in 2013 from ENIEG Buea under MINESEC. Her research interest covers aspects such as Culture and Childhood development, Institutions and Land conflict Resolution. Email: nformisc@gmail.com

**Njilin Adela Njamnjubo** obtained her BSc in Geography from the University of Buea in 2009, and a Secondary School Teachers Grade II Diploma (DIPES II) in 2018 from the University of Bamenda. She is presently a Geography teacher and researcher in Government High School (GHS) Jiyane (Oku), North West Region of Cameroon.

**Eyongeta N Telma** and **Nkongho C Ayuk** are final year Postgraduate students in the Women and Gender Studies Programme in the University of Buea, Cameroon.

*For the staff of University Health Ophthalmology Clinic, Hoxworth Centre for saving my eyes.*

# Table of Contents

## Theoretical and Methodological Framing

# Land Rights and Land Conflicts

# The Gender Dimension of Natural
# Resources and Development

# Natural Resource, Development Challenges and Policy Options

# Acknowledgements

The idea of this book was borne out of my frustration and failure to organize a conference at the University of Buea to discuss the findings of a three-year project on women and large-scale land acquisitions in sub-Sahara Africa, of which I was the principal investigator. In 2016 the Anglophone socio-political crisis broke out resulting to insecurity. After several postponements of the conference we decided in 2017 to work on a book project with those who had submitted papers for the conference and widened our call. The response was an exceptional success as we received over forty submissions. I want to sincerely thank all the contributors who braved the rigor of the peer review process and cooperated with me in the interactive process to arrive at the final product.

We are sincerely grateful for the editorial suggestions and inputs from Professor Njimanted Geoffrey, Professor of Economics and Deputy Director of the School of Transport and Logistics, University of Bamenda, Dr Charles Fonchingong, Senior Lecturer at Canterbury Christ Church University UK, Dr. Kenneth C. Asongwe, St Cloud University, Professor Molem, Vice-Dean for Programs and Mr Marx Ntangsi, Head of Short Courses both in the Faculty of Social and Management Sciences, Dr. Che Tita, former Head of Journalism and Mass Communication, Dr. Christiana Abonge, Head of Gender Studies, Dr. Justine Ayuk, Head of Administration, Dr. Dorothy Forsac, Head of Cooperation, and Dr. Ethel Nangia, Head of Research, all at the University of Buea, Cameroon.

Many thanks also go to Ms Tabitha Samje for editing the manuscript Dr. Mojoko Fiona, Isaih Adamu and Regina Ndip Zama for secretarial assistance.

Finally, immense thanks to Ms Ramata Thiuone, Senior Project Office at the IDRC office in Nairobi for the technical and financial supervision of the grant under which this project was funded and to the funding agency-International Development Research Centre, IDRC Canada under grant No. 107590-1 awarded to the University of Buea.

# Preface

*Lotsmart Fonjong*

It is an indisputable fact that Cameroon is richly endowed with natural resources but what is controversial is how significantly the resources have contributed to the development of the country. The current state of poor basic infrastructures, high rates of poverty, unemployment, instabilities, among others suggests that the country needs to reconsider its current path to development and reflect on other possible routes to national prosperity. Njimanted et al, strongly articulate this need for alternative and better economic option that can deliver development to majority of Cameroonians in their chapter. These authors use the example of colonial powers who develop Europe from the same resources exploited out of Africa to argue that the problem is not the natural resources themselves but those incharge of them and where they are found. Thus, natural resources are as important as well as where they are found in analysing their benefits to growth and development. Njimanted et al. based their argument on an analysis of Cameroon time series data from 1970 to 2017 using several economic models. The authors concluded the existence of the Dutch Disease Syndrome in the Cameroon economy. Cameroon needs to enhance agricultural, social, industrial and cultural transformation by eliminating the waste from external debts, natural resource rents, and structural rigidities.

In this regard, the presence of abundant natural resources does not represent a curse to any country; but rather, it is the attitude of the governing elites, mechanisms of governance and other policy inadequacies that are responsible for the present poor economic performance of Cameroon. Only a return to an effective management and proper policy formulation in Cameroon can reverse the current underdevelopment curse and build a resilient economy. Natural resource rents need to be redirected into more productive sectors of the economy for effective usage. Research and development, technical and vocational education, good governance and infrastructural development are among these sectors that should be prioritized.

The huge deposit of natural resources in Cameroon is reaffirmed by Nkwetta et al. Natural resources (huge deposits of energy, mineral, forest, etc.) represents a major source of revenue (about 29% of GDP) and should naturally lead the country to growth and development. However, as a typical natural resources-based economy where there is increasing exploitation and depletion of these resources, Cameroon needs to worry about the future and the chances of achieving long-term economic growth and emergence by 2035. The authors ran some regression and auto regression analysis on World Bank and other international partners' growth data for Cameroon from 1980 to 2017 to obtain varying results across sectors. For example, energy depletion will only significantly affect growth in the long but not in the short-run. Deforestation will neither affect growth in the immediate or long run. However, Cameroon's economic growth cannot be sustainable if it must rely solely on the resources. Accordingly, in addition to the promoting sustainable exploitation of nonrenewable and renewable resources, currents rent from these resources should be channelled to more productive activities. This is only possible where government, international parthers and the civil society can intensify the fight against corruption in the resource sector and decelerate activities that put unnecessary pressure on natural resources in Cameroon.

Theories give rise to policies and policies to the type of development we get. It is from this premise that Amungwa attempts a reflection on public sector understanding and application of development theories and the resulting underdevelopment of the agricultural sector in Cameroon. The author opines that the failure in the agricultural sector to transform and promote growth is because national agricultural policies have been inspired by both the modernization and dependency theories rooted in the free market. As such, he advocates for another path to agricultural transformation and growth for Cameroon contrary to liberalization and call for direct government control of the sector through conscious planning, protection, subsidization, pricing, modernization of extension services and improvement of rural life.

Yet, the population should be able to benefit from the exploitation of their natural resources directly (through corporate social responsibility) and indirectly (through taxation). Yungong's study provides a framework for understanding the latter through corporate social investments (CSI) which are voluntary programs lunched by companies involved in the exploitation of these resources to promote the welfare of host countries and communities. Where CSI policies are well conceived and executed, the projects realized are community impacted and the benefits reach a larger population because these projects have the potentials to avoid corruption and delays from the trickle-down effects of taxation. Yungong provides a theoretical understanding of CSI and how it can serve as an effective model for redistributing the wealth from natural resources in Cameroon.

Management defines the extent to which the population is positively affected by its natural resources. Good management is derived from the existence of good functional institutional and legal frameworks with clear mandates and mechanisms to demand accountability and render justice. The papers of Wanki et al. and Ngeh et al. are rooted on issues related to macro and micro management of land resources. Both papers look at the tension in the ownership and exploitation of land in the North and South West Regions. While Wanki and Ndi focus on international actors of land grabbing in Cameroon and the resulting conflict and resistance from the local population, Ngeh et al. describe the sources, nature and effects of local land conflicts on the development of Ndu, a sub division where farmer-grazier conflicts over land have been exacerbated by ecological fragility and the presence of corrupt officials and institutions posing as arbiters. Wanki and Ndi believe that although affected population from land dispossession by foreign agro-businesses in Nguti sub Division many have the same grievances against land grabbing, they do not necessarily have the same response based on their different strategic interests. As such, some segments of this population have opted for collaborations and compromises, others maintain outright opposition against any land grabbing, while others continue to clamour for compensation and improved development dividends and opportunities within established plantations. Such competing grassroots responses must be well articulate by researchers to inform policy and decision making on issues relating to large-scale land acquisitions in Africa.

The Majority of Cameroon's population is female thus making gender consideration very important in analysing the development impact of natural resource exploitation and development in the country. The chapters authored by Nangia, Tema and Ayuk; Akem and Molua; and Fonjong introduce the gender perspective to the debate by focusing on gender and water, agriculture and land grabbing. Water is one of the most abundant natural resource in the country. In concrete terms, almost all the fifty-two divisional administrative units derive their names from a water source. Yet, majority of Cameroonian do not have access to portable water. Women, because of their triple roles, play a key role in developing countries in the harvesting, management and conservation of water. As such, Nangia et al. observe that building the capacities of women in water provision and management is important. The authors use the example of the locality of Bomaka-Buea to illustrate the general poor situation of water provision, the difficulties endured by women in accessing water and the likely health effects. As those directly impacted, it is important for the authorities in Cameroon to involve women in the water solution by providing opportunities to build their capacities through technical assistance. Meanwhile, in the short term, they should address some of the technical lapses of the sole water company for better coverage and effective water provision.

The negative impact of gender inequality in economic development has been highlighted by many scientific studies. Atem and Molua queue from this foundation to reiterate how the gender gap in agriculture presents a challenge to Cameroon's economic emergence. The authors focus on maize farmers and use several economic models to analyse the effects of gender differential access to production resources on the productivity levels for both male and female farmers. They conclude that where there is a gender gap in accessing agricultural production resources, technical efficiency and productivity for the female farmers is negatively affected. This, of course, has a multiplier effect on national development when one considers the fact that women constitute the bulk of these farmers.

Fonjong believes that gender mainstreaming is the key to achieving gender equality for development in natural resource management, especially in the water and agricultural sectors mentioned above by Nangia and Atem, just as in any other domains in Cameroon. Using the example of large-scale land acquisition by corporate bodies for commercial agriculture, he argues that gender mainstreaming in any sector will ensure that women's just like men's voices are considered in the process of consultation, negotiation and compensation paid for losing their land. Many important agro-investments have failed to impact local communities in Cameroon because women were either left out or considered as mere passive beneficiaries. Women play an important role in agriculture and no true development initiative on land can achieve its objective without engendering the process. Mainstreaming gender in natural resources management in Cameroon is seen not only good for window dressing used simply to attract multinational funding, but a policy option that can no longer be avoided and need to be institutionalized.

The impact of natural resources on the population and ability to serve both the present and future generations depend on the national policies and instruments guiding their exploitation and management. Cameroon policy on logging, land ownership, mineral and petroleum exploitation for example, have been criticized for lack of transparency and strong enforcement as well as favouritism towards foreign powers and companies. The last chapters are focused on the policy environment as they affect conservation, water, and rural communities.

With the help of its international partners, the government of Cameroon has embarked on biodiversity conservation through the creation of conservation projects. The Mount Cameroon National Park in the South West Region falls in line with this government policy. It was created in 2009 but the conservation project came with the displacement of thousands of food crops farmers operating in the area. Fonjong and Nyanbo note that the loss of over 8000 hectares of farm land by farmers in some ways turned out to be a blessing as farmers productivity and output, overall, increased above what they used to produce prior to the park. The increase in production is attributed to the survival strategy adopted by the displaced farmer which includes the change from extensive to intensive farming with the adoption of improved seeds and farming techniques to compensate for land scarcity. The success of the new farming dispensation lies in farmers willingness to learn new skills and embrace change in the face of their challenges. The success story of the displaced farmers of the Mount Cameroon National Park area provides reasons to believe that conservation as a policy option is feasible where it is well thought out and accompanied by viable alternative livelihood packages for the affected population.

Nonetheless while CSI as observed by Yungong is beneficial to poverty reduction and development at community levels, these communities themselves can also fight poverty and underdevelopment by transforming some of these resources into economic assets. Such is the view of Fonchingong and others who have provided examples of the importance of non-farm activities in fighting poverty in rural Cameroon. Non-farm activities such as grazing, exploitation of non-timber forest products, beekeeping, local artisanal craft, charcoal harvesting among others that reflect the diversity of rural population can serve as important sources of rural income, energy, medicine and local materials to the population when managed sustainably. This population will need measures from government to accompany their efforts to achieve targeted results.

Fonchingong's rural policy analysis focuses on two of these groups; the aged and pastoralists. The Fulani pastoralists are largely considered in north-west Cameroon as a marginalized group with a unique kinship system tied to their pastoral activities and economy. The economy of these livestock farmers is currently being threatened by the combined effects of climate change, ecological fragility, changing farming practices and land conflicts with their food crop counterparts. This leaves the social security condition of old age Fulani cattle herders of region under study in jeopardy because it is originally conceived around pastoralism. Fonchingong argues that under these changing circumstances, rural development policies in the region should capture some of the fundamental aspects of pastoralists' traditions, so far missed by government and other agencies to achieve well-intentioned social security and development in rural areas.

Cameroon does not only need a comprehensive rural development policy but also a comprehensive water policy. Defo examines the policy framework guiding the establishment of water institutions and provision of water in Cameroon and used the example of water pollution to decry their failures in the management of water resources. He came to the same conclusion as Nangia et al. that poor policies and management are responsible for the generalized malfunctional water installations and services across the country that have plunged the population into infinite water crisis. The result is that the already impoverished and water-deprived population further suffers additional health costs from water borne diseases brought about by the type of water they are served. Policy deficiency in water management has thus turned Cameroon from physical water abundance to economic water scarcity and crisis.

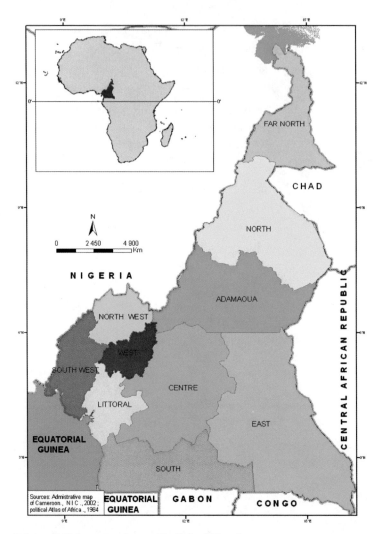

**Map of Cameroon's ten Political Regions**

# Introduction

## Natural Resources and Underdevelopment in Cameroon: Untangling a Puzzle

*Lotsmart Fonjong and James Emmanuel Wanki*

Cameroon like several other African countries is richly endowed with natural resources. Alao (2011) describes natural resources as non-artificial materials/products which can be used to generate income or serve other functional purposes benefiting mankind. Land, water, forest, minerals, oil, biodiversity, landscape, etc. constitute what is broadly referred to as renewable and non-renewable natural resources. Natural resources are thus the product of nature's benevolence which a country really does nothing special to receive. As gifts of nature to humanity, natural resource deposits anywhere are not a function of military, technological, financial or spiritual might. Rather, the availability of these resources can make a country an economic, financial or military giant.

While the availability of natural resources does not depend on humanity and its civilization, there is a strong relationship between civilization, exploitation and the benefit from natural resources. In other words, not all countries endowed with natural resources are well developed and not all developed societies (for example Japan) enjoy economic development because of enormous natural resources endowment. African countries south of the Sahara are glaring examples where natural resources have somehow failed to lead to economic and social transformations that benefit the entire population. In most of these countries, natural resources are increasingly being 'captured', owned, controlled and exploited by foreign capitalists and powerful national 'elites' for selfish ends, leaving the continent and most of its population in a development crisis. Important natural resources such as water, land, forest and minerals, remain entrenched within the control of these capitalists whose water, agribusinesses, power or mining companies (national, foreign or multinational) operate mostly without leaving concrete and sustainable development impacts on the population. Not only are these resources grabbed and exploited without visible development attention in the host countries/communities, but those involved often ignore the rights of local communities and indigenous peoples whose livelihood chances have depended solely on these resources since time immemorial. Such dispossession of local inhabitants partly explains why despite their resource endowment, most African countries including Cameroon remain poor and underdeveloped. Mawuna Koutonin in 2014 aptly sums up the situation in these words: "...Africa is not poor. Africa is a rich continent inhabited by poor people..." By inference, Cameroon as a country is not poor. But its natural resources do not really translate to much developmental outcomes for its inhabitants. Cameroon largely remains a natural resource-rich country at the heart of the central African region inhabited mostly by poor people who neither directly nor indirectly benefit from the wealth of its resources.

The inherent paradox presented by natural resources is well established in scholarship. On the one hand, natural resources have amounted to significant blessings for Gulf States like Qatar and Dubai which have used oil rents to completely modernise and transform their development outlooks, moving from the doldrums of underdevelopment to global industrialised centres of innovation and progress. However, natural resources could as well serve as a curse, as amply demonstrated by the role natural resources such as oil, diamond and coltan have played in perpetuating wars in the Sudans and in the Democratic Republic of Congo, and in plunging already impoverished populations further into generalised despondency. In Cameroon and in the townships of South Africa, pockets of dispiriting poverty further illustrate the baffling respects to which these resource-rich countries continue to be mired in profound misery. Taking the analogy of a child with fire in his hands, one could surmise of natural resources as the building blocks for progress, if well managed, or implements of disaster, in the case of poor management. Simply put, the child could either use the fire, figuratively speaking, to prepare food, warm the house and live well or to set the house ablaze and be destroyed together with it. Any of these two outcomes depends on the capacity of the child to make the right or utmost decision with the fire. The implication of the abovementioned analogy is that natural resources alone cannot create development, jobs, or lead to emergence and economic prosperity in a country. They do have the potentials to do all these, if combined well with prudent management and visionary leadership.

The nexus between leadership and governance has been well-established in scholarship and both concepts are key determinants of the type and level of socio-political and economic development a country like Cameroon can achieve (Mbaku and Takougang, 2003). Leadership and governance are ultimately key determinants of the types and levels of development and prosperity that accompany natural resource endowments. Leadership generally embodies the vision and capacity to make the right investments, enter into profitable partnerships and create an enabling environment for national and international businesses that can create jobs, wealth and prosperity to a people. Therefore, a country's prosperity does not solely depend on the amount of its natural resources alone but beyond that, it depends on the nature and capacity of its human resources to transform these natural endowments into development dividends and basic needs for the majority of the population through sustained growth. Capacity and governance are thus as important as natural resource endowment, and this is where most African countries including Cameroon are obviously lagging behind.

**Natural resource endowment as both sides of the same coin**

Cameroon with a population of over 24 million inhabitants in 2014 is a development myth. It is geographically well situated with access to the Atlantic Ocean to its south. Cameroon also spans several ecological regions with a varied landscape which account for its rich natural resource endowment. It is often described as Africa in miniature; a country richly endowed with a wide variety of natural resources and nestled within an enterprising regional market environment, with significant demand potentials from neighbouring Nigeria and the rest of the Central Africa Economic Monetary States (CEMAC). As a microcosm of Africa, Cameroon's natural resources are very diverse; consisting of a dense drainage network, rich vegetation system of flora and fauna, iconic geology and landforms, with beautiful touristic sceneries of mountains, lakes, and water falls.

Cameroon's rich and diverse natural endowment is no secret. It counts several water basins including the Lake Chad basin in north Cameroon, the Niger basin, Congo basin and the Atlantic basins. Several crater lakes (Lake Nyos, Noun, and Barombi amongst others) and water reservoirs (the lagdo, mbakaou, mapé, bamendjin reservoir, nyong basin and the Sanaga River) are bound. The southern forests (in the central, eastern, and south-western regions) are characterized by dense vegetation, a vast hydrographic network and hot, humid climate with abundant rainfall (Ngnikam and Tolale, 2009). The rich soil and great climate favour the commercial cultivation of oil palm, rubber, cocoa, and tea along the coastal areas, tobacco, sugar cane and coffee in the southern plateau, and coffee in the western highlands. Offshore oil production first began in Cameroon in 1977 before its rise to the 6th largest oil producer in sub-Sahara Africa producing 667,000 barrels daily with over 400 million barrels of estimated reserve in 2004 (World Atlas). There is also a vast deposit of unexploited crude oil and natural gas especially in the oil-rich Bakassi area. Nickel, gold, nepheline, iron ore, cobalt, syenite, granite, bauxite, rutile, and many others constitute part of the mineral deposits dotted across the country. From a historical point of view, European scramble for Cameroon during colonization and today's neo-colonialism cannot be dissociated from the country's resource endowments.

When one looks at Cameroon's abundant mineral, petroleum, water, forest (timber, non-timber and wildlife), touristic attractions and of course, fertile land that is backed by favourable climatic conditions, one would expect at least a country with a minimum level of development: a country that is self-sufficient, with basic social infrastructures (of water, schools, hospitals, roads, electricity supply), a booming economy with acceptable low levels of unemployment and poverty or unemployment that can attract the finest qualified migrants from all over African and beyond. This is unfortunately not the reality as Cameroon has emerged as a "donor darling to foreign partners and a site for external programmatic experimentation"

(Ingram et al, 2015) – a sort of embarrassment both to its international development partners and its people.

According to the World Bank, 30% (8.1 million) of Cameroonians live below the poverty line. The country is currently ranked 163 out of 190 economies in the world and 153 out of 188 in the Human Development Index. Gauthier and Zeufack, (2009) add that:

> '...an analysis of development outcomes reveals a very bleak picture and suggests that Cameroon did not harness its oil resources for sustained growth and development. Since the mid-eighties, the already poor physical, social and human capital indicators have deteriorated dramatically. Development outcomes have continued to free fall. Life expectancy has decreased from 56 to 50 years between 1996 and 2005. Over the same period, infant mortality increased from 61 to 78 per thousand and child malnutrition increased from 14 to 22 %. The education system once one of the best in Africa has collapsed. Primary school enrolment decreased from 101 % to 91% between 1996 and 2005. Secondary education gross enrolment rates declined to 25% in 2000 from 28% in 1990 and poverty has increased. The question, therefore, is not if oil has contributed or not to growth, but what factors explained aggregate savings and spending decisions from the oil rent that led to such poor development outcomes...'

## Sharing from Africa's development misfortune

There is no gainsaying that natural resources have the potentials of delivering sustainable livelihood chances and improved prosperity for Africans. Accordingly, one would expect cocoa in Cote d'Ivoire, oil in Nigeria, Sudan, Gabon, Equatorial Guinea, Ghana and Cameroon; gold and diamond in Ghana, Burkina Faso, Liberia, and Sierra Leone; or mining in the Congo, etc. to have a visible impact on the lives of their population. This is not to suggest that these natural endowments are not exploited, sold and bought as the figures below indicate. The puzzle is instead why these interesting figures have not transformed the current misery, poverty and underdevelopment of these countries into basic social wellbeing (water, food, health, and shelter), jobs, growth or outright prosperity.

**Table 1: A compilation of the development potentials of some natural resources in Africa**

| Natural resource and impact | Examples of contributions to some national economies in Africa. |
|---|---|
| **Petroleum** key sources of foreign earnings and revenue | - Nigeria is 13th world oil producer in 2017.<br>- Account for 97% of export earnings for Equatorial Guinea.<br>- Represent 95% of export and 60 % of revenue for Sudan in 2008.<br>- Represent 98% of public revenue for South Sudan in 2008. |
| **Minerals** As a source of revenue | - Guinea is among the top five producers of bauxite in the world<br>- Ghana is 10th world producer of gold in 2018. |
| **Forest** Revenue | - Represent 30% of GDP in Angola.<br>- Gabon is the 3rd exporter of tropical log.<br>-Timber is the 2nd primary export for Equatorial Guinea.<br>- Over 25% of total revenue of many come from beekeeping in Zambia.<br>- About 10% of GDP for Ethiopia in 2009. |
| Job creation | - Over 62,000 workers in Burkina Faso.<br>- Some 33,662 workers in Cote d'Ivoire.<br>- About 12,700 in Senegal (FAO, 2005). |
| **Non-timber forest products** Health provision | - About 90% and 60% of rural and urban dwellers respectively in Ghana rely on traditional herbs for treatment.<br>- Over 60% of children suffering from fever in Ghana, Mali, Nigeria and Zambia are treated at home with herbal medicine (WHO, 2002). |
| **Rivers** Energy (Hydro-electricity) provision | The Inga hydroelectricity facility on River Congo is expected to generate between 1,115 to 39,000MW power to supply central, northern and southern Africa. |
| Natural scenery/ wildlife Tourism development | Represent 8.5% of GDP and provides 7.5% employment in South Africa. |

The irony here is that these figures have instead brought about indescribable underdevelopment, poverty and misery rather than wealth, growth, and development to Africa. The oil-rich State of Equatorial Guinea for example, has the highest per capita income in the continent but its life expectancy and infant mortality are below the mean figures for sub-Sahara (Bekele, 2017). One is therefore tempted to agree with Karl, (1997) that natural resources have created a dependency syndrome in Africa where states seem to be contented with revenue from these resources without any initiative or plans for investments and economic diversification. African leaders seem to believe (unfortunately wrongly) that oil and mineral wealth will last forever instead of labouring to invest the current wealth into infrastructural, economic, research and technological development needed to create future wealth while the boom from these resources last.

Many studies have revealed the mixed fortunes that national resources have on the continent's prospects, and especial focus has been directed at the ways in which certain selfish neo-capitalistic and unpatriotic political elite instigate development reversals in resource-rich countries. Such groups continue to milk the continent to either maintain their grip over power and wealth as in the case of the political elites through tyranny, dictatorship and bloody wars or sustain their access and control over the exploitation and profits from African rich natural resources in the case of global capitalists. Weak or complete absence of legal frameworks regulating mining, oil or land concessions have further facilitated the displacement of farmers and communities both without their informed consent, and in the absence of any resettlement plans in place. Bad governance and corruption are thus at the centre of the multiple bloody natural resource-driven conflicts that have together kept these natural resource-rich African countries in a state of perpetual underdevelopment, abject poverty and misery.

Natural resources have amplified the penchant for corruption and embezzlement by African political elites, leading to the deprivation of the masses and the syphoning of natural resources, leading to economic alienation and the resurgence of 'natural resource-driven bloody conflicts' in countries such as Liberia, sierra

Leone, Nigeria, the Congo, and Angola. In Angola, Jonas Savimbi's UNITA rebel group exercised brutal control over huge amounts of diamond mines, using their proceeds to acquire arms, effectively funding and sustaining his war for the total independence of Angola against the Russian-backed Luanda government until 1998 when the UN imposed a diamond embargo on the rebels. The war spelt a disaster for the oil rich country of Angola where more than 1 million people were killed, 4 million displaced, entire cities destroyed and millions continue to depend on food assistance (Harden, 2000). Laurent Kabila' rebel group was also able to translate their control over the rich diamond reserves in eastern Congo into arms and alliance with neighbouring Uganda, Zimbabwe and Burundi, leveraging these to overthrow President Mobutu of Zaire. Similar examples have been recorded with Charles Taylor's Liberia Revolutionary United Front, and the Niger Delta Avengers militant group in Nigeria, where minerals have been bartered for arms to finance political and ideological struggles. (ibid).

It is perhaps the stark absence of developmental outcomes for the common masses in the midst of natural resource abundance due mainly to predatory governance that best symptomizes the resource curse in Africa. Wanki, (forthcoming) adds that embattled communities in resource rich Democratic Republic of Congo, Sierra Leone and Liberia, have for instance experienced the more poignant illustrations of the resource curse through the ravages of resource-driven conflicts that incentivize the organised predation of priceless natural resources like diamond and coltan, often accompanied by a near apocalyptic decree of dispiriting violence and atrocities perpetuated against civilian populations. The consequences of the resource-based conflicts unfortunately incite other tragic ramifications that extend far beyond the macabre slaughter of civilan populations or ecological destruction that occur, as epitomized by the conflicts in Darfur. They equally incentivize the widening of black markets for trafficking that sap legitimate trade revenue from the coffers of affected countries, which is why illegal mineral trade has been highlighted as constituting an enormous leakage from the economy of affected countries. Furthermore, these conflicts provide ample opportunity for especially Western, Asian and Latin American countries and corporations to take advantage of the fragility and exploit Africa's resources. They often negotiate resource exploitation agreements on terms that grossly underrepresent the actual value of such resources, and frequently accompanied by *quid pro quo* agreements for arms sales that further inflame conflicts and deepen their tragic consequences.

During the Angolan civil war for example, the government traded huge quantities of natural resources with the United States and Cuba at give-away prices to secure their constant geostrategic support.

Unfortunately, most contemporary African political elite continue to focus more on the preservation of their power rather than seeking innovative ideas on leveraging their countries' natural resource endowments to initiate economic growth and sustainable development. This is evident in the type of international diplomacy and partnership they labour after. Neither the trade deals nor most bilateral alliances seek to advance human rights and development but rather to enlist favours that secure their power at the helm of a stagnant state, as was the case with Mobuto's Zaire. No wonder, African dictators are increasingly turning away from their traditional western allies to China and Russia who are ready to support their eternal zeal to clinch to power and to continue syphoning their nation's wealth, often without recourse to human rights considerations, accountability and transparency.

The examples from some of the current hot spots in Africa tell a more illustrative story: Sudan's imports come from China, Saudi Arabia and Russia while China is only second to UAE as the principal destination of its export consisting mostly of gold and crude oil. China tops the chart of importers from the mineral rich Democratic Republic of Congo and is only second to South Africa as the country's main source of importation. Although Equatorial Guinea trades with Spain and the United States as principal sources of import, China is among the top two destinations of exports from this predominantly oil rich country. China is today Cameroon's primary market for import, pushing France to the second place, although Italy and France still remain among the top destinations for the country's exports (https://atlas.media.mit.edu/en/profile/country/).

Like other African countries, Cameroon remains stuck in the natural resource curse. The imposing figures of Cameroon's natural resources revenue unfortunately represent little impact in the lives of ordinary citizens. The following few examples put these observations in context:

- Cameroon is the 5th top producer of tropical wood in the world. The forest accounts for 9% of GDP and 20% of jobs (Reed and Miranda, 2007) but the East which is one of the regions from where the timber comes from is the least developed with one of the highest rates of unemployment in the country.

- Cameroon's rich soils make her the 5th world producer of cocoa, producing 275,000 metric tons in 2013 (World Atlas). Yet, most of Meme and Fako Divisions, localities in the South West Region where most of this is produced is enclaved and poverty-stricken.

- Forest exploitation and ancillary engagements account for about 8.9% of GDP between the period 1992 and 2000 and contributing to 28.2% of total non-oil exports in the same period.

- Petroleum resources may account for more than half of the export earnings, about 24% of government revenue, and approximately 6% of GDP (Reed & Miranda, 2007). Similarly, Cameroon may be producing about 32 million bbl/year of crude oil, yet extractive industries account for just 8 to 10% of Cameroon's GDP (Dominguez-Torres and Foster, 2011) but beyond the generalized state of chronic poverty in the country, Ndian Division from where the oil comes from is not only poor and enclaved but also abandoned.

The above paints an illustrative picture of some facets of the paradox of natural resources and underdevelopment in Cameroon and provides provisional explanations to Cameroon's slothful growth and the extremely high poverty rates of 40 to 55%, particularly in the rural areas. Several explanations could be advanced as to why Cameroon's enormous natural wealth has instead triggered development reversals in the country, reasons which could best be summed up under the theory of managerial capacity. Consider the fact that most of these resources (be it energy, land, timber, oil or minerals) are in the hands of foreign companies. These companies are able not only to fix the terms of exploitation but beyond all economic norms, also play key roles in setting price and quantity of resources to be exploited. This has led to a national outcry against natural resource grabbing. Supporters of the state will argue that this is not managerial or capacity lapses on the part of the state which in the absence of technology is forced to work with external partners who have the necessary capital and technology. No one can that say international partnerships are in themselves bad. What is of concern pertains to how these partnerships are negotiated and the levels of the states' transparency and accountability to its population on the management of revenue thereof and how these serve the interest of the country and its people. These concerns will remain in the public debates for a long time if the state continues to demonstrate basic instinct of aloofness that speaks volumes in terms of its ineptitude to fight against state capture.

Considering the situation in the tourism sector, the government's default argument that the absence of technological capacity explains the preeminent place given to foreign investors in the exploitation of the country's natural resources does not hold much sway. Managerial ineptitude is clearly implicated in the underdevelopment of the Cameroon tourism sector where technological intensiveness is out of question. The World Bank observes that tourism is a promising sector in sub-Sahara Africa. It attracted over 33.8 million visitors alone in 2012 which brought in US$36 billion worth of revenue, representing 2.8% of the region GDP (Christie, et al 2013). Some countries like Tanzania, Namibia and Zimbabwe benefited from this new market with tourism revenue increasing to more than 8% of GDP, it represented between 2-3.9% of GDP for Senegal and Ghana while despite its huge rich potential, tourism represented just between 1-1.9% of GDP for Cameroon (ibid). Cameroon therefore lacks the necessary managerial competence and leadership to compete for a fair share of Africa's new tourism market. She is unable to translate its huge touristic potentials that require sheer entrepreneurship with little or no technology into viable economic assets just as other countries like Senegal have done.

By and large, natural resources have not just been a curse to Africa; some countries have made significant progress on the governance side of the equation and used natural resources to unlock widespread development dividends for their peoples. Botswana for instance, is a world-leading producer of diamonds, and because to rigorous management, the diamond industry accounts for 66% of government revenue, employing 25% of its population. Thanks to diamond revenue, Botswana has upped its standard of living to a level that is higher than that of South Africa, Africa's second largest economy, as well as Turkey (Harden, 2000). Acemoglu et al., (2003) also observes that Botswana has successfully escaped the resource curse by providing property rights, political checks and balances, health care, education and investments in infrastructure. This should serve as a propitious example for other countries like Cameroon to emulate. Good leadership remains the key reason why Botswana has succeeded where others failed. Political leadership in many oil-rich countries tend to embezzle resource wealth thereby undermining accountability, neglecting inequality or the interest of the poor (Djafari, 2016). Under such circumstances, these countries cannot achieve growth that will create jobs, development and prosperity.

## Conclusion

Competing theories have tried to explain the present predicament of natural resources and underdevelopment in Africa. Some of these arguments may hold true for Cameroon. The unstable and volatile international market for some natural resources like oil may contribute in making planning difficult. However, it's too naive to always attribute Africa's failure or challenges to some external linkages and misfortunes. The era of blaming colonization and slave trade for Africa's predicaments are over. Africa must be able to look inwardly and figure out its problems. For example, Cameroon's diverse natural resources makes the country most suited to weather the shocks of volatility in the international market (e.g. for oil, timber etc.), unlike most of her African contemporaries. Until recently (2016), the country enjoyed relative peace and stability for most of its post-independence period which should have served to attract significant foreign direct investment if the business climate was right and corruption curtailed. It was perhaps the ability to take advantage of favourable factors like those listed above that gave Botswana its advantage. As Harden (2000) observes:

"...In stark contrast to the rulers of Angola and Congo, they [Botswana] created an African nation devoted to improving the lives of its people. In 1965, only about half of primary school-aged children attended school. Today, 90 percent of that group is enrolled. Life expectancy, which was less than 50 at independence, is now near 70. Phones work in Botswana, potholes get repaired, garbage gets picked up, and a lively press pokes fun at the government without fear..."

By and large, Cameroon is blessed with a variety of natural resources which should serve to engineer its superb economic growth. Unfortunately, this has not been the case as the country's "...growth performance since independence has been very mixed and the country has become one of the best examples of the resource curse..." (Gauthier and Zeufack, 2009). So what could be the problem with Cameroon's natural resources that it cannot propel the country to the same level of expected prosperity? The question is so preoccupying even to the country's President Biya whose worries and frustrations were expressed in his 2013 End of Year Message when he noted that:

"...In 2013, our growth rate stands at 4.8%, and thus below our forecast of 6.1%. ... It will be absolutely imperative that we address the causes of our weaknesses by removing sticking points, areas of dispersion and duplication. Would we be unable to do what some other countries comparable to ours have done or are doing? I do not think so. We have talented, resourceful, well-trained and enterprising men, women and youth, who are capable of meeting these challenges. We have abundant and diverse natural resources as well as modern and democratic institutions. Our country is peaceful and stable. What then do we lack? ..."

Part of the problem may be with the accuracy of President Biya's diagnosis. He might have failed to capture in his speech, the biggest albatross around the nation's neck. If not what does Cameroon lack that it cannot reap the dividends and prosperity that other African countries have?

## Bibliography

Alao, A (2011): Natural Resources and the Dynamics of Conflicts in West Africa. https://www.codesria.org. ECOWAS and the Dynamics of Conflict and Peace-building. ECOWAS.pmd 28/10/2011

Alpha B. and Ding Yibing (2016). A Study on the Impact of Natural Resources Endowment on Economic Growth: Empirical Evidence from Mali. *Journal of Economics and Development Studies*, 4(4)81-103.

Auty, R. (2001), "Resource Abundance and Economic Development". Oxford: Oxford University Press Bekele, D. Africa's Natural Resources: From Curse to a Blessing. https://www.hrw.org/news/2017/04/21/africas-natural-resources-curse-blessing.

Biya, P. (2013). Head of State's New Year message to the Nation. https://www.prc.cm/en/news/speeches-of-the-president/525

Christie, I. et al (2013. Tourism in Africa: Harnessing Tourism for Growth and Improved Livelihoods. The World Bank

Djafari, N. (2016). Oil and Development in the Middle East: A Two-edged Sword https://en.qantara.de/content/oil-and-development-in-the-middle-east-a-two-edged-sword?nopaging=1

Dominguez-Torres, C. and Foster, V. (2011): Cameroon's Infrastructure: A Continental Perspective. Africa Infrastructure Country Diagnostic (AICD) Country Report. Washington, DC, www.worldbank.org

Gauthier, B., and Zeufack, A. (2009). Governance and Oil Revenues in Cameroon, Oxcarre Research Paper 38, Oxford Centre for the Analysis of Resource Rich Economies, University of Oxford

Harden, B. (2000). Africa's Gems: Warfare's Best Friend By Blaine *New York Times*. April 6, 2000.
https://atlas.media.mit.edu/en/profile/country/cod/
https://www.globalpolicy.org/component/content/article/190/33886.html

Karl, T. (1997) *"The Paradox of Plenty-Oil Booms and Petro-states"*, *London*

Koutonin, R (2014). Africa Top 10 Problems: Not the ones You were thinking about! https://www.kimpavitapress.no/africa-top-10-problems-not-the-ones-you-were-thinking-about-by-mawuna-remarque-koutonin/ retrieved March 18, 2019

Mbaku, J.M., and Takougang, J., eds. (2003). The leadership Challenge in Africa: Cameroon under Paul Biya. Africa World Press, Trenton.

Ngnikam, E. and Tolale E. (2009): Energy Systems: Vulnerability, Adaptation, Resilience (VAR). Regional Focus: sub-Saharan Africa. www.helio-international.org

Reed, E. and Miranda, M. (2007): Assessment of the Mining Sector and Infrastructure Development in the Congo Basin Region. World Wide Fund for Nature (WWF) Washington, DC, http://www.panda.org/mpo

Resource Governance Index (2017) Cameroon: Oil and Gas, Natural Resource Governance Institute Country Profile, https://resourcegovernanceindex.org/country-profiles/CMR/oil- gas [retrieved 23 June 2019]

United Nations Economic Commission for Africa, UNECA (2013): Managing Africa's Natural Resource Base for Sustainable Growth and Development. Sustainable Development Report on Africa IV, Addis Ababa, Ethiopia. www.uneca.org

Wanki, J.E., (forthcoming) Whose country? Deconstructing the Governance Mystique in Cameroon's development conundrum

World Atlas. https://www.worldatlas.com/world-facts/

World Bank, (2019). Poverty & Equity Brief Cameroon. povertydata.worldbank.org Cameroon www.worldbank.org/poverty

World Bank, (2019). The World Bank in Cameroon https://www.worldbank.org/en/country/cameroon/overview

# Theoretical and Methodological Framing

# Chapter 1

# Natural Resource Endowment, a Curse or a Blessing on Economic Growth: The Cameroon Experience

*Njimanted Godfrey Forgha, Forbe Hodu Ngangnchi and Mukete Emmanuel Mbella*

**Abstract**

This study is designed to evaluate the extent to which natural resource rents have influenced the economic growth of Cameroon using time series data from 1970 to 2017; as well as investigate whether the Dutch Disease Syndrome had existed in the economy of Cameroon within the period of the study. Using the Distributive Dynamic Lag Model under the Co-integration Error Correction Mechanism, the natural resource curse is observed to have been established in Cameroon. This means that natural resources are more of a curse than a blessing to the country. The findings also confirm the existence of the Dutch Disease Syndrome in the economy. Based on the above findings, it is recommended that the natural resource rents need to be redirected into more productive sectors of the economy for effective usage such as in research and infrastructural development, technical and vocational education and the enhancement of good governance practices. The study provides for the elimination of waste from external debts, natural resource rents, and structural rigidities, thereby enhancing agricultural, social, industrial and cultural transformation. However, the presence of natural resources does not create a curse; rather, elite's attitude, governance mechanism and other policy issues are responsible for the present performance of the nation in relation to its natural resources. Effective management and proper policy formulation can reverse the curse to build a resilient economy.

**Key Words:** Natural Resource Curse, Dutch Disease Syndrome, Economic Growth, Good Governance, Transformations, and Pragmatic Education.

# Introduction

Natural resource endowments are important sources of national wealth which enhances countries' potentials for economic growth around the world. Yet, the vast availability of these rich endowments through a number of empirical studies, have shown that they are neither necessary nor sufficient for economic prosperity. This negative relationship between natural resource intensity in the composition of a country's output and the growth rate of per capita income has been dubbed the curse of natural resources. This paradox of plenty phenomenon has been shown empirically based on cross-country and panel studies. Theoretically, there are three channels of causation from natural resources abundance to poor economic performance. Firstly, there is the institutional impact of natural resources which explains that natural resources generate rents which lead to rapacious rent-seeking and increased corruption which adversely affects long-term growth. Secondly, natural resource endowments expose countries to volatility, particularly in commodity prices, which could have an adverse impact on growth through increased inflation. And thirdly, natural resource endowment makes countries susceptible to Dutch Disease, that is, the tendency for the real exchange rate to become over appreciated in response to the positive shocks-which leads to a contraction in the tradable sector. As such, the country concerned is seen as a trader of just few products.

Natural resources according to Ewubare and Kakain (2017) generally include the land area, nature and quality of the soil, richness and quality of the forest, minerals, river, good bracing climate and hydrocarbons. This implies that natural resources refer to all resources that exist in the natural state and systems that are or can be useful to man in the actual technological, economic and social circumstances. A country is natural resource dependent when accords for more than 23% of the value of its total export. Warner (1995) argues that the success story of Great Britain and Germany were principally because of their huge deposits of ore and coal. However, others believe that an increase in natural resource revenue possesses a negative effect on economic growth (Mehlum et al.,

2006). Sustained and rapid growth in today's global economy requires the formulation of policies that integrate domestic as well as imported resources for the creation of utility (Kehinde and Adebimpe, 2012).

According to the UNCTAD (2012), between 2006 and 2012, 74% of the world GDP was generated in developing countries with mostly domestically mobilized resources compared to about 22% in developed countries, contrary to the past when developed countries accounted for 75% of global growth between the 1980s and 1990s. Among the developing regions, East, South and South - East Asia experienced the highest growth rates of 6.1%, 4.3% and 4.7% respectively in 2013. Growth in most of these countries was driven by demand and domestic resources mobilization. Previous studies on the link between natural resource endowment and economic growth especially in developing economies have shown that many natural resource-rich countries have performed poorly contrary to countries with scarce natural resource. Among countries which have fallen victims of a resource-curse are Nigeria, Angola, Congo, Bolivia, Sierra Leone and Venezuela (Arezki and Ploeg, 2010).The only natural resources-rich countries cited with long-term investment of above 25% of GDP on average from 1970-1998, which equates that of successful industrial countries poor in natural resources were Botswana, Indonesia, Malaysia, and Thailand (Glyfason, 2001).

Empirically, countries share of natural resource rent to GDP have mixed blessing. In Malaysia and Qatar for instance, the share of natural resources rents to GDP stood respectively at 5.3% and 49.3% in 1970. While in 1980, the share of total natural resources rents to GDP were 22.2% and 79.3% for Malaysia and Qatar respectively. These figures were 13.1% and 48.4% in 2000 and 9.8% and 24.2% in 2012. On the average, natural resources rent as a share of GDP was 13.7% and 44.6% for Malaysia and Qatar respectively between 1970 and 2012, indicating that natural resources account for a greater share of GDP in Qatar relative to Malaysia. Similarly, in Germany total natural resources rents as a share of GDP was 0.4% on the average. In Belgium, it was only 0.04% from 1970-2012. In Nigeria, the share of natural resources rents to GDP stood at about 35.6% on average between 1970 and 2012 and in Sudan, statistics show that natural resource rents as a share of GDP stood at 5.4% on average from 1980-2012 (World Development Indicators, 2014). We can observe from the above statistics that countries with high share of natural resources rents to GDP are less developed than those with least share of natural resource rents to GDP.

The economy of Cameroon is said to be endowed with numerous natural resources, but the economy continues to show low growth in recent years from a growth rate of 4.1% in 2011 to 4.4% in 2012, increasing fairly to 4.9% in 2013 and to approximately 5.0% in 2014. The fastest growing sectors are trade, hotels and restaurants (19.9%), agriculture (16.9%), manufacturing (14.5%), and the extractive industries (8.2%). The total natural resource rent to GDP in Cameroon was 3.3% in 1970 and ten years after, it increased to 17.2%. Though it increased to 23.2% in 1984 due to the oil boom, it later decreased to 7.4% in 1988 because of the fall in international prices of cocoa, coffee and oil. In the year 2000, natural resource rent to GDP was 13.3% which was slightly higher than the case of 1990 which was approximately 12%. In 2012, 2013 and 2014, the total natural resource rent to GDP stood at 11.6%, 11.9% and 12% respectively (World Development indicators, 2016). Cameroon still struggles to achieve sustainable economic growth and development despite her huge natural resource endowments and efforts put in place to revamp the economy since the early 1990s. The resulting achievement and progress made by Cameroon has been very unsatisfactory.

Most studies on natural resources and economic growth are cross sectional in nature, thus failing to give an in-depth situation about the problem. Again, most of them adopted the Ordinary Least Squares (OLS) as estimation technique. This technique is unable to eliminate simultaneous equation bias, the endogeneity accounted for by the interdependency of the variables and non-linearity of the variables. Though there are few specific cases of some countries, none of such studies have been conducted in Cameroon. To the best of our knowledge, only the study of Njimanted, et al (2015) which concentrated on Timber Extraction is focused on Cameroon. None of such studies tested the natural resource curse or blessing in line with the Dutch disease syndrome. In this light, this study is out to investigate whether the natural resource curse or blessing phenomenon exists in Cameroon and to examine whether the Dutch disease holds in Cameroon. After this introduction, section two reveals the literature review with section three devoted to the analytical methodology of the study. While section four presents and discusses the findings, section five provides the recommendations and conclusion of the work.

## Literature Review

The natural resource curse can be defined as natural resource abundance in a country which rather has an adverse effect on its growth. According to Sachs and Warner (1995), who have done several pioneering empirical studies on the issue, "a natural resource curse is a reasonably solid fact." Other scholars like Lederman and Maloney (2007), maintain that "natural resource exports seem to have a positive rather than a negative effect on subsequent economic growth" based on an extensive empirical study of the relationship between various structural aspects of international trade, ranging from natural resource abundance to export diversification and subsequent economic growth.

There exist a number of channels through which natural resource utilisation is a curse to a country's growth performance. Firstly, the curse is associated with all primary commodities: agricultural, petroleum, forest resources, minerals, etc. When an economy has a large and profitable primary commodity sector, it tends to crowd out the development of manufacturing and other industrial activities (Sachs and Warner, 2001). This is a generalized case of the "Dutch disease" in which foreign exchange revenues from primary commodity exports would cause real appreciation of the exchange rate, which then would adversely affect the international competitiveness of manufacturing and other tradable goods produced. Under these circumstances, entrepreneurs and investors would not have incentives to invest in manufacturing activities, which would stifle growth. Secondly, the nature of the natural resource curse is different. The extraction activities of oil, gas and other minerals generate rent revenue to the state, which is normally the ultimate owner of the country's subterranean resources. Agricultural commodities such as coffee, rubber, palm oil, cocoa, etc., while using natural resources as important factor inputs, are less likely to create sizeable rent and attracting rent seeking activities. These rent-seeking activities have a bearing on the government socio-political and economic policies. Revenue abundance, especially if it comes about in the form of a windfall, tends to make it easy for politicians and bureaucratic policymakers to waste it on uneconomic investments and ostentatious expenditures. Often, it induces corruption. This may be called the "voracity effect" that causes the retardation of growth through misuse and abuse of public funds (Collier, 2007). Thirdly, a country with rich natural resource endowments tends to depend on them for production and exports. International prices of primary commodities (including petroleum products, minerals and agricultural commodities) are notorious for their volatility in the business cycles, in response to rampant supply difficulties due to natural disasters and political disturbances in the supplier countries.

Brunnschweiler and Bulte (2008) have fundamentally assessed the observational premise for the natural resource curse syndrome utilizing two-stage least squares (2SLS) estimator for a cross country test of 60 nations making use of information from 1970 to 2000. They discover that regardless of the ubiquity of the natural resource curse, it might be a distraction after all. They contend that the most normally utilized measure of the resource plenitude can be explained as a proxy for resource reliance which is endogenous to the fundamental basic variables of an economy. In various estimations that consolidate resource abundance and reliance, using constitutional variables, Brunnschweiler and Bulte (2008) demonstrate that resource plenitude, constitutions and institutions decide resource reliance. Again, the study shows that resource reliance does not change economic development compared to resource plenitude which emphatically impacts development and institutional quality. The constructive outcomes on development of natural resources have been affirmed in studies conducted by Ding and Field (2005), and Butkiewicz and Yanikkaya (2010). These findings may be true in the case that, natural resource abundance as

8

in most African countries leads to weak institutional and governance framework.

According to Van der Ploeg (2011), natural resources are either a curse or a blessing. His empirical findings imply that either outcome is possible. The study investigates a diversity of hypotheses and supporting facts regarding the reason why some nations are able to reap maximum benefits from natural resource plenitude while others fail to gain it. Van der Ploeg debates that resource plenitude causes a rise in the real exchange rate, de-industrialization, and negatively impacts growth prospects, and that these unfavourable effects are more extreme in volatile countries with weak institutions, the absence of law and order, corruption, and under-developed financial set-ups. Another assumption is that; resource abundance reinforces rent seeking and civil conflict especially if institutions are weak, incites corruption especially in undemocratic nations, and brings along unsuitable policies. Finally, resource abundance economies are unable to effectively transform these weary resources into other profitable assets.

Collier and Hoffler (2002) have demonstrated that natural resources significantly expand the conceivable outcomes of civil clash in a nation. As per their assessment, the impact of natural resources in creating clashes is severe and nonlinear. They demonstrate that a natural resource-poor nation confronts a likelihood of 0.5% civil clash, whereas a richly endowed natural resource nation characterized by a ratio of 0.26 to GDP faces a likelihood of 23 percent. Just like Van der Ploeg concluded, this is true of Sub-Saharan African countries endowed with great natural resources.

Arezki and Ploeg (2010) provide cross-country empirical evidence for the effect of resources on income per capita. Using the Ordinary Least Squares (OLS) and the Instrumental Variable (IV) techniques, their findings show that natural resource dependence (resource exports) has a significant negative effect on income per capita, especially in countries with bad rule of law or bad policies, but results weaken substantially after allowing for endogeneity. However, the more exogenous measure of resource abundance, the natural stock of capital has a significant negative effect on income per capita even after controlling for geography, rule of law and de facto or de jure trade openness.

Chong-Sup Kim and Yeon-silkim (2008) revisit the Natural Resource Abundance and Economic Growth in Latin America and Developed countries from a comparative perspective. They use the basic framework of Sachs and Warner (1995) in examining the consistency of their results within the longer period of 1970 to 2005 instead of 1970-1990. Their findings once more highlighted the views of Sachs and Warner that there is a negative relationship between economic growth and a high ratio of natural resource exports. Thus, the study supports the idea of Dutch Disease.

Adu (2011) in investigating the relationship that exists between long run economic growth and natural resource abundance in Ghana with time series data from 1962 to 2008 used the Phillips-Hansen Fully-Modified Least Squares estimator which corrects for non-stationarity and endogeneity. With the help of nine different indicators that could proxy for resource abundance in nine alternative specifications, the results rejected evidence of the resource-curse hypothesis.

Gylfason (2000) reviews the reasons behind the inverse relationship between natural resource abundance and economic growth. He concludes that the heavy reliance on natural resources and agriculture may result in corruption and policy failures. He also maintains that resource reliance may discourage human capital accumulation, external trade and genuine savings. In a related study, Gylfason (2001) provides empirical evidence for the inverse relationship between natural resources and growth through the human capital channel using public expenditure on education as an indicator.

From the above studies that have been carried out on natural resource endowment and economic growth, we observe that some support the resource curse hypothesis while others oppose it. For instance, studies of Sachs and Warner (1997), Gylfason and Zoega (2006), Gylfason (2001), Sachs & Warner (2001), Atkinson & Hamilton (2003), Salmani &Yavari (2004), Ding and Field (2004), Malik et al (2005), Papyrakis and Gerlagh(2006), Fan et al (2012) support the resource curse hypothesis while those for resource blessing hypothesis include the works of Sala-i-Martin & Subramanian (2003), Lederman & Melony (2003) and Adu (2011). This therefore gives mixed conclusions about the issue. Most of these studies were again based on cross sectional findings which failed to provide an in-depth situation of the issue at hand.

## Methodology

This study employs the use of time series data from 1970 to 2017which is long enough to test the natural resource curse or blessing hypothesis in Cameroon; since it covers the period when Cameroon highly depended on agricultural products and petroleum exploitation as major sources of domestic income. Data for this study was gotten from World Bank development indicators on Cameroon. In this study, a causal research design is adopted.

Following the neoclassical growth model, we observed that labour and capital inputs are able to explain the bulk of a country's growth performance. It is this input-output relationship that has assisted in the adoption of a technical analysis whose starting point is based on aggregate production function expressed as;

$$Y_t = f(A, L, K)(1) \dots \dots \dots \dots \dots \dots \dots . . (3.1)$$

Where $Y_t$ is the real GDP at a period of time (t), $L$ is labour input, $K$ is capital input and $A$ is the index of technological efficiency. Based on further theoretical and country specific characteristics, other explanatory variables were included. In addition, the new endogenous growth theory holds that the$A$ in equation (3.1) is endogenously determined by economic factors. The case of Cameroon is given as;

$$A = \bar{g}(NR, EXP, XDEBT) \dots \dots \dots \dots \dots \dots \dots \dots (3.2)$$

Where NR is natural resources, EXP is exports of goods and services as a ratio of economic growth, and XDEBT is external debt. Therefore, substituting equation (3.2) inequation(3.1) gives us;

$$GDP_t = (NR_t, EXP_t, XDEBT_t, L_t, K_t) \dots \dots \dots \dots \dots . (3.3)$$

Due to unavailability and inconsistency of data, the variable labour was dropped. Therefore, our estimation models for the natural resource curse and the Dutch Disease of this study, logged to linearize the variables and also to enable us to interpret the coefficients of the estimates as elasticity is given as;

$$lnGDP_t = \beta_0 + \beta_1 lnNR_t + \beta_2 lnEXP_t + \beta_3 lnXDEBT_t + \beta_4 lnGCF_t + \varepsilon_t \dots\dots (3.4)$$

The a priori of this model are that $\beta_0 \neq 0$, $\beta1 > 0$, $\beta2 > 0$, $\beta_3 > 0$, $\beta_5 > 0$.

$$lnREXR_t = \alpha_0 + \alpha_1 lnNR_t + \mu_t \dots\dots\dots\dots\dots (3.5)$$

$\alpha_0 \neq 0$, $\alpha_1 < 0$

Where $\beta_0$ to $\beta_4$ and $\alpha_0$ to $\alpha_1$ indicate the elasticity of natural log of identified resources within the period of study, natural log of real gross domestic product ($lnGDP_t$), natural log of Natural resources ($lnNR_t$), natural log of exports of goods and services as a ratio of economic growth ($lnEXP_t$), natural log of external debt stock total ($lnXDEBT_t$), natural log of gross capital formation ($lnGCF_t$), $lnREXR_t$ is the log of official exchange rate and $\varepsilon_t$ is the stochastic error term.

In determining the presence or absence of the natural resource curse hypothesis, the following conditions were considered following Sala-i-Martin and Subramanian (2008), and Rocha, (2010) approach. This is presented in table 3.1.

**Table 3.1: Conditions for Natural Resource Curse and Dutch Disease**

| Case | Conditions | Description |
|------|-----------|-------------|
| 1 | $\dfrac{dGDPt}{dNRt} < 0$ | **Natural Resource Curse:** That is, if an increase in natural resources lead to a fall in Economic Growth. |
| 2 | $\dfrac{dGDPt}{dNRt} > 0$ | **Natural Resource Curse Absence** That is, if an increase in natural resources lead to a rise in Economic Growth. |
| 3 | $\dfrac{dREXR}{dNRt} < 0$ | **No Dutch Disease** That is, if an increase in natural resources leads to a depreciation of real effective exchange rate |
| 4 | $\dfrac{dREXR}{dNRt} > 0$ | **Dutch Disease** That is, if an increase in natural resources leads to an appreciation of real effective exchange rate |

**Source: Adopted from the work of Pirezki and Ploeg (2010)**

In estimating equation(3.4), we employed the Autoregressive Distributed Lag (ARDL) bounds testing approach developed by Pesaran, Smith, and Shin (2001). ARDL models are linear time series models in which both the dependent and independent variables are related not only contemporaneously, but across historical (lagged) values as well. The term "autoregressive" shows that $x_t$' (independent variables), $y_t$ (dependent variable) also get explained by its own lag. Unlike the Johansen and Juselius (1990) co-integration procedure, Autoregressive Distributed Lag (ARDL) approach to co-integration helps in identifying the co-integrating vector(s). That is, each of the underlying variables stands as a single long run relationship equation. If one co-integrating vector (i.e. the underlying equation) is identified, the ARDL model of the co-integrating vector is re-parameterized into ECM. The re-parameterized result gives short-run dynamics (i.e. traditional ARDL) and long run relationship of the variables of a single model and ARDL (m, n) becomes;

$$y_t = \beta_0 + \beta_1 y_{t-1} + \cdots + \beta p y_{t-m} + \alpha_0 X_{t-1} + \alpha_1 X_{t-2} + \alpha_2 X_{t-2} + \cdots + \alpha_q X_{t-n} + \varepsilon_t - (3.6)$$

Here, m and n are the number of years for lag, $\varepsilon_t$ is the disturbance terms and $\beta_i$'s are coefficients for short run and $\alpha_i$'s are coefficients for long run relationship.

One of the conditions for the applications of the ARDL model is that underlying variables are I(0) or I(1) or a combination of both. Also, if the F-statistics (Wald test) establishes that there is a single long run relationship and the sample data size is small or finite, the ARDL error correction representation becomes relatively more efficient. Under such circumstances, the ARDL procedure can distinguish between dependent and explanatory variables. That is, the ARDL approach assumes that only a single reduced form technical relationship exists between the dependent variable and the exogenous variables (Pesaran et al. 2001). The major advantage of this approach lies in its identification of the Co integrating vectors especially where there are multiple Co integrating vectors. Furthermore, since each of the underlying variables stands as a single equation, endogeneity is less of a problem in the ARDL technique because it is free of residual correlation (i.e. all variables are assumed endogenous). In addition, the Error Correction Model (ECM) can be derived from ARDL model through a simple linear transformation, which integrates short run adjustments with long run equilibrium without losing long run information. The associated ECM model takes a sufficient number of lags to capture the data generating process especially in the formulation of the modelling frameworks.

In estimating the ARDL technique, the issue of finding the appropriate lag length for each of the underlying variables in the ARDL framework is very important because we want to have Gaussian error terms (i.e. standard normal error terms that do not suffer from non-normality, autocorrelation and Heteroscedasticity). To determine the optimum lag length, we employed the Akaike Information Criterion (AIC) and the Schwarz Bayesian Criterion (SBC). By alternating the lags of the variables and estimating the result, we selected the model with the smallest AIC and SBC estimates. The stability of the model was carried out using the CUSUM test.

To determine the long run relationship between the variables, the study employs the Bound F statistic (Bound test for co-integration).

In practice, testing the relationship between the forcing variable(s) in the ARDL model leads to hypothesis testing of the long-run relationship among the underlying variables. The ARDL model approach to co-integration testing is modelled as follows;

$$\Delta X_t = \delta_{0t} + \sum_{t=1}^{k} \alpha_1 \Delta X_{t-1} + \sum_{t=1}^{k} \alpha_2 \Delta Y_{t-1} + \delta_1 X_{t-1} + \delta_2 Y_{t-1}$$
$$+ V_{1t} \ldots \ldots \ldots \ldots (3.7)$$

$$\Delta Y_t = \delta_{0t} + \sum_{t=1}^{k} \alpha_1 \Delta Y_{t-1} + \sum_{t=1}^{k} \alpha_2 \Delta X_{t-1} + \delta_1 Y_{t-1} + \delta_2 X_{t-1}$$
$$+ V_{2t} \ldots \ldots \ldots \ldots (3.8)$$

Where, k is the maximum lag order in the model. The F-statistic is carried out on the joint null hypothesis that the coefficients of the lagged variables ($\delta_1 X_{t-1}$ $\delta_1 Y_{t-1}$ or $\delta_1 Y_{t-1}$ $\delta_1 X_{t-1}$) are zero. The differences ($\delta_1 - \delta_2$) correspond to the long-run relationship, while ($\alpha_1 - \alpha_2$) represent the short-run dynamics of the model. The null of non-existence of the long-run relationship is defined by;

Ho: δ1 = δ2= 0 (null, i.e. the long run relationship does not exist)
H₁: δ1 ≠ δ2 ≠ 0 (Alternative, i.e. the long run relationship exists)

**Discussion of Findings**

This research makes use of time series data in testing for natural resource curse or blessing and the Dutch disease expectation in Cameroon. As a tradition, we first test for stationarity of the variables using the traditional unit root tests (Augmented Dickey Fuller (ADF) and Phillip Perron Test (PP)) to avoid spurious results. The reason for performing two unit root tests is to make a strong point about the order of integration of the variables. The findings are presented as shown below.

## Table 4.1: Unit Root Test

| Variables | ADF Test Statistics | Critical Values | PP Test Statistics | Critical Values | Remark |
|---|---|---|---|---|---|
| Economic Growth (GDP) | -7.0173* | 1% = - 3.581 <br> 5% = - 2.927 <br> 10% = - 2.602 | -7.0173* | 1% = - 3.584 <br> 5% = - 2.928 <br> 10% = - 2.602 | Stationary I (1) |
| Exports (EXP) | -3.349* | 1% = - 3.581 <br> 5% = - 2.926 <br> 10% = - 2.601 | -3.390** | 1% = - 3.581 <br> 5% = - 2.926 <br> 10% = - 2.601 | Stationary I (0) |
| Natural Resource (NR) | -3.677* | 1% = - 3.581 <br> 5% = - 2.926 <br> 10% = - 2.601 | -3.839* | 1% = - 3.581 <br> 5% = - 2.926 <br> 10% = - 2.601 | Stationary I (0) |
| Gross Capital Formation (GCF) | -7.606* | 1% = - 3.581 <br> 5% = - 2.926 <br> 10% = - 2.601 | -12.090* | 1% = - 3.581 <br> 5% = - 2.926 <br> 10% = - 2.601 | Stationary I (1) |
| External debt stock (XDEBT) | -6.188* | 1% = - 3.581 <br> 5% = - 2.926 <br> 10% = - 2.601 | -6.1916* | 1% = - 3.581 <br> 5% = - 2.926 <br> 10% = - 2.601 | Stationary I (1) |
| Real Effective Exchange rate (REXR) | -6.033* | 1% = - 3.581 <br> 5% = - 2.926 <br> 10% = - 2.601 | -6.0343* | 1% = - 3.581 <br> 5% = - 2.926 <br> 10% = - 2.601 | Stationary I (1) |

Source: Computed by the Authors from Eviews version 7. 2018 = *Significant at 1% level.*

## Table 4.2: ARDL Results

Dependent Variable: D(GDP)
Included observations: 41 after adjustments

| Variables | Coefficient | Std. Error | t-Statistic | Prob. |
|---|---|---|---|---|
| C | -2.037716 | 0.492238 | -0.695409 | 0.5178 |
| D(GDP(-1)) | -2.590215 | 0.730261 | -2.977599 | 0.0314 |
| D(GDP(-2)) | -0.779535 | 0.193872 | -3.652947 | 0.0026 |
| D(GDP(-3)) | -1.614779 | 1.165920 | -1.384983 | 0.2247 |
| D(GDP(-4)) | -0.763637 | 0.812616 | -2.939726 | 0.0205 |
| D(GDP(-5)) | -0.690615 | 0.654255 | -1.055574 | 0.3395 |
| D(GDP(-6)) | 1.287606 | 0.805757 | 1.598007 | 0.3409 |
| D(NR(-1)) | -0.353952 | 0.002259 | 3.151351 | 0.0017 |
| D(NR(-2)) | -0.883503 | 0.357274 | 4.030596 | 0.0030 |
| D(NR(-3)) | -0.772936 | 0.270415 | 3.152922 | 0.0311 |
| D(NR(-4)) | -0.847767 | 0.442742 | 2.009258 | 0.0592 |
| D(NR(-5)) | -0.948138 | 0.385347 | -5.099182 | 0.0001 |
| D(NR(-6)) | -0.982397 | 0.340574 | 2.758176 | 0.0425 |
| D(XDEBT(-1)) | -0.391474 | 0.190373 | -2.056353 | 0.0949 |
| D(XDEBT(-2)) | -0.064944 | 0.132454 | -0.490313 | 0.6447 |
| D(XDEBT(-3)) | -0.025861 | 0.187609 | -0.137847 | 0.8957 |
| D(XDEBT(-4)) | 0.755974 | 0.776325 | 0.317451 | 0.6037 |
| D(XDEBT(-5)) | -0.613062 | 0.162716 | -3.923981 | 0.0004 |
| D(XDEBT(-6)) | -0.591986 | 0.170187 | -3.080679 | 0.0092 |
| D(GCF(-1)) | 0.860129 | 0.374025 | 3.237571 | 0.0016 |
| D(GCF(-2)) | -0.512737 | 0.447010 | -1.147037 | 0.3033 |
| D(GCF(-3)) | 0.904916 | 0.350904 | 2.868944 | 0.0246 |
| D(GCF(-4)) | 0.754403 | 0.318121 | 3.742742 | 0.0011 |
| D(GCF(-5)) | 0.454009 | 0.117372 | 4.430525 | 0.0000 |
| D(GCF(-6)) | 0.320960 | 0.137282 | 3.733990 | 0.0012 |
| D(EXPORT(-1)) | -0.912834 | 0.385563 | -4.162013 | 0.0010 |
| D(EXPORT(-2)) | -0.966243 | 0.392252 | -3.962429 | 0.0021 |
| D(EXPORT(-3)) | -1.014084 | 0.007424 | -3.922712 | 0.0001 |
| D(EXPORT(-4)) | -0.848840 | 0.423783 | -2.295098 | 0.0519 |
| D(EXPORT(-5)) | -0.845527 | 0.370466 | -3.392820 | 0.0003 |
| D(EXPORT(-6)) | 0.725691 | 0.671054 | 0.832643 | 0.0002 |
| GDP(-1) | 0.944704 | 0.417260 | 4.065771 | 0.0003 |

17

| | | | | |
|---|---|---|---|---|
| NR(-1) | -1.682288 | 0.395169 | -3.879296 | 0.0010 |
| XDEBT(-1) | -0.075389 | 0.103555 | -1.728008 | 0.4993 |
| GCF(-1) | 0.042146 | 0.673643 | 2.062564 | 0.0525 |
| EXPORT(-1) | -0.756992 | 0.300603 | 3.445151 | 0.0080 |

| | | | |
|---|---|---|---|
| R-squared | 0.719714 | Mean dependent var | 2.863239 |
| Adjusted R-squared | 0.693641 | S.D. dependent var | 0.234665 |
| S.E. of regression | 0.129887 | Akaike info criterion | -1.145976 |
| Sum squared resid | 0.725434 | Schwarz criterion | -0.951060 |
| Log likelihood | 32.50343 | Hannan-Quinn criter. | -1.072317 |
| F-statistic | 27.60365 | Durbin-Watson stat | 1.289793 |
| Prob(F-statistic) | 0.000000 | | |

**Source: Compute by the Author from Eviews Version 7, 2018.**

The unit root test results from Table 4.1 above shows that exports and natural resources were stationary at that level [that is 1(0)] while economic growth, gross capital formation, external debt stock and real effective interest rate only gained stationarity after their first difference [that is 1(1)]. This meets the condition for applying the Autoregressive Distributed lagged (ARDL) Bound Testing since the variables have different level of stationarity but none of them is stationary after second difference. We then proceeded to determine the number of lags in the model, the Akaike information criterion and the Schwarz criterion settled at six lags implying that our model makes use of six lagged. We then proceeded to estimate the ARDL model as shown in Table 4.2.

From Table 4.2, we observed that the coefficient of multiple determination indicates that about 69 percent variation of the current growth rate is explained by the current and lagged values of economic growth, natural resources, exports of goods and services, external debt stocks and gross domestic capital formation. The significance of this is confirmed by the F-statistics. The findings show that the lagged one, two, three, four, five have negative influence on the

18

current state of economic growth while lagged six indicates a positive influence. However, from these, only lagged one, two, and four are significant. This implies that, a percentage increase in the one year, two year and four-year lags of economic growth has reduced the current level of economic growth by 2.590, 0.779 and 0.7636 percent respectively. All the lags values of natural resources as observed from the table exert negative influence on economic growth in Cameroon. This demonstrates that it is not a must that the more endowed a country is in natural resources, the more its ability to accumulate growth potentials. This can only be possible if the natural resource rents are put into productive use. It follows that the natural resource curse is a pitfall into which Cameroon has fallen because its policies and management framework is not robust enough to direct the economy to its desired expectation. The under-development of such a framework is as a result of the absence of good governance, and institutional weaknesses. These findings are in line with those of Fan et al (2012), Arezki and Ploeg (2010), and Sachs and Warner (1995) which supports the natural resource curse phenomenon.

The lagged values of external debt denote that they exert negative influence on current economic growth except for the lagged four years. However, only the five and six lags are significant. This implies that a percentage increase in the fifth and sixth lag values of external debt will reduce current economic growth by 0.613 and 0,591 percent respectively. The negative effect is justified by the fact that, the debt which Cameroon has contracted over the years is not put into productive projects but on deadweight projects which only help to increase the incidence of the debt on the tax payers. These findings are in line with the debt overhang hypothesis and the study of Mbanga and Sikod (2001). Except for the two-year lag, all the lag values of gross domestic capital formation indicate a positive significant effect on the current economic growth of Cameroon over our period of the study. This is also in agreement with the money a study, among which is that of Pirezki and Ploeg (2010).

Table 4.2 shows that the lagged values of exports grossly reduce the current state of economic growth in Cameroon. Precisely, they are negative over our period of study with the exception of the lag four-year value. This influence is due to the fact that Cameroon's exports are mostly agricultural which are not stable and therefore cannot foster growth. Also, exports are low in relation to global trade due to administrative bottlenecks and the fact that majority of the exports are raw materials as opposed to the imports which are mainly manufactured goods. This finding is not in line with the export led growth hypothesis, but it is in agreement with findings associated with most studies in developing countries.

From the ARDL results, the long run terms are GDP (-1), NR(-1), XDEBT(-1), GCF(-1) and EXP(-1). The long run effect shows that the one period lag of GDP and GCF positively affect the current level of economic growth in the country while the one period lagged of XDEBT, EXP, and NR negatively affect the current level of economic growth in Cameroon. They are all significant at less than 10 percent level, meaning that they are instrumental for long-term policy formation.

We then proceeded to test for serial correlation and stability of the model which is in line with the Bound Testing procedure. The Breusch-Godfrey serial correlation LM test for serial correlation is presented in table 4.3.

### Table 4.3: Breusch-Godfrey Serial Correlation LM Test:

| F-statistic **0.321094** | **Prob. F(2,7) 0.7355** |
|---|---|
| Obs*R-squared **3.445315** | Prob. Chi-Square(2) 0.1786 |

**Source: Computed by the Authors using Eviews Version 7, 2018.**

It is observed from table 4.3 that the null hypothesis of no serial correlation is accepted since the probability of the Chi square value is not significant at 5 percent. Hence our model is free from serial correlation. The next was for us to test for stability of the model using the CUSUM test as presented.

**Figure 4.1: CUSUM Stability Test**

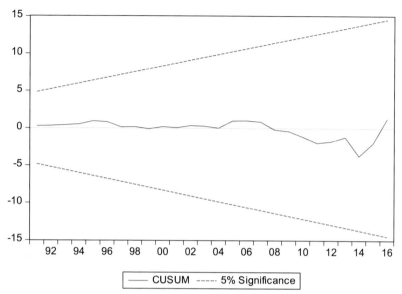

Source: Computed by the Author Using Eviews Version 7, 2018.

The CUSUM test of stability presented above shows that our variables are stable since they stayed within the critical bounds indicating the stability of the economic growth equation. Also the functional form of the model was checked with the help of the Ramey test but the findings are not presented here due to space. The results show that the model is correctly specified by failing to reject the null hypothesis. To test for heteroscedasticity, we employed the ARCH test. The test for constant variance as presented in table 4.4 shows that homoscedasticity exists in the variables included in the model.

**Table 4.4: Heteroscedasticity Test: ARCH**

| F-statistic **0.172682** | Prob. F(2,7)**0.6800** |
|---|---|
| Obs*R-squared **0.180737** | Prob. Chi-Square(2) 0.6707 |

Source: Computed by the Authors using Eviews Version 7, 2018.

The above ARCH test denotes the presence of homoscedasticity and has empowered us not to reject the null hypothesis of equal variance since the probability of the chi square is greater than 5 percent. Therefore, our model is homoscedastic. Hence, since the model has no serial correlation, it is homoscedastic and stable. We therefore proceeded to do bound testing to see if our variables were stable in the long run. That is checking whether GDP(-1), NR(-1), EXP(-1), GCF(-1) and XDEBT(-1) have long run association. This is done by applying the Walt Statistics as presented in table 4.5.

## Table 4.5 Wald Test

| Test Statistic | Value | Df | Probability |
|---|---|---|---|
| F-statistic | 4.803783 | (5, 5) | 0.1412 |
| Chi-square | 14.01892 | 5 | 0.0155 |

Source: Computed by the Authors using E-views Version 7

Table 4.5 Wald Test of Long Run Relationship
Null Hypothesis: C(32)=C(33)=C(34)=C(35)=C(36)=0
Null Hypothesis Summary:

| Normalized Restriction (= 0) | Value | Std. Err. |
|---|---|---|
| C(32) | 0.444704 | 0.417260 |
| C(33) | -1.682288 | 0.895169 |
| C(34) | -0.075389 | 0.103555 |
| C(35) | -0.042146 | 0.673643 |
| C(36) | 1.156992 | 0.800603 |

Restrictions are linear in coefficients.

Source: Computed by the Authors using Eviews Version 7

From the above Walt test, with four explanatory variables, the F-statistic is 4.803 which has to be compared with the Paseran critical value at 5 percent in the case of unrestricted intercept and no trend. Since the coefficient of the F-statistics obtained is greater than the upper bound critical value of 4.544, we reject the null hypothesis of no long run relationship. This implies that economic growth, Natural Resource Endowment, External Debt, and exports of Goods and services have long run association when interacted. Based on the above, we proceeded to obtain the speed of adjustment in the short run for the long run equilibrium using the Enger and Granger cointegration and error correction analyses presented below.

## The Error Correction Model

$$DGDP = 0.2236DGDP(-1) + 1.1064DGDP(-2)$$
$$+ 0.3607DGDP(-3) +$$

(0.5689) (1.4404) (0.8194)

$$0.3692DGDP(-4) + 02776\,DGDP(-5) +$$
$$1.2744DGDP(-6) ** -0.9013DNR(-1) -$$

(0.9745)(0.8066)　(2.2885)　(-1.512)　$0.8782DNR(-2) **$
$$-0.6437DNR(-3) * -0.6301DNR(-4) **$$
$$-0.8334DNR(-5) *$$

(-2.838)(-3.733)(-2.913)(-3.633)

$$-0.2625DNR(-6) - 0.0319DXdebt(-1)$$
$$- 0.0011DXdebt(-2) + 0.0774DXdebt(-3)$$

(-3.150) (-0.225)(-0.006) (0.539)

$$+0.0532DXdebt(-4) - 0.2328DXdebt(-5)$$
$$+ 0.2517DXdebt(-6) + 0.0118DGCF(-1) *$$

(0.3266) (-1.227) (1.2291) (3.2832)

$$-0.2860DGCF(-2) * +0.1018DGCF(-3)$$
$$* +0.1937DGCF(-4) * -0.0316DGCF(-5) *$$

(-3.176) (3.4233) (3.7427) (-3.1033)

$$-0.0757DGCF(-6) * +0.9306DExport(-1)$$
$$+ 0.9680DExport(-2) **$$

(-3.2596)(1.444) (2.988)

$$+0.3025DExport(-3) * +0.5155DExport(-4)$$
$$+ 0.6792DExport(-5) *$$

(3.116) (2.232) (3.219)

$$+0.4619DExport(-6) * -0.6286ECT(-1)$$
$$* \ldots \ldots \ldots \ldots \ldots (4.1)$$

(3.4019) (2.851)

The values in the brackets represent the t-statistics. * = significant at 1 percent, ** = significant at 5 percent and *** = significant at 10 percent.

**Source: Computed by the Authors Using E-view Version 7**

From the above result, the error correction term (ECT) is the speed of adjustment towards achieving long run equilibrium. From the findings, it is observed that the ECT is negative and significant. This demonstrates that the whole system can be adjusted to long run equilibrium at the speed of 63 percent. This means that about 63 percent departures from the equilibrium is being corrected each period. We then proceeded to check whether this error correction model is serially correlated and stable. The Breusch-Godfrey serial correlation and CUSUM stability tests which are not presented here due to space, indicate that the model is not only free from serial correlation but it is also stable.

To check for short run causality between the variables, the wald Test was conducted with the following findings.

**Table 4.6: Wald Test Equation: Short Run causality running from NR to GDP**

| Test Statistic | Value | Df | Probability |
|---|---|---|---|
| F-statistic | 2.468711 | (6, 9) | 0.1077 |
| Chi-square | 14.81227 | 6 | 0.0218 |

**Wald Test Equation: Short Run causality running from GCF to GDP**

| Test Statistic | Value | Df | Probability |
|---|---|---|---|
| F-statistic | 0.312804 | (6, 9) | 0.9146 |
| Chi-square | 1.876822 | 6 | 0.9307 |

**Wald Test Equation: Short Run causality running from EXPORT to GDP**

| Test Statistic | Value | Df | Probability |
|---|---|---|---|
| F-statistic | 1.464642 | (6, 9) | 0.2911 |
| Chi-square | 8.787850 | 6 | 0.1859 |

**Source: Computed by the Authors Using E-Views Version 7**

It is observed from the Chi Square value on table 4.6 that there exists a short run causality running from natural resource endowment to economic growth in Cameroon while there is no short run causality running from export or gross capital formation to economic growth in Cameroon.

In testing for the Dutch disease in Cameroon, equation (3.5) was estimated using the Generalised Method of Moments and findings are presented thus;

$$lnREXR_t = 1.941 + 0.732lnNR_t \dots \dots \dots \dots \dots \dots \dots \dots \dots \text{(4.2)}$$
(12.35) (3.932)
Adj. R-square =0.23 Durbin- Watson statistics = 1.909

From the exchange rate equation, we observed that natural resource endowment exerts a positive significant influence on the official exchange rate in Cameroon over our period of study. On the average, an increase in the natural resource endowment will appreciate the exchange rate in the country. This goes to confirm the fact that there exists the Dutch Disease syndrome in Cameroon. This implies that natural resource exploitation has significant impact on the official exchange rate. This is not in line with the study of Bannor (2016).

**Conclusion and Policy implications**

This study set out to test the natural resource curse hypothesis and the Dutch Disease Syndrome in Cameroon from 1970 to 2017. Based on the findings, it is observed that the natural resource curse hypothesis holds in Cameroon as natural resource endowment is observed to exert a significant negative effect on economic growth. Testing for the Dutch Disease Syndrome, the findings indicate that natural resource exploitation has a great impact on the official exchange rate in Cameroon. This means that the Dutch Disease Syndrome exists in Cameroon.

The country generates significant amount of wealth from its natural resources both sub-soil and top-soil. Given that the resource curse hypothesis exists in Cameroon despite the fact that the bulk of national wealth is generated from the natural resource endowments such as the deep sea and associated ports, the thick evergreen forests with quality timber and the oil deposits that have permitted the setting up of an oil refinery, adequate attention should be given to policies around the use of natural resources.

Based on the above, this study recommends that natural resource rents need to be put into effective use such as in research and development, training in technical and vocational education and good governance. Infrastructural development such as the construction of farm to market roads, hospitals, educational facilities, air and sea ports among others are strongly recommended. Cultural transformation, regional balance, women empowerment, industrial development, export promotion and industrialisation should be areas of concern. There is therefore need for the government to provide checks and balances against corruption and natural resources mismanagement to reverse the resource-curse hypothesis in Cameroon. This study advocates for the elimination of wastage, external debts, natural resource rents, structural rigidities, thereby enhancing agricultural, social, industrial and cultural transformation. Research on innovations in all sectors of the economy of Cameroon should be prioritized. In this way, the much-treasured resources can be freed-up to enhance the competitiveness of the agricultural, social, industrial sectors, as well as the cultural framework for the development of the nation.

The study also strongly recommends that the performance capacity of the resources in Cameroon should be enhanced by improving upon the coordination of key sectorial ministries such as the Ministry of the Environment, Nature Protection and Sustainable Development (MINEPDED), the Ministry of Mines, Energy and Technological Development, Ministry of State Property and Land Tenure, Ministry of Agriculture and Rural Development, Ministry of Forestry and Wildlife, the Ministry of Trade and Commerce and the civil society. This can be done by setting up institutional frameworks that allow for effective and efficient management of the country's natural wealth. There is need to reform the mining code and revise the law regulating timber and other natural resource extraction in the country by eliminating unnecessary waste, structural rigidities to increase the competitiveness and overall performance of the extractive or sector. By doing so, the Dutch disease syndromes will be eliminated.

# References

Adu, G. (2011). *Natural resource abundance and economic growth: The case of Ghana.* Environmental and Resource Economics Unit, Department of Economics, Swedish University of Agricultural Sciences: Uppsala, Sweden.

Atkinson, G., and Hamilton, K (2003). Savings, growth and the resource curse hypothesis. *World Development, 31(11), 1793-1807.*

Arezki, R. and Ploeg, F. (2010). Do natural resources depress income per capita? *Cesifo Working Paper No. 3056*

Bannor, F. (2016) Investigating the natural resource curse syndrome: A case of Ghana's oil production (Master's thesis). School of Graduate Studies, Kwame Nkrumah University of Science and Technology.

Brunnschweiler, C. and Bulte, E. (2008). The resource curse visited and revised. *Tale of Paradoxes and Red Herrings. 55(3) 248-264.*

Butkiewkz J. and Yanikkaya, H. (2010). Minerals, institutions, openness and growth: An empirical analysis. *Land Economics, 86 313-328.*

Chong-Sup K. and Yeon-sil K. (2008). Natural resource abundance and economic growth revisited: Latin America and developed countries from a comparative study. *AJLAS, 21(102).\*

Collier, P. (2007). *The bottom billion – Why the poorest countries are failing and what can be done about it.* Oxford University Press, Oxford

Collier, P. and Hoffler, A. (2002). Greed and grievance in African civil wars. *Oxford Economics Papers,* 56 (4), 563-596.

Ding, N. and Field, B. (2005). Natural resource abundance and economic growth. *Land Economics,* 81(4), 496-502.

Ewubare, B and Kakain, S. (2017). Natural resource abundance and economic Growth in Nigeria. *Global Journal of Agricultural Research,* 5(3), 1-11.

Forgha, G., Wujung, A. and Nkwetta, A. (2015). Natural Resource abundance and economic growth: Cameroon Experience.

Gylfason, T. and Zoega, G. (2006). Natural resource and economic growth: The role of investment. *World Economy, 29(8), 1091-1115.*

Gylfason, T. (2001). Natural resources, education and economic development. *European Economic Review, 45, 847-859.*

Gylfason, T. (2000). Resources, agriculture and economic growth in economies in transition. *Kyklos, 53(4), 546-580.*

Johansen, S. and Juselius K. (1990). Maximum likelihood estimation and inference on cointegration with application to the demand for money. *Oxford Bulletin of Economics and Statistics, 52, 162-210.*

Ledermann, D., and Melony, W. (2003). Trade structure and growth. *World Bank Policy Research Working Paper, 3025.*

Malik, S., Chaudhry, S., and Hussain, S. (2005). *Natural resource management and economic growth in Pakistan.* A Time Series Analysis.

Mbanga, G. and Sikod, F. (2001). The impact of debt and debt service payment on investment in Cameroon. *AERC Final Report, Nairobi, Kenya.*

Mehlum, H., Moene, K., and Torvik, R. (2006). Cursed by resources or institutions? *The World Economy, 29 (8), 1117-1131.*

Papyrakis, E. and Gerlagh, R. (2006). Resource windfalls, investment and long term income. *Resources Policy,* 31(2) 117-128.

Pesaran, H., Shin, Y., and Smith, R. (2001). Bounds testing approaches to the analysis of level relationships. *Journal of Applied Econometrics, 16, 289-326*

Rocha, F. (2010). Natural resource curse and externalities from natural resource exports. *Av.Pasteur,* 250, 290-240.

Sachs, D. and Warner, M. (2001). Natural resources and economic development: The curse of natural resources. *European Economic Review,* 45, 827-838.

Sachs, D. and Warner, A. (1997). Natural resource abundance and economic growth. *Working Paper, Institute for International Development, Harvard University, 1-50*

Sachs, J.D. and Warner, A.M. (1995), "Natural resource abundance and economic growth", NBER *Working paper, No. 5398,* Cambridge, Massachusetts.

Sala-i-Martin, X. and Subramanian, A. (2003). Addressing the natural resource curse: An illustration from Nigeria", NBER *Working Paper Series, No. 9804,* Cambridge, Massachusetts.

Salmani, B. and Yavari, K. (2004). Economic growth in oil exporter countries. *Journal of Business Researches,* 3, 1-24.

The Dutch Disease (1977). The economist. Pp. 82-83. Retrieved from www.economist.com

28

UNCTAD. (2012). World investment report. Published by United Nations Conference on    Trade and Development.

Van der Ploeg, F. (2011). Natural resources: Curse or blessing?" *Journal of Economic Literature*, 49(2), 366-420.

WDI (2018). World Development Indicators on Data on Cameroon. Retrieved from *http://data.worldbank.org/country/cameroon*.

# Chapter 2

## Natural Resources Depletion and Economic Growth: Implications and Prospect for Cameroon Economic Emergence by 2035

*Nkwetta Ajong Aquilas, Njimanted Godfrey Forgha[1],
Mbohjim Mobit and Mbu Sunday Agbor*

### Abstract

Cameroon no doubt possesses huge deposits of energy, mineral and forest resources, which are a major source of revenue for the country's economic growth and development. With an increase in the exploitation and the consequent depletion of these resources, in addition to the "paradox of the plenty" that operates in most natural resources-rich economies, the fundamental question of whether long term economic growth can be achieved becomes inevitable. It is on this basis that the current study is designed to investigate into the effects of natural resources depletion on the economic growth of Cameroon and to evaluate the implications and prospect of resource depletion on the country's long-term economic vision by 2035. The study employs the Vector Auto regression (VAR) technique and Autoregressive Distributed Lag (ARDL) approach to co-integration and establishes the causal relationship between resource depletion and economic growth and the long run relationship respectively. Data for the study was obtained from the World Bank database and United Nations Conference on Trade and Development (UNCTAD) statistics from 1980-2017. The results reveal that while in the short run energy depletion affects growth significantly, in the long run, the effect is insignificant. Also, deforestation affects growth insignificantly both in the short run and long run. Economic growth also has a significant effect on energy and forest depletion. With the increasing rate of resource depletion, it is obvious that Cameroon's economic growth cannot be sustained, and the long-term vision may be jeopardized if

---

[1] Corresponding author

growth were to solely rely on the resources. Based on these results, the study recommends that besides depleting non-renewable resources steadily and renewable resources sustainably, rents from these resources should be channelled to more productive activities such as infrastructure, education and health. In this regard, government, international organizations and the civil society must intensify the fight against corruption in the resource sector to mobilize revenue from the resources. We also recommend the reduction of activities that put unnecessary pressure on natural resources.

**Key Words:** Economic Emergence, Gross Domestic Product Growth, Renewable and Non-Renewable Resources, Resource Depletion

## Introduction

Natural resources have been considered an important input in to production (Barbier, 2003) and a contributor to the growth of many developing economies. Oil for example has fuelled growth in some developing economies such as Iran and Russia. For instance, between 2006 and 2012, the share of oil revenue to gross domestic product (GDP) and oil exports to total exports for Iran was 21% and 74% respectively (Farzanegan, 2013). The contribution of the forest to GDP has been negligible, with rates averaging only about 0.4% of GDP respectively between 1980 and 2017. Between 2006 and 2012, oil revenues accounted for about 10.5% of Russia's GDP with a negligible contribution of forest and mineral resources (World Bank, 2018).

Most African countries have depended on oil resources for their growth. For instance, Sudan recorded an average real economic growth rate of 9% from 2005-2006 due to its dependence on oil (Nour, 2011). Oil sector GDP growth was 36.1% in 2012 (International Monetary Fund [IMF], 2012) and only about 0.7% of Sudan's GDP in 2016 (World Bank, 2018). For Nigeria, the share of oil to GDP were 38.87% in 2005, 37.44% in 2009 (Akinlo, 2012) and 29.1% in 2010 (Takebe and York, 2011). Oil rents as share of GDP fell from 17% in 2011 to 3% in 2016 (World Bank, 2018). The cumulative economic growth rate for Angola reached 67.5% from 2003-2006 due mainly to oil production, with oil rents as share of GDP rising steadily from 35% in 2003 to 54% in 2006. Oil rents fell steadily from 41% in 2013 to 11% in 2016. In Cameroon, the share of oil rents to GDP increased from about 6.8% in 2009 to about 8.3% in 2012 before falling steadily from 7% in 2013 to 1% in 2016 (World Bank, 2018).

Cameroon's economy grew by nearly 5.6% between 1970 and 1977, with natural resources contributing about 4% to GDP and depleting by a negligible 0.0007% on the average (World Bank, 2018) due to dependence on primary products. Petroleum became the main source of growth from 1978-1986, annual real GDP growing by 8.8% (Ghura, 1997). Oil production rose from less than 5 million barrels in 1978 to more than 66 million barrels in 1986. On the average, GDP grew by 21% between 1978 and 1986 (Ghura, 1997), and the share of natural resources to GDP averaged about 16% with degradation averaging about 6% of GNP (World Bank, 2018). From 1987-1993, economic crisis set in, leading to a negative growth rate of -5% on the average from 1987-1993. Natural resources contributed 9% to GDP on the average within this period compared to the 16% to GDP share from 1978-1986 and depleted by about 6% of GNI (World Bank, 2018).

Following the FCFA devaluation in 1994, real GDP increased to about 2% from 1994-1996. Private investment also increased from 11% to 13% of GDP between these periods. Natural resources contributed about 11.8% to the GDP and depleted by about 5.5% of GNI on the average. From 1997-2000, average GDP growth was 4.6% (Ghura, 1997). Natural resources made up 10% of GDP and depleted on the average by 6% of GNI (WDI, 2017). From 2000 to 2003 when the Poverty Reduction Strategy Paper (PRSP) was formulated, the GDP growth rate stood at 4% (Ghura, 1997) and natural resources degraded by 7% of GNI (World Bank, 2018). From 2003-2007, GDP growth on the average was 3.3%. Energy depletion was 7% of GNI on the average from 2008-2010. Growth grew on the average by 4.6 % from 2010-2017 while resources depleted by 4.6% of GNI (World Bank, 2018).

Cameroon's economic performance has not been very stable from the early 1970s to date. The country's desire to achieve sustainable growth and reduce poverty levels, coupled with a growing population has thus imposed pressure on natural resources, leading to their eminent depletion. This has likely implication on economic growth, as the resources may increasingly become unavailable for future use. The concern therefore, in this work is whether economic growth can be sustained given the rate of resources depletion. It is within this context that the current study is out to investigate the impact of natural resources depletion on economic growth in Cameroon and its implications and prospect for Cameroon economic emergence by 2035.

The long-term economic vision of Cameroon is to become a newly industrialized economy by 2035. The specific objectives of the vision include meeting targets for the macroeconomy, education and training, population and living conditions as well as the infrastructure. At the macroeconomic level, GDP growth is expected to reach 9.9%. The objective in the health sector is to move from 7 to 70 medical doctors for every 100,000 people and for education, it is to increase the student enrolment rate in scientific and technological courses in secondary school and higher education, from 5% to 30% (Ministry of Economy, Planning and Regional Development [MINEPAT], 2009). The objective for population and living conditions are first is to reduce the rate of population growth to less than 2% and second target is to increase life expectancy from 50 to 70 years, thereby reducing overall mortality (MINEPAT, 2009). Five targets are involved with infrastructure objective. First is to increase the length of tarred roads to 32%; second to achieve a digital access index of 0.47 in 2035; third to increase the number of people with portable water to 70% and fourth to increase energy consumption per GDP to 45% by 2035 (MINEPAT, 2009).

Amongst the risk factors, threats and the obstacles to the accomplishment of the 2035 agenda is the over-exploitation and consequent depletion of natural resources which exists at the social level (MINEPAT, 2009). Cameroon's objective of achieving a GDP growth target of 9.9% by 2035 is one that poses significant threats to the natural resource base and hence growth, reason why this study investigates the effects of natural resources depletion on the economic growth of Cameroon and evaluates its implications and prospect for economic emergence by 2035.

Notwithstanding the contribution of natural resources to the GDP of Cameroon, the problem remains that of the overexploitation and depletion of these resources which potentially can limit economic growth. Over the past four decades (1975 to 2015) natural resources depleted on the average by about 4%. The loss resulting from depletion of natural resources amounted to about 4.5% of GNI from 1976 to 1984, 6% from 1985 to 1995, 4% from 1996 to 2005 and 5% from 2006 to 2015 (World Bank, 2018). To counter this threat, environmental laws have been put in place by the government in an attempt to ensure efficient management of natural resources. Law No. 96/12 of 5th August 1996 lays down the general legal framework for environmental management in Cameroon. The law lays down the procedures for protecting the atmosphere, continental waters and flood plains, the coast and marine waters, soils and subsoil and human settlements. However, most of these laws express what authorities are yet to do to protect the environment. From 1960 to date, the Ministry of Environment, Nature Protection and Sustainable Development along with allied ministries are responsible for natural resources management. These are some efforts towards managing natural resources to ensure sustainable economic growth, in addition to international, continental and regional conventions ratified by Cameroon. Natural resources depletion remains a major issue of concern for Cameroon despite these measures. It is against this backdrop that this study sets out specifically to;

1) Determine the nature of causality between energy depletion, deforestation and GDP in Cameroon.

2) Evaluate the long-term implications of energy and forest depletion on the economic growth of Cameroon.

This study is organized in five sections. Section one introduces the work. In section two, the literature review is presented. The analytical methods are presented in the third section. The fourth

35

section is reserved for results and discussion, while recommendations and conclusions are made in section five.

## Literature Review

Selden and Song (1993) identified four air pollutants that followed an inverted-U relationship between pollution and growth. Specifically, the authors examined per capita emissions and per capita GDP in thirty countries. They found that carbon dioxide emissions did not follow the inverted-U relationship, but rather appeared to rise monotonically with income.

Grossman and Krueger (1995) examined the relationship between economic growth and the environment by estimating a reduced-form relationship between income per capita and various indicators of environmental degradation. Four environmental indicators including urban air pollution, faecal contamination of river basins, state of the oxygen regime in river basins, and contamination of the river basins by heavy metals were used. Panel data from the Global Environmental Monitoring System's (GEMS) tracking of urban air and water quality for developing and developed countries in the world was used. After estimating a random effects model, enough evidence was found to show that economic growth initially destroys the environment but later improves it. This suggests the existence of EKCs for the pollutants.

Using environmental indicators such as sulphur and carbon emissions for Asia, Taguchi (2005) tested whether the race to the bottom and revised EKCs follow the conventional analytical EKC framework. The study used panel data starting from 1950-2009 and adopted dynamic panel Generalized Method of Moment (GMM) as the analytical method. From the findings, sulphur dioxide emissions follow the inverted U-shaped EKC pattern while carbon dioxide emissions turn to increase with an increase in GDP per capita over the time period considered. The revised EKC scenario was verified in the case of sulphur dioxide emissions while the race to the bottom EKC is verified neither in sulphur nor in carbon dioxide emissions. It was recommended that advanced technologies which are capable of trapping and storing carbon emissions should be adopted;

emissions charge and greenhouse taxes be instituted to internalize externalities.

Using panel data for the provincial-level from 1985 to 2005, Jiang et al. (2008) investigates the relationship between economic growth and the sustainability of the environment in China by empirically estimating EKC models. For waste gas from fuel consumption and waste water, the findings showed that there is an inverted U-shaped relationship between per capita income and per capita emissions with a turning point at the per capita GDP of $12,903 and $3,226, respectively, confirming the EKC hypothesis. The EKC hypothesis does not however hold in the case of waste gas from production or solid waste. The results also reveal that the EKCs of more developed coastal regions in China have a fatter but rising portion with turning points which occur at higher income levels than those of less developed central and western regions.

The relationship between economic growth and environmental degradation was examined by Phimphanthavong (2013) for Laos using time series data spanning from 1980-2010. Carbon dioxide (CO2) emissions per capita were adopted as the proxy for environmental degradation. Tests for stationarity were carried out using the Augmented Dickey-Fuller unit root test. The study was especially out to test the validity of the EKC hypothesis which suggests an inverted U-shaped relationship between environmental degradation and economic growth. The results show evidence of the EKC hypothesis. Environmental quality first falls in the early stages of economic growth but starts rising at some point along the growth path of the country. Factors such as trade openness, industrial extension, and becoming a full member of ASEAN were amongst important and significant determinants of environmental degradation in Laos. Strong environmental and natural resource protection policies were strongly recommended to be put in place for the current and future development of Laos.

Steer (2014) evaluates the relationship between depletion of natural resources, climate change and economic growth. After recognizing that natural resources, marketed and non-marketed are important inputs in to production, the study argues that productivity and economic growth will fall as current patterns of resource use, agriculture and urbanization are unsustainable and would lead to increased environmental costs. If these patterns are not checked, they will result to climate change, reduced productivity and growth. Besides costs of climate change, environmental costs constitute about 10% of GDP in many emerging countries.

Mittal and Gupta (2015) carried out an exploratory analysis of the relationship between natural resources depletion and economic growth in the present era. Though these resources contribute to a country's economic development, the study argues that current patterns of the consumption of natural resources, agricultural practices and urbanization seem unsustainable and this can trigger economic downturn. The quest for developing countries to grow leads to land abuse, generating pollution of all types, soil erosion and natural resources depletion. Population explosion and increase in economic activities are the main catalysts for resources depletion besides an increase in the exploitation technology, excessive demand and the non-equitable distribution of resources. The study recommends sustainable exploitation of natural resources in order to protect the resource base, environment and ensure future growth.

One of the main weaknesses in empirical studies on the relationship between environmental indicators and growth is that that growth is an exogenous variable that is always assumed to affect environmental degradation unilaterally, thus ignoring the interdependence between the economy and the environment. This defect is taken in to cognizance in this study by applying the VAR methodology which allows all variables to be endogenous and exogenous. Another shortcoming is the absence of studies which have employed natural resources depletion as an environmental indicator in the study of the relationship between environment and economic growth. This study also closes that gap. Another recurrent problem with studies on economic growth and environmental degradation is the use of cross-country regressions based on panel data. Studies based on individual countries are limited. Panel data studies, especially those of the panel random effects model have been criticized for not adequately taking in to consideration the country-specific characteristics such as differences in the level of economic development. This accounts for the increasing number of country-specific studies of the economic growth-environment relationship.

Endogenous growth theory provides the theoretical base for this study. This theory explains long-run growth in terms of endogenous factors. Endogenous growth theory has modified the neoclassical growth theory by introducing endogenous technical progress (Jhingan, 2011). The proposition of endogenous growth theory is that factors within the production process account for economic growth. The new growth theory is motivated by the need to explain factors that determine GDP growth that couldn't be explained exogenously in the neoclassical model, that is, Solow residual. These models aim at explaining differences in growth rates across countries (Jhingan, 2011). Crafts (1996), cited in Snowdon and Vane (2005) notes that endogenous growth models broadly define investment to include research and development (R&D) expenditures and human capital development unlike physical capital accumulation in the national income accounts. These models assume that the production function experiences increasing returns to scale resulting from public and private investments in human capital that generate productivity gains which offset the possibility of diminishing returns. In this sense, endogenous growth models turn to explain divergent growth among countries. The theory assumes that; market has many firms; technological advancement or knowledge is considered a non-rival good; all factors of production, taken together exhibit increasing returns to scale but individual factors experience constant returns to scale; human beings are the producers of technological advancement and individuals and firms have market power and derive profits from what they discover (Jhingan, 2011).

The first economist to introduce the idea of learning by doing as an endogenous variable in economic growth was Arrow (1962), who hypothesized that at all times, knowledge is part of new capital goods because of accumulated experience (Jhingan, 2011). Arrow demonstrated that as worker's experience increases, labour productivity also increases. A simplified form of Arrow's model is presented on equation 2.1;

$$Y_i = A(K)F(K_i, L_i)\ldots\ldots (2.1)$$

From equation 2.1, $Y_i$ is output by firm i, $K_i$ is capital stock, $L_i$ is the stock of labour, K is the aggregate capital stock and A is technology. He showed that if the stock of labour is constant, growth would be slowed because socially, very little is invested and produced. Building on Arrow's model, Romer (1986) defined capital in broad terms to include investment in knowledge and physical capital accumulation. Romer modifies the production function to include technology as an endogenous variable such that;

$$Y = F(K, L, A) \ldots\ldots\ldots\ldots (2.2)$$

In equation 2.2 above, knowledge is said to depend on capital growth since capital deepening fosters technological spill overs that increase marginal productivity of capital in the economy. In Romer's (1986) endogenous growth model, learning externalities among firms account for aggregate knowledge expansion. In effect, via learning by doing, an increase in capital stock increases the productive capacity of each firm.

**Analytical Methodology**

This study covers a period of 37 years, from 1980-2017 inclusive. This period is long enough to enable the establishment of a meaningful relationship between resources depletion and economic growth. The data for the study was also available within this period. It is not the aim of this study to investigate the effects of natural resources abundance on economic growth in Cameroon by directly considering the effects of resources revenue on economic growth, a topic that has been highly researched in the literature. However, by focusing on the effects of natural resources depletion on growth, the study provides more insights in to the resource-curse hypothesis in Cameroon, as positive growth is expected to precede resource depletion at least in the short run. The data for gross domestic product, gross fixed capital formation, energy depletion and openness of the economy are obtainable from the World Bank data base. Total labour force data is from United Nations Conference on Trade and Development (UNCTAD) statistics, human development index data is from Human Development Reports of the United Nations Development Programme (UNDP).

Endogenous growth theory provides the theoretical foundation for modelling the relationship between natural resources depletion and economic growth. The theory recognizes that factors within the production process account for economic growth. These theories are motivated by the need to explain factors that determine unexplained growth, (Jhingan, 2011). In the context of these theories, Crafts (1996), cited in Snowdon and Vane (2005), notes that investment is defined to include research and development (R&D) and human capital expenditures unlike physical capital accumulation in neoclassical theory. A simple version of endogenous growth model by Romer (1986) and Arrow (1962) is shown on equation 3.1.

$$Y = F(K, L, A)\dots\dots\dots\dots\dots\dots \quad (3.1)$$

Recognizing that both energy and forest resources depletion are utilized as separate factor inputs gives rise to a production function represented by equation 3.2;

$$Y = F(K, L, A, ED, FD)\dots\dots\dots\dots \quad (3.2)$$

In equation 3.2, growth of knowledge or technology represents human capital development, HK which is important for economic growth, as technological spill overs raise productivity of capital across the economy. By incorporating trade openness as a fundamental determinant of economic growth, the econometric model is specified thus;

$$\Delta lnGDP_t = \delta_0 + \delta_1 \Delta lnL_t + \delta_2 \Delta lnK_t + \delta_3 \Delta HK_t + \delta_4 \Delta lnED_t + \delta_5 \Delta FD_t + \delta_6 \Delta OPEN_t + \infty_t$$
$$\dots\dots\dots\dots\dots\dots\dots\dots \quad (3.3)$$

A priori $\delta_1 > 0$; $\delta_2 > 0$; $\delta_3 > 0$; $\delta_4 < 0$; $\delta_5 < 0$; $\delta_5 > 0$

The variables are defined as follows;

$GDP_t$ = Gross domestic product in constant local currency at time t, defined as the sum of gross value added by all resident producers in the economy.

$L_t$ = Total labour force at time t, defined as supplier of labour services aged 15 and above. It includes those currently employed and the unemployed of the working age seeking for work.

$K_t$ = Gross fixed capital formation in constant local currency at time t, defined to include land improvements; machinery, plant and equipment purchases; roads and railways construction and other investments such as hospitals, schools, offices, commercial and industrial buildings and private residential dwellings.

$HK_t$ = human capital formation at time t, measured by the human development index

$ED_t$ = Energy resources depletion at time t, defined as the ratio of the value of the stock of energy resources to the remaining reserve lifetime. It covers coal, crude oil, and natural gas.

$FD_t$ = Forest resources depletion/deforestation at time t, defined as the difference between forest cover for the previous period t-1 and current period t expressed in terms of t-1.

$OPEN_t$ = openness of the economy at time t, defined as trade to GDP ratio

$\delta_1, \delta_2, \delta_3, \delta_4, \delta_5, \delta_6$ are coefficients to be estimated, $\infty_t$ is error term and $\Delta$ is the difference operator. Non-ratio variables are logged to permit the interpretation of estimated coefficients as elasticity.

From the econometric model of equation 3.3, though GDP, which is endogenous, depends on energy depletion and deforestation, which are exogenous, energy depletion and deforestation also depend on GDP, due to the economy-environment interaction. This simultaneity causes an endogeneity problem which makes estimation using Ordinary Least Squares yield biased and inconsistent results. An estimation procedure that fully accounts for such simultaneity problems is required. In this regard, the VAR technique developed by Sims (1980) is found to be relevant. The VAR model is an $n$-equation; $n$-variable linear model in which each variable in the model is explained by its lagged values plus current and past values of the remaining $n-1$ variables (Stock and

Watson, 2001) cited in Njimanted et al (2016). This model treats all variables symmetrically without distinction between endogenous and exogenous variables. In practice, an equation of the form shown below is estimated for each variable in the economic growth model.

$$Y_t = a_0 + a_1 Y_{t-1} + a_2 Y_{t-2} + a_3 Z_t + a_4 Z_{t-1} + a_5 Z_{t-2} + a_6 X_t + a_7 X_{t-1} + a_8 X_{t-2} + a_9 R_t + a_{10} R_{t-1} + \mu \dots\dots\dots\dots\dots (3.4)$$

In equation 3.4, $X, Y, Z$ and $W$ represent the variables, $a_1$ to $a_{10}$ are coefficients to be estimated and $\mu$ is the error term. This study also employs the ARDL-bounds test approach to cointegration to estimate the long run coefficients of the models because the method imposes no restriction that all the variables must be integrated to the first order, that is, I (1). It only requires that variables are either I (0) or I (1) or both but not I (2).

Prior to estimating the econometric model, pre-tests such as stationarity and multicollinearity were carried out. Formal tests of stationarity such as the augmented Dickey-Fuller (ADF) and Phillips-Perron (PP) unit root test were used to test for stationarity. Multicollinearity was tested by the correlation matrix table of all variables. Results of the study are validated on the basis of economic (a priori) test which verify whether the sizes and signs of estimated coefficients are in line with economic theory. Also, statistical tests such as the adjusted $R^2$, t-statistics and F-ratio test are applied to determine the reliability of estimated coefficients. Lastly, econometric tests were used to verify the assumptions of the distribution of the error term such as tests for autocorrelation and Heteroscedasticity. While the VAR serial correlation LM test was used to test for autocorrelation, VAR White's Heteroscedasticity test was used for Heteroscedasticity

**Findings and Discussion**

A graphical relationship between resources depletion and GDP growth over time (presented on figure 1) in Cameroon provides a preliminary understanding of the likely effects of energy and forest depletion on growth.

**Figure 1: Relationship between energy depletion, deforestation and GDP growth, Cameroon**

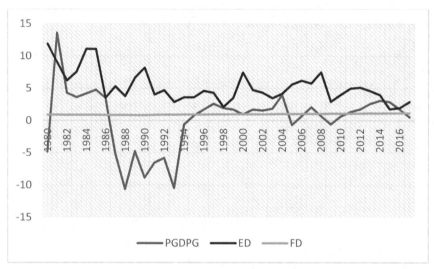

**Source: Drawn by Author from World Bank Data using Excel 2013**

From figure 1, on the average from 1980-2017, energy depletion (% of GNI) exceeds growth in GDP. In other words, the proportion of gross national income (GNI) allocated for oil and natural gas depletion exceeds the rate of economic performance on the average between 1980 and 2017, implying energy depletion is likely to hamper economic progress even in the long run as energy consumption increases. Furthermore, with the decrease in the world market price of oil in the late 1980's and the liberalization of the economy in the early 1990's, forest resources, particularly timber became a main source of foreign earnings. This has resulted in increased deforestation over time. And despite this increasing trend, economic performance has turned to lag behind especially since the 1990s.

In terms of the trend analyses of variables, real GDP and energy depletion (figure 1), human capital and trade openness (see appendix) are white noise stochastic processes with positive drift parameters, indicating they are non-stationary processes. Graphs of deforestation (figure 1) and total labour force (appendix) indicate a positive linear deterministic trend with positive drift terms. For these variables, the Hodrick-Prescott filter was applied to de-trend the series before formally testing for unit roots. Results of the ADF and PP unit root tests are presented on Table 1.

**Table 1: Augmented Dickey-Fuller and Phillips Unit Root Test Results**

| Variables | ADF Test Statistic | | | PP Test Statistic | | |
|---|---|---|---|---|---|---|
| | Test Statistic | P- Value | Remark | Test Statistic | P-Value | Remark |
| lnGDP | -3.483920 | 0.0143** | I (1) | -3.520098 | 0.0131** | I (1) |
| lnTLF | -3.058379 | 0.0387** | I (0) | -3.241839 | 0.0254** | I (0) |
| HK | -5.964966 | 0.0000* | I (1) | -5.966874 | 0.0000* | I (1) |
| lnK | -4.554411 | 0.0008* | I (1) | -4.586504 | 0.0008* | I (1) |
| lnED | -6.558109 | 0.0000* | I (1) | -10.39087 | 0.0000* | I (1) |
| FD | -3.327269 | 0.0207** | I (0) | -3.329822 | 0.0206** | I (0) |
| OPEN | -5.569752 | 0.0000* | I (1) | -5.562990 | 0.0000* | I (1) |

**\* = significant at 1%, \*\*=significant at 5%,**
**Source: Computed by Authors (2018) using Eviews 10**

The ADF and PP unit root test results of table 1 indicate that except for total labour force and deforestation which have achieved stationarity at their levels, that is I (0) processes, the rest of the variables are stationary at first difference, meaning they are I (1) processes. Prior to presenting these results, a test of multicollinearity based on the pairwise correlation matrix table (see appendix) is done. The weak correlation between all the independent variables suggests the absence of multicollinearity in the regression model. The empirical results of this study based on VAR are presented on table 2. This includes results of the economic growth model, energy depletion model and deforestation models.

## Table 2: Vector Auto regression Results

| | D(lnGDP) | D(lnED) | FD |
|---|---|---|---|
| Sample (adjusted): 1983 2017 | | | |
| Included observations: 35 after adjustments | | | |
| D(lnGDP(-1)) | 0.434463 (0.0891) | 7.962809 (0.0231) | 0.088883 (0.3945) |
| D(lnGDP(-2)) | 0.106288 (0.6455) | -0.857177 (0.7800) | 0.192486 (0.0577) |
| D(lnED(-1)) | -0.004661 (0.7956) | -0.235983 (0.3296) | -0.005562 (0.4644) |
| D(lnED(-2)) | 0.037575 (0.0422) | 0.154511 (0.5101) | 0.008596 (0.2512) |
| FD(-1) | -0.259974 (0.5987) | -0.104046 (0.9873) | 0.516864 (0.0199) |
| FD(-2) | 0.492550 (0.0996) | 2.731689 (0.4799) | 0.034596 (0.7757) |
| lnTLF(-1) | 0.838237 (0.5351) | 6.203619 (0.7292) | 3.641093 (0.0000) |
| lnTLF(-2) | 1.372351 (0.5023) | 11.80723 (0.6634) | -1.362708 (0.1220) |
| D(lnK(-1)) | 0.042421 (0.6010) | -2.987674 (0.0107) | -0.033884 (0.3243) |
| D(lnK(-2)) | 0.011298 (0.8950) | -1.073369 (0.3510) | -0.033188 (0.3609) |
| D(HK(-1)) | 0.131243 (0.6839) | 3.738971 (0.3869) | 0.122044 (0.3714) |
| D(HK(-2)) | 0.190557 (0.7021) | 6.542370 (0.3286) | 0.332817 (0.1223) |
| D(OPEN(-1)) | 0.066382 (0.5345) | 0.508692 (0.7196) | 0.060221 (0.1874) |
| D(OPEN(-2)) | -0.137948 (0.0806) | 2.782316 (0.0113) | -0.000715 (0.9821) |
| C | 0.004371 (0.3073) | -0.053022 (0.3509) | -0.004413 (0.0204) |
| **Diagnostic Tests** | | | |
| Adj. R-squared | 0.577783 | 0.307239 | 0.794637 |
| F-statistic Prob (F-statistic) | 4.323375 (0.001557) | 2.077071 (0.066021) | 10.39715 (0.000003) |
| VAR Heteroscedasticity Prob (Chi-squared) | 796.4653 (0.3707) | | |

Source: Computed by Authors (2018)

Results from the economic growth model reveal that gross domestic product (lnGDP), total labour force (lnTLF), gross fixed capital formation (lnK) and human capital development (HK) in the previous years have positive effects on current economic growth in Cameroon. Specifically, a 1% increase in labour force in the previous years would lead to an increase in economic growth by 0.8% and 1.4% respectively. Similarly, economic growth increases by 0.04% and 0.01%, 0.13% and 0.19% for a 1% increase in fixed capital formation and human capital development in the past years respectively. However, the effects of total labour force, fixed capital formation and human capital development in all the lag periods as well as gross domestic product in the lagged two-year period on current economic growth are insignificant since their p-values exceed 0.05 at 5% level of significance. Previous year economic growth has a significant effect on the current level of economic growth at 10% level of significance given a p-value of 0.08. Furthermore, energy depletion and deforestation in the previous year both have insignificant negative effects on economic growth and positive significant effects on growth in the previous two-year period. This shows that an increase in energy depletion and deforestation in the year adversely effects growth while in the previous two-year period, the effect is positive and also significant. Specifically, a 1% increase in previous year energy depletion and deforestation would reduce growth by 0.005% and 0.26% respectively while in the previous two-year period, it will increase growth by respectively 0.04% and 0.49%. Trade openness also affects growth positively in the lagged one-year period and negatively in the lagged two-year period but both effects are insignificant.

The VAR Granger causality test results for the growth model (see appendix) show significant causality from energy depletion to economic growth in Cameroon, given the p-value of the chi-square test for lnED of 0.06 which is less than 0.1 at 10% level of significance. In order words, previous year's energy depletion jointly affects economic growth significantly within the period of the study. Though no significant causality exists from labour force, gross fixed capital formation, human capital, forest depletion and trade openness to economic growth, causality test results reveal that these variables jointly affect economic growth significantly. Moreover, the VAR granger causality test results for the energy depletion and deforestation models show that significant causality runs from gross domestic product to energy depletion and deforestation respectively with p-values of 0.0451 and 0.046 respectively.

The multiple coefficient of determination for economic growth, energy depletion and forest depletion models are respectively 0.58, 0.31 and 0.79 meaning that about 58%, 31% and 79% of variations in economic growth, energy depletion and deforestation models are explained by variations in the lagged GDP, energy depletion, deforestation, total labour force, physical capital, human capital and economic openness, with the remaining 42%, 69% and 21% due to factors not included in the models. The values of the F-statistic for the economic growth, forest and energy depletion models and their p-values show that these results are reliable and can be used for policy recommendation. In addition, the p-value of VAR heteroscedasticity test (0.37) shows that the hypothesis of no heteroscedasticity in the models cannot be rejected. The results of the VAR serial correlation LM test (see appendix) also reveal the absence of autocorrelation in the estimated regression models.

To evaluate the implications of energy and forest resources depletion on long term economic growth, a long run relationship between GDP, energy depletion and deforestation was tested based on the autoregressive distributed lag approach to cointegration. The results, presented on table 3 suggest that in the long run energy and forest resources depletion has the tendency to drive economic growth positively, given that the coefficients of lnED and FD are positive and equals to 0.04 and 2.13 respectively. This finding is however still insignificant given p-values of 0.13 and 0.15 respectively, which are greater than 0.05 at 5% level of significance.

**Table 3: Long run Coefficients**

| Variable | Coefficient | Std. Error | t-Statistic | Prob. |
|---|---|---|---|---|
| lnTLF | 10.20522 | 8.997924 | 1.134175 | 0.2808 |
| HK | 0.519747 | 0.723885 | 0.717997 | 0.4877 |
| lnK | 0.718897 | 0.205946 | 3.490702 | 0.0051 |
| lnED | 0.043165 | 0.026399 | 1.635132 | 0.1303 |
| FD | 2.130159 | 1.391671 | 1.530648 | 0.1541 |
| OPEN | 0.581291 | 0.200307 | 2.901998 | 0.0144 |
| C | 0.968510 | 0.423924 | 2.284631 | 0.0432 |

**Source: Computed by Authors (2018) using Eviews 10**

The first key finding of the study is that energy depletion affects growth significantly while deforestation has an insignificant effect on growth. But in the long run, both energy depletion and deforestation have insignificant effects on growth. The increasing dependence on revenue from oil, natural gas and timber to finance development projects in the country only points to the fact that, over the years, these resources are degraded and gradually become unavailable for exploitation, hence limiting any growth that ultimately depends on it. These results are in line with the findings of Mittal and Gupta (2006) who argue that though resources contribute to a country's economic development, the current pattern of their consumption, agricultural practices and urbanization seem unsustainable and this can trigger economic downturn. The quest for developing countries to grow leads to abuse of their lands, generating pollution of all types, soil erosion, consequently leading to natural resources depletion. In addition, after evaluating the relationship between natural resources depletion, climate change and economic growth and recognizing that both marketed and non-marketed resources are important inputs in to production, Steer (2013) holds that productivity and growth is bound to fall as current patterns of resource use, agriculture and urbanization are unsustainable. Without controlling these patterns, climate change, and a decrease in productivity and economic growth would be inevitable. Furthermore, studies such as those of Kerr et al (2004), Aliyuet al (2014) and Doupé (2014), argue that though tropical deforestation is driven by the desire of people to achieve economic progress, it has detrimental effects on agricultural productivity and growth.

Another important finding of this study is that economic growth is a significant driver of both energy and forest degradation. Increased economic performance is at the expense of increased degradation of natural resources especially the non-renewable resources. This finding is in line with those of most empirical studies on the relationship between economic growth and the level of environmental degradation; even though most of them argue that the relationship is nonlinear indicating that at some point, growth cannot harm the environment. Some of these studies are those of Shafik and Bandyopadhyay (1992), Panayotou (1993), Grossman and Krueger (1995), Taguchi (2005), Kubatko (2008), Yaduma et al. (2013), Phimphanthavong (2013) and Wolde (2015) for many different types of indicators. A study by Nkwetta A. A. (2018) showed that growth will always ever lead to the depletion of natural resources using a panel data of 26 sub-Saharan African countries. Population increase as well as an increase in the level of economic activities is the main catalysts for resources depletion besides an increase in exploitation technology, excess demand and non-equitable distribution of resources.

**Conclusions**

Based on the results of this study, we conclude that energy depletion has a significant effect on economic growth in Cameroon while deforestation has an insignificant effect on growth all in the short run. In the long run, energy depletion and deforestation have an insignificant effect on growth in Cameroon. It is also concluded that economic growth significantly affects energy and forest depletion. There are therefore no prospects that the increased depletion of energy and forest resources are capable of driving Cameroon to economic emergence where it is expected to achieve a marked increase in infrastructural development, education and health thereby achieving an economic growth rate of more than 9%. However, as a source of revenue generation, its contribution towards achieving the country's long run vision cannot be undermined. For natural resources to create the expected impact on the economy, a steady depletion of energy resources and a sustainable exploitation of forest resources are first and foremost recommended to guarantee their continued existence and utilization. In addition, natural resources revenue should be continuously mobilized and directed towards productive investments in infrastructure, education and health. This cannot be achieved without ensuring that accountability and transparency are achieved in the management of resources revenue. It is also recommended that the level of economic activities should be checked to ensure that it does not exert unnecessary pressure on the natural resource base. This can be achieved by reducing activities that put more pressure on natural resources.

# References

Akinlo, A. (2012). How important is oil in Nigeria's economic growth? *Journal of Sustainable Development, 5 (4), 165-179*. Retrieved from www.ccsenet.org/jsd.

Amin, A. (1998). *Cameroon's fiscal policy and economic growth*. AERC Research paper No. 85, Nairobi: AERC

Amin, A. (2002). *Sources of economic growth in Cameroon*. African Economic Research Consortium, Nairobi, Kenya. African Economic Research Paper 116.

Arrow, J. (1962). The economic implications of learning by doing. Review of Economic Studies.

Barbier, E. (2003). The role of natural resources in economic development. *Australian Economic Papers*. Blackwell Publishing Ltd

Crafts, N. (1996). Post-neoclassical endogenous growth theory: What are its policy implications? *Oxford Review of Economic Policy*, 12(2), 30-47.

Farzanegan, M. (2013). *Oil and the future of Iran: A blessing or a curse?* Future of Iran Economy. Global Transitions.

Ghura, D. (1997). *Private investment and endogenous growth: Evidence from Cameroon*. International Monetary Fund Working paper. WP/97/65

Grossman G. and Krueger A. (1995). Economic growth and the environment. *Quarterly Journal of Economics*, 110 (2), 353-377.

IMF. (2012). Sudan. Staff report for the 2012 Article IV Consultation. IMF Country Report No. 12/298. Washington, D.C. http://www.imf.org.

Jhingan, M. (Ed.). (2009). *The economics of development and planning* (40th ed.). Vrinda Publications (P) Ltd.

Kubatko, O. (2008). *The environmental Kuznets curve: evidence from Ukraine* (Master's thesis). National University Kyiv-Mohyla Academy Economics Education and Research Consortium.

MINEPAT (2009). Cameroon, Vision 2035

Mittal, I. and Gupta, R. (2015). Natural resources depletion and economic growth in the present era. *SOCH-Mastnath Journal of Science & Technology*, 10(3).

Njimanted, G., Sama, M. and Nkwetta, A. (2016). An econometric investigation in to Financial Intermediation, Domestic Investment and Economic Growth in Cameroon. *Journal of Finance and Economics*, 4(1), 1-9.

Nour, S. S. O. M. (2011). Assessment of the impact of oil: Opportunities and challenges for economic development in Sudan. *African Review of Economics and Finance*, 2(2), 122-148.

Phimphanthavong, H. (2013). The impacts of economic growth on environmental conditions in Laos. *Int.J.Buss.Mgt.Eco.Res., 4(5), 766-774.*

Romer, M. (1986). Increasing returns and long-run growth. *Journal of Political Economy*, 94(5), 1002-1037.

Romer, D. (Ed.). (2012). *Advanced macroeconomics* (4th ed.). McGraw-Hill, New York, United States.

Selden, T. and Song, D. (1994). Environmental quality and development: Is there a Kuznets curve for air pollution emissions? *Journal of Environmental Economics and Management*, 27, 147-162.

Shafik, N. and Bandyopadhyay, S. (1992). *Economic growth and environmental quality: time series and cross section evidence.* World Bank Policy Research Working Paper, No.WPS904 Washington, DC.

Snowdon, B., & Vane, R. (2005). *Modern macroeconomics: its origins, development and current state.* Edward Elgar Publishing, UK.

Steer, A. (2014). Resource depletion, climate change, and economic growth. Towards a Better Global Economy: Policy Implications for Citizens Worldwide in the 21st Century, 381.

Taguchi, H. (2012). The environmental Kuznets curve in Asia: The case of sulphur and carbon emissions. *Asia-Pacific Development Journal*, 19 (2), 77-92.

Takebe, M. and York, R. (2011). *External sustainability of oil-producing Sub-Saharan African countries.* IMF Working Paper, WP/11/207. African Department.

Wolde, E. (2015). Economic growth and environmental degradation in Ethiopia: An environmental Kuznets curve analysis approach. *Journal of Economics and International Finance, 7(4), 72-79.*

World Bank (2018). World Bank open data. Retrieved from https://data.worldbank.org.

Yaduma, N., Kortelainen, M. and Wossink, A. (2013). The environmental Kuznets curve at different levels of economic development: A counterfactual quantile regression analysis for $CO_2$ emissions. *Economics Discussion Paper Series EDP-1322,* the University of Manchester.

# Appendix

|  | D(lnGDP) | lnTLF | D(lnK) | D(HK) | D(lnED) | FD | D(OPEN) |
|---|---|---|---|---|---|---|---|
| D(lnGDP) | 1.000000 |  |  |  |  |  |  |
| lnTLF | 0.000789 | 1.000000 |  |  |  |  |  |
| D(lnK) | 0.758658 | 0.286156 | 1.000000 |  |  |  |  |
| D(HK) | 0.243815 | -0.030138 | 0.188198 | 1.000000 |  |  |  |
| D(lnED) | 0.002722 | -0.102866 | -0.143306 | 0.310183 | 1.000000 |  |  |
| FD | 0.397432 | 0.320466 | 0.353573 | -0.193175 | -0.147174 | 1.000000 |  |
| D(OPEN) | 0.021817 | 0.142207 | 0.190458 | -0.253041 | 0.379726 | 0.084492 | 1.000000 |

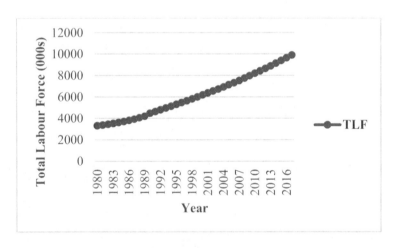

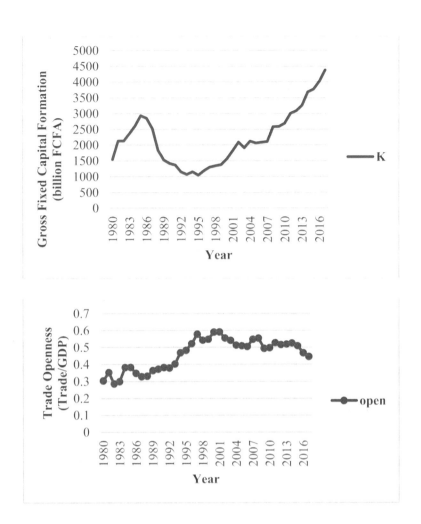

# VAR Granger Causality Test

VAR Granger Causality/Block Exogeneity Wald Tests
Date: 10/04/18 Time: 12:44
Sample: 1980 2017
Included observations: 35

Dependent variable: D(LNGDP)

| Excluded | Chi-sq | df | Prob. |
|---|---|---|---|
| TLF | 3.815717 | 2 | 0.1484 |
| D(LNK) | 0.282687 | 2 | 0.8682 |
| D(HK) | 0.251655 | 2 | 0.8818 |
| D(LNED) | 5.566092 | 2 | 0.0618 |
| FD | 3.003107 | 2 | 0.2228 |
| D(OPEN) | 3.733629 | 2 | 0.1546 |
| All | 20.42725 | 12 | 0.0594 |

Dependent variable: D(LNED)

| Excluded | Chi-sq | df | Prob. |
|---|---|---|---|
| D(LNGDP) | 6.198748 | 2 | 0.0451 |
| TLF | 1.390549 | 2 | 0.4989 |
| D(LNK) | 8.027259 | 2 | 0.0181 |
| D(HK) | 1.401495 | 2 | 0.4962 |
| FD | 0.541412 | 2 | 0.7628 |
| D(OPEN) | 7.971577 | 2 | 0.0186 |
| All | 19.57881 | 12 | 0.0755 |

Dependent variable: FD

| Excluded | Chi-sq | df | Prob. |
|---|---|---|---|
| D(LNGDP) | 6.150773 | 2 | 0.0462 |
| TLF | 71.93783 | 2 | 0.0000 |
| D(LNK) | 1.551373 | 2 | 0.4604 |
| D(HK) | 2.839167 | 2 | 0.2418 |
| D(LNED) | 2.682015 | 2 | 0.2616 |
| D(OPEN) | 1.863256 | 2 | 0.3939 |
| All | 97.03479 | 12 | 0.0000 |

# Chapter 3

## Application of Major Development Theories to Agricultural Transformation in Cameroon: Recurring Crises and Future Prospects

*Fonteh Athanasius Amungwa*

### Abstract

Development theories applied to agriculture have long advocated a break from reliance on single crop exports and imported foods and the promotion of crop diversification. The agricultural sector in Cameroon is today still underdeveloped, as the food import bill keeps rising. This paper employed archival and observational research methods to evaluate the Cameroon government's promotion of agriculture following modernization and dependency paradigms. The different challenges to agricultural transformation are rooted in the conventional linear method of agricultural research and development which believes in the generation of technologies by researchers and their transfer by extension agencies to farmers. This method has likely limitations in that the technologies may not easily translate to meaningful socio-economic benefits. Thus, an alternative construct is needed to commit economic resources to agricultural development, stressing the need to adopt a sufficiently shared vision of a desired future state in order to 'navigate' the pathway towards its attainment. This study concludes that both modernization and dependency theories have failed to transform Cameroon's agriculture positively and recommends adoption of a sustainable development path with continuous government support and protection, judicious planning, employment of qualified staff, and favourable market prices for improvement in the quality of rural life for present and future generations.

**Keywords**: Development theories, Plantation agriculture, Smallholder agriculture, Mode of production, Development poles, and Medium-sized enterprises.

## Introduction

At the opening ceremony of the Scientific Conference on Food Production and Agriculture in Africa on December 8, 1986 in Lomé, Togo, Nicholas Kittrie observed that "Europe has gone beyond post-World War II food deficiencies into food surpluses, but in Africa shortages and hunger persist" (Professors World Peace Academy, 1988, p. xii). In Europe and the USA, increasingly, declining numbers of farmers are being subsidized through their national treasuries; the many are subsidizing the few. In Africa, on the contrary, the large farming communities are not deriving sufficient benefits from their investment and work in agriculture. Indeed, it is the relatively small number of urban workers whose food needs are being subsidized through government policies that maintain low farm prices. Agriculture is the backbone of Cameroon's economy, accounting for about 32% of GDP and 75% of the employment opportunities (World Bank, 2007). Although agriculture remains the mainstay of the Cameroon economy; there has been declining contributions of this sector to the GDP in the past three decades due to gross neglect and over dependence on the oil sector and importation of food products, which could be produced at home (Amungwa, 2015). Farm production in Cameroon is inadequate, but the economic incentives for farmers to do better are also insufficient. One of the most remarkable events in the political economy of Cameroon has been the government's promotion of agro-industrial estates, believed to be good revenue generators and agents of socio-economic development (Kimengsi and Lambi, 2015). However, a critical analysis of the agricultural situation in Cameroon shows that the plantation economy has been characterized by growth that does not benefit the majority of the population but the political elite and neo-colonial interests. If development implies ensuring that the basic necessities for human survival are made available to everyone, then it is obvious

58

that the development path adopted by the post-independent state in Cameroon is yet to fully achieve its objectives.

Development is viewed as 'the nation's human resources acting on its natural resources to produce tangible and intangible goods in order to improve the condition of the average citizen of the nation-state' (Chumbow, 2005, 167). The link between Africa's domination and techno-economic backwardness did not escape the early African nationalists. The 'founding fathers' of pan-Africanism, were keenly aware of the imperatives of 'modernization' if Africa were to escape the domination and humiliation it had suffered in the hands of the West and attain 'self-reliance and independence' (Blyden, cited in Mkandawire, 2005,13). Self-reliance advocates the need for people to improve their condition using local initiatives and resources at their disposal (Fonchingong & Fonjong, 2003). The eradication of the 'unholy trinity of ignorance, poverty and disease' was a central component of the African nationalist agenda. Indeed, one of the major indictments of colonialism was its failure to provide colonies with access to knowledge and other means that were available for dealing with these issues. The objective of development in the broad sense of structural change, equity and growth was popular and internally anchored (Mkandawire, 2005, 13-14). Development also implies "movement from a set of conditions (social, material, political, cultural) defined as undesirable or detrimental to well-being to another set deemed necessary for promoting well-being" (Yenshu, 1997, 129). Amartya Sen defines development as "increasing human choices and freedom to achieve valued outcomes" (Sen, 1999, p. 291). This implies removing "unfreedoms" that leave people with little choice and little opportunity of exercising their reasoned agency (Selwyn, 2011, p. 69). Development entails some deliberate policies, strategies and actions through instruments like programmes and projects sustained by some powerful agency (Amungwa, 2013, 267). It involves putting a particular ideological orientation into action to restructure the social and economic order for desired ends. Porter et al. (2004) posit that it is based on attributes such as economic growth and enhanced freedoms, increasing incomes and material goods, redistribution of resources, empowerment, increased participation, and enhanced human rights that we could measure development.

Before annexation in 1884 by Germany, the economy of Cameroon was based on subsistence agriculture. Plantation agriculture was introduced by the Germans, to provide raw materials for European-based industries. When Germany lost the First World War (1914-1918), Cameroon was administered as a condominium by the Allied Military Forces for a brief period and partitioned by the League of Nations between France and Great Britain. In 1946 this arrangement was converted to a United Nations Trusteeship. During the colonial period, there was strong dualism between European-owned large-scale plantations and Cameroonian peasant small-holdings. Agricultural policies were closely linked to the politics of colonialism with emphasis placed exclusively on export crops. Development of the indigenous food sector received little attention or was actively discouraged because it conflicted with the labour needs of the European-owned large-scale plantations.

After independence, Cameroon directed a substantial proportion of its agricultural investment to plantation agriculture. From the late 1960s onwards, this sector became one of the main pillars of the government's agricultural policies (Courade, 1984). The Third and Fourth Five-Year Plans (1971-1981) allocated not less than about 60% of public funds for development of the agro-industrial sector (Konings, 1993). With a population of 23.3 million people, Cameroon is rated as a poor and highly indebted country (World Bank, 2015). The country has remained underdeveloped since independence, despite huge natural and human resources. The perpetuation of underdevelopment in the midst of these riches is largely blamed on the type of development politics that have been practiced" (Fomin, 2005, p. 163).

From the mid-1970s to the mid-1980s, the economy grew at about 7% per annum and achieved a per capita income of about $800, nearly two times that of most sub-Saharan African countries (Amin, 2008). This boom was short-lived as the economy slipped into a crisis in 1986 due to changes in the international economy and domestic policy environment. For more than a decade since 2001, Cameroon's poverty rate has been alternating. Poverty decreased from 40% in 2001 to 37.5% in 2014, but this decrease was more urban than rural. Urban poverty declined from 18% in 2001 to an estimated 9% in

60

2014 while rural poverty increased from 52% in 2001 to 56.8% in 2014 (World Bank, 2015). Some studies attribute this decline to poor soil nutrient conditions and to global environmental change related variables such as population growth and the inherent expansion of agricultural land through forest clearance, which results in reduced soil organic carbon and nitrogen, essential elements in crop growth (Nkamleu, 2004). Other potential causes of the decline are inadequate access to farm inputs, inadequate funding and training of extension personnel, ineffective research and extension linkages, insufficient agricultural technologies for farmers, and lack of clientele participation in development. Agriculture's central role in the economy, combined with its importance for food security and the persistence of low rural living standards make the agricultural sector a prominent focus for research. The central question that this study seeks to address is how do major development theories influence agricultural transformation in Cameroon?

The objectives of this study were thus to: i) evaluate the Cameroon government's promotion of agriculture with the help of major development theories, ii) identify the characteristics of Cameroon's agriculture and development priorities, and iii) assess the new orientations in agricultural policy.

**Theoretical framework and literature review**

Some of the salient features of Cameroon are poverty and underdevelopment, manifested at the national level by low per capita GDP, unequal income distribution, poor infrastructure, and limited use of modern technology in agriculture. Questions about the underlying causes of underdevelopment and the pathways to development elicit very different responses from social scientists. For several decades, two competing paradigms have shaped scholarly analysis of underdevelopment in developing countries. The first, modernization theory, emerged in the post-World War II as American Political Science's mainstream interpretation of underdevelopment. The second, dependency theory, offered a more radical perspective on development that is more sensitive to the concerns of African and Latin American scholars (Handelman,

2000). Each theory suggests a different path towards relieving poverty, suffering and hunger in the world.

## Modernisation Theory

Historically, pre-colonial African societies were never static and isolated systems requiring the dynamics of the colonial system in order to make progress. The people had achieved "a very high degree of integration and self-reliance in the use of local human talent and ingenuity to harness local resources to the needs and consumption habits of the population" (Mentan, 1996, p. 19). In parts of Cameroon like Oku, Babungo and Foumban, iron foundries existed and served local industries which forged tools for household use and for husbandry and hunting. Some of "the first European travellers to the Bamenda Grassfields, who have left a record of their impressions, were struck by the house-building, domestic crafts and manufactures of the area" (Chilver & Kabbery, 1967, p. 41). The people harnessed natural resources from their immediate environment communally, and nobody waited for imported European materials to secure shelter and the other basic necessities of life for their families. They practiced a variety of agricultural methods and most of the yields from oil palm, kola, shea, cocoa, coconut, rubber, banana and cotton cultivation were exchanged in inter-ethnic or distant trade (Fanso, 1989).

The treaty of Berlin, in 1878, granted any "civilized state" occupying a coastal African region, the right to claim the hinterland (Graniage, 1969, p. 199), and so the scramble for Africa had begun, with a massive outpouring of European explorers and missionaries to Africa. In 1885, the jurisdictional disputes between rival European countries over Africa were settled with the recognition of territorial claims and Africa became an integral part of the world's economic system, supplying raw materials. The European colonization of Africa brought about a paradigm shift on Africa's development trajectory and ushered in the phenomenon of 'underdevelopment' with which African countries are now preoccupied.

As the demise of European colonialism produced a host of newly independent nations in Africa and Asia, Western social scientists began to look for explanations of 'underdevelopment' characterized within the newly-independent societies by a depressing cycle of unemployment, illiteracy, diseases, and poverty. These countries had to be set on the path of "development", with the assistance of theory and empirical studies of their problems. A post-World War II vision of social change was the "developmentalist perspective" or the modernization paradigm, which held that development and economic growth were synonymous. Inversely, underdevelopment was a product of lack of capital. Consequently, to promote development meant to work towards economic prosperity by the "infusion of capital" and this, in turn would lead to industrialization.

Modernization theory explains global inequality in terms of technological and cultural differences among societies (Handelman, 2000). This development path often saw traditions as obstacles to economic growth, while assuming that, with financial and technical assistance, for instance, traditional societies can be transformed in the same manner as the more developed countries. This theory advocates the diffusion of western capital, know-how, technology and values as a necessary pre-requisite for 'development' and capital accumulation in developing countries (Long, 1977). During the 1950s and early 1960s modernization theorists, saw agricultural advancement as contributing to general economic development in four principal ways, notably by: (a) increasing the supply of food and raw materials to the urban, non-agricultural sectors; (b) providing a surplus of *capital* (through taxation and/or savings) which may then be invested in urban non-agricultural sectors, and transfer of *labour* out of agriculture into other sectors; (c) increasing foreign exchange earnings (through expanding exports) or saving foreign exchange (through import-substitution of foodstuffs and raw materials) which makes possible an increased import of capital goods for the expansion of local non-agricultural production; and (d) raising rural incomes, thus providing an expanding market for local non-agricultural sectors.

Modernization theory assumed that the potential for economic growth and hence for human development throughout the world was infinite and could be pursued by any country. In the late 1960s and early 1970s, however, several factors combined to corrode that assumption. The turn of the decade saw an end to the long period of post-war economic boom. An economic recession began to hit the industrial countries, sending reverberations throughout the developing world. The post-war economic boom which had trebled the world's industrial product had succeeded in doing so only by rapacious use of the world's natural resources (Hoogvelt, 1985). The ability to accumulate capital so as to introduce new techniques or exploit new resources is seen as one of the keys to agricultural growth. Whether agriculture is regarded as a source of capital or labour, or a growing market for industrial goods (farm tools and agro-chemicals), its transformation was seen as simply underpinning the modernization process, through capital transfer from agriculture to industry for eventual alleviation of poverty. The collusion of interests between Western capitalists and the ruling elites of the ex-colonial territories that dictated the goal of development to be economic, the adoption of Western socio-cultural and political values became agreed official policy in African countries. Modernization theory became the dominant ideology legitimating the wholesale adoption by developing countries of 'Western patent solutions to basic human needs' (Kahn, 1979, p. 54).

Most studies on Cameroon's agriculture have been written from a modernization perspective (Epale, 1985; Fossung, 2001). Epale argues that "the introduction of a modern plantation enclave in the relatively backward and inarticulate economy of Cameroon's South West region at the turn of the last century and the development of that enclave to its present state, had, in balance, a salutary effect on the economy" (ibid, p. 7). The claim was that plantations are economically efficient units of production, benefiting from considerable economies of scale and technical progress, and should be looked upon as agents of development and capital accumulation (Kimengsi et al., 2016; Goldthorpe, 1985). The government assigns a crucial role to agriculture in stimulating growth and poverty reduction. This role is articulated in a variety of political and strategic documents like the Cameroon Vision 2035, the Growth and Employment Strategy Paper and the Rural Sector Development Strategy (MINADER, 2014).

## Dependency Theory

Discontentment with modernization theory precipitated new strands of thinking which resulted in dependency theory, a development path, which locates the cause of 'underdevelopment' of developing countries, within the world capitalist system (Jeffry, 2013; Baran, 1967; Frank, 1967). Underdevelopment, it was claimed, is not an 'original state of affairs' but the result of the same world historical process through which the now developed capitalist countries became developed (Hoogvelt, 1985). From the very beginning, the dependency path has been a world-system, defined by Wallerstein as 'a single division of labour comprising multiple cultural systems, multiple political entities and even different modes of surplus appropriation' (Wallerstein, 1980, p. 5). The globe, for Wallerstein, is grouped into core nations and peripheral nations and the determining features of capitalism emphasize 'production for sale in a market to realize maximum profits' (ibid, p. 15). Appropriation of this profit is either on the basis of individual or collective ownership. Neither the development nor underdevelopment of any specific territorial unit can be analysed nor interpreted without fitting it into the trends of the world economy (Ritzer, 2007). The prosperity or poverty of any country is the product of a global economic system, in which rich nations constitute the core. Colonialism enriched this core by funnelling raw materials from around the world to Western Europe, where they fuelled the Industrial Revolution. The process continues today, through multinational corporations, which operate profitably worldwide, channelling wealth to the developed countries. Plantation agriculture in Africa is seen by dependency theorists as an agent of underdevelopment and exploitation, since it is dominated by external forces, which drain capital from the periphery. Thus, poor countries are impoverished, and the rich ones enriched by the way the poor states are integrated into the world system (Matunhu, 2011).

Samir Amin (1976) adopts both a determinist and voluntarist perspective (a world system and a national liberation approach) in his writings arguing that unequal exploitation leads to unequal exchange. For him, the prime-mover of the world system is the contradiction which capitalism has created in the periphery since the advent of imperialism, leading to rebellions which have forced world capitalism to reorganize, reaching ever higher stages of capital accumulation in the core countries. This is manifested in the simultaneous development of the production of consumer goods and of capital goods, as well as the simultaneous development of agriculture and industry. Yenshu (2018) situates Amin's research and writings within dependency theory, world systems theory, historical materialism and critical theory, which are closely related to the Marxist paradigm that held sway as a competing alternative to liberalism and modernization theory within social science.

Dependency theory has been criticized for its equation of underdevelopment with dependency on the West and world capitalist system (Bernstein & Campbell, 1985). However, it would be grossly unfair to think that Africa has always been a victim of external influence. Some African leaders have allied with developed countries to continue to exploit their natural resources, not for national development but to serve the interests of neo-colonial powers. Dependency theory has not paid enough attention to the various changes that have occurred in plantation production in the wake of transformations in the world capitalist system and the achievement of independence of colonial states. It can be observed that multinational corporations now control the capitalist world market and trade in plantation products. They also control much of the necessary processing, though they have tended to disinvest in the (risky) production of plantation crops *per se* (Barker, 1984). The post-colonial state in Cameroon has increasingly intervened in the control and stimulation of plantations and tries to integrate smallholders further into the system. In some cases, post-colonial states in Africa have taken measures that have led to either complete or partial nationalization of plantations and in other cases, they have acted as partners in joint ventures with foreign or local private capital (Bolton,1985). The Cameroon government has continued to allocate a substantial proportion of the agricultural budget to the expansion of plantation agriculture (Courade, 1984). This sector constitutes an economic stronghold that enables the ruling class to consolidate its power (Geschiere, 1986).

For dependency theorists, pre-capitalist societies tend to be destroyed or fully transformed following their incorporation into the world capitalist system. However, Binsbergen & Geschiere (1985) argue that the pre-capitalist modes of production have at least been partially preserved, albeit in subordination to the dominant capitalist mode of production. Contrary to the modernization and dependency schools, the articulation of modes of production school demonstrates the problems which accompany the subordination of pre-capitalist societies to the imperatives of capital accumulation, thus providing another picture of the impact of plantation agriculture. For Taylor (1979, p. 101), "we cannot understand the contemporary reality in underdeveloped countries unless it is analysed from within historical materialism as a social formation, dominated by an articulation of (at least) two modes of production, a capitalist and a non-capitalist mode, in which the former is, increasingly dominant over the other." This perspective has often assumed that state intervention was only required in the initial process of the articulation of modes of production, which helps to establish the supremacy of the capitalist mode of production and the ultimate subordination of the pre-capitalist mode to the imperatives of capital accumulation, supply of land, labour and raw materials. This was thought to be a more reliable trajectory of maximizing capital accumulation in the short-term and as a major device for integrating the relatively autonomous domestic communities further into the capitalist system.

## Methodology

The study area, Cameroon, lies between latitudes 2° and 13° north of the equator, extending from the Gulf of Guinea to Lake Chad over about 1,200 km and between longitude 8° and 16° east of the Greenwich Meridian and extends over a distance of 800 km at the widest portion. It has a total surface area of about 475,650 km2 (Neba, 1999; NIS, 2001). There are three main climatic zones in Cameroon: the equatorial climate extending from the coast to the Southern Plateau; the equatorial transition climate extending from the Southern Plateau (latitude 6° N) to the Adamawa Plateau; and the tropical climate extending from the Adamawa Plateau to Lake Chad. Rainfall distribution in the country is a function of the climate type.

Precipitation diminishes from a maximum of more than 9,000 mm/year in the south to less than 300 mm/year in the extreme north.

Valuable data for this study were gathered from bibliographic sources, administrative records and reports, and informal personal observations in the field, covering both small farms and the agro-industrial estates, particularly in the South West and Littoral Regions. Previous studies of other researchers from the 1960s to the 1990s and beyond on the agricultural economy in Cameroon, were reviewed in an effort to drive this analysis forward. Based on the data from documents, complemented by the field observations, this study employed content analysis to examine the issues of underdevelopment in Cameroon's agriculture. The annual reports of the CDC and the Ministry of Agriculture and Rural Development were perused to advance the research goals. Content analysis is an 'empirical method for systematic, inter-subjectively transparent description of substantial and formal features of messages' (Flick, 2011, p. 133).

## Results and Discussions

### Development theories and agricultural transformation

The Cameroon government's promotion of agriculture reveals persistent distrust of the development potential of the 'traditional sector' and its belief in the superiority of the agro-industrial sector (Henn, 1989). Although being the mainstay of Cameroon's economy, agriculture is still poorly organized and of low productivity. During the 1960s and 1970s, the state created a variety of organizations aimed at the improvement of peasant farming (Amungwa, 2015; Kamdem, 2015). With the passing of years, peasant output has been declining and this requires increased investments by the state and private sector in the modernization of smallholder agriculture. In Cameroon, modernization is about getting Cameroonians to follow the developmental path of Europe and the USA. Accordingly, agricultural modernization often consists of disseminating information about more efficient techniques of production. This involves encouraging farmers to adopt high yielding crop varieties and animal species, new production methods and marketing skills, the green house technology, genetically modified food, artificial fertilizers, insecticides, tractors and scientific knowledge in traditional agriculture (Ellis & Biggs, 2001). Experience in the diffusion of technology has shown that it is the above-average farmers, who have access to non-farm resources and capital and are able to take the risk of investing in new technology. Small farmers follow only when the technology has been well proven. The agro-industrial sector is therefore expected to be best placed to take the risks of adopting new technology. The diffusion model provides the intellectual foundation of much of the research and extension effort in farm management. Diffusion of innovations rests on the empirical observation of substantial differences in land and labour productivity among farmers and regions (Amungwa, 2017; Udemezue & Osegbue, 2017; Rogers, 2003). The route to agricultural transformation thus, is through effective dissemination of technical knowledge and a narrowing of productivity differences among farmers.

Modernization theorists attribute the political elite's option for agro-industrial expansion to the influence of western values and to pressures on the part of international development agencies and financial institutions (Dinham & Hines, 1983). Thus, development strategies and finances, packaged by the developed nations and sent to Cameroon, entrench the country more into debt and misery. The pillage of Cameroon's natural resources continues to exacerbate the poverty situation. Specialization in exporting raw materials while importing industrial products from the developed countries enables those countries get richer the more they exchange with Cameroon, which in turn gets poorer. The colonial agenda in Cameroon was impelled first and foremost by the profit motive of exploiting cheap labour and raw materials rather than a desire for socioeconomic development of the country. German, British and French colonial policies in Cameroon encouraged the economy to develop with "enclaves" or dual sectors, where one urban or rural area was heavily involved in export or cash crop production, while the rest of the country lagged far behind (Mentan, 1996). The enclave-nature of plantations creates a 'chronic dependency syndrome', which causes a few biases, including restriction of peasant expansion through the engrossment of land, and easier access to capital resources (Beckford,

1972, p. 215). Studies on the CDC support this assessment of the consequences of plantation systems for the local economy (Molua, 1985; Kimengsi *et al.*, 2016).

Dependency theorists attribute the poverty in Cameroon to the continuous pillage of resources from this satellite to the metropolis. They try to explain the continuing government support for agro-industrial expansion in terms of the political elite's vested interests in the agro-industrial sector and the latter's potential for subordinating the peasantry to the imperatives of capital accumulation (Matunhu, 2011). This argument has some backing in the Cameroonian context because the agro-industrial sector is known as one of the most illustrious fields of 'predendal politics' (Joseph, 1983). The highly privileged top positions in this sector are used by the regime in power either to reward loyal members of the political elite for services or to co-opt new members into the 'hegemonic alliance' (Bayart, 1979). Other reasons for the continued policy to expand the agro-industrial sector include: i) to diversify agricultural exports, and, consequently, the state's sources of foreign exchange; ii) to add value to agricultural raw materials by their local transformation; iii) to halt the growing importation of certain foodstuff such as wheat, rice, sugar and industrial palm oil; iv) to create employment opportunities in the rural areas and reduce the rate of rural out-migration; v) to promote a more balanced regional development pattern; and vi) to enlarge the rural base of support for the regime in power (Bates, 1981).

The economic crisis of the mid-1980s, led to reformulation of agricultural development priorities. The crisis triggered a sharp slowdown in the expansion of export crop production, due to the drastic fall in the prices of agricultural exports in the world market. In particular, the abandonment of input subsidies and the progressive withdrawal of the State from productive activity chiefly affected export crops, which had been the main beneficiaries of government assistance. Unlike the experience of other large producer countries, the coffee and cocoa yields in Cameroon have declined. In the early 1990s, many African countries adopted the Structural Adjustment Programme (SAP), imposed by the World Bank and IMF. SAPs were founded on neo-liberal orthodoxy, which prioritized economic liberalization (Amin, 2008; IFAD, 2007; FAO, 2014). Its outcomes in many African countries have been generally disappointing. Deterioration of the economic situation in Cameroon has transformed the country from a medium to a low income country (Kamgnia & Timou, 1999). The idea of modernization, associated with development aid, was borrowed from the Marshall Plan of the post-World War II era. Apparently, aid can be negotiated either bilaterally or multilaterally, but it must be noted that, aid (except humanitarian aid) has strings attached to it and tends to benefit the metropolitan states more than the recipient countries. Consequently, there has to be a paradigm shift if Cameroon is to reclaim its right to chart a new development path.

## Characteristics of agriculture and development priorities

Two broad farming systems characterize Cameroon's agriculture. These include the smallholder/family farm system and the plantation or agro-industrial system. The family farms are generally less than 2 ha, and represent 80% of all farms, and contribute up to 90% of the production (MINADER, 2010; Amungwa, 2013). On the family farms, food and cash crops are combined with livestock like fowls, pigs, sheep and goats, and cattle are also raised. Where farm sizes are large the people generally go beyond the use of family labour to employ the work-group system, a useful practice for enhancing cooperative endeavours in agriculture.

The agro-industrial sector differs from the family farms in the way in which factors of production are combined. The system employs a relatively large number of unskilled labourers and specializes in the production of a few marketable products like tea, rubber, oil palms, and bananas. Agro-industrial enterprises provide social amenities like housing, schools and healthcare. The system is characterized by an industrialized management system involving specialized management methods, and production systems, well-defined responsibilities and close delineation of purpose, hierarchical authority and a supervised labour force (Graham & Floering, 1984). The agro-industrial sector in Cameroon may be differentiated according to the organization of commodity production. The Cotton Development Authority and the Rice Development Company in the

Far North Region rely exclusively on peasant production. The CDC relies predominantly on large-scale plantations (Abina, 1989). CDC has estates in the South West, the Littoral, West and North West Regions, and employs about 22,431 workers, the second largest employer in Cameroon after the government (Kimengsi & Lambi, 2015).

A second characteristic of plantation agriculture is its predominant location in the coastal region. Plantations usually require extensive land, and the Cameroonian government has been faced with the problem of selecting vast lands in those regions suitable for plantation agriculture with easy access, particularly to the railways. The policy has been to select lands in lowly populated areas so as to forestall the large-scale expropriation of peasant lands, except the case of Djuttisa Tea Estate, located in the densely populated West Region, which may foreshadow future developments (Konings, 1986b).

A third characteristic is that plantation agriculture is either wholly or partially owned by the state. The Cameroon government seeks to establish a certain degree of state control over the operations of multinationals in the country by advocating state participation in these enterprises. This policy has stifled multinational investment in plantation production as it poses a problem to the 'free movements' of foreign capital (Courade, 1984). While the government has always strongly encouraged foreign investments, it has never made it a secret that it will not allow foreign partners to set up autonomous industrial and commercial enterprises which operate outside the scope of the state. The government's participation is affected directly through parastatal organizations like the National Investment Corporation and the National Social Insurance Fund. The Oil Palm Company - SOCAPALM's share capital is divided between the government (76%), the National Produce Marketing Board (18%), and the National Investment Corporation (6%) (Agbor, 1982; Konings, 1993). Although state officials continue to portray Cameroon as being primarily an agricultural country, there is increasing dependence on oil revenues, which account for more than 60% of foreign earnings.

The state has been compelled to resort to external borrowing from financial institutions like the World Bank, the Commonwealth Development Corporation, the European Development Fund, and the European Investment Bank in order to proceed with the costly expansion of the agro-industrial sector, and this has increased Cameroon's external debt considerably (Dessouane & Verre, 1986). It was once hoped that average productivity would increase if enough state-run agricultural enterprises were created, since these would utilize modern technology and trained personnel. However, whilst it is true that in certain areas like palm oil and sugar cane, the productivity of land and labour is indeed higher, it remains a fact that returns on capital is very low, despite a huge level of investment. The state-owned enterprises have a deleterious effect on peasant farming since they divert resources from it, and uproot the peasants themselves, turning them into simple labourers (Konings, 1993). Fewer than 50,000 jobs have been created in the agro-industrial enterprises and the kind of employment has been largely unskilled and semi-skilled. Such employment attracts particularly the young, uneducated men from the densely populated and marginalized areas of Cameroon. The contribution of the agro-industrial sector to total domestic agricultural output and the creation of employment opportunities have remained marginal, and failed in substituting national products for food imports (Willame, 1986). Wages on the plantations are usually insufficient to raise the living standards in rural areas and to modernize production techniques. Low productivity and high costs of production make it impossible for Cameroon's agro-industrial enterprises to compete with foreign imports in the domestic market and problems have been aggravated by low prices for exports in the world market (Ndzana, 1987). Plantations have hardly been subject to technological innovations and have largely preserved their labour-intensive production techniques (de Silva, 1982).

A considerable proportion of the surplus extracted from the peasantry by the National Produce Marketing Board has never been used for the stabilization of producer processes and the industrial sector (Jua, 1986; Henn, 1989). Government priorities have shifted to the introduction of smallholders' schemes in the agro-industrial sector although their scope has remained limited. The CDC and SOCAPALM began to develop 2,000 hectares of rubber and oil palm smallholder plantations in 1977 and were joined by the Cameroon Rubber Corporation, whose programme (1979-1985) included trials of 250 hectares of smallholder rubber. The expansion of the agro-industrial sector activities has been sometimes questioned. Yet, the government has continued to supply large annual subsidies and grants to the parastatals and agro-industrial enterprises, irrespective of their economic performance. Total public subsidies and grants to the state enterprises attained FCFA 150 billion (US $272.7 million) in 1984, representing 50 % of public oil revenues and 18% of total public expenditure during that same year (Konings, 2011; 1993).

Since the mid-1980s the Cameroon government has strongly encouraged the setting-up of private medium-sized plantations in the hope that these will not only capture an important intermediate position between peasant farms and agro-industrial enterprises, but also create new economic outlets for the elite population (Bates, 1981). This programme was launched during the 1985/86 Budget to encourage the elite to participate in modern farming. It was boosted by the government through the supply of land, free extension services, and special credit facilities, channelled through the National Fund for Rural Development, which reserved FCFA 27, 680 million (US $50,181) for the scheme during the Sixth Five-Year Plan (1986-1991).

One of the beneficiaries of this policy remarked: *"...I was able to acquire up to 60 hectares of land in Nwa sub-Division in Donga Mantung, to invest in oil palm cultivation..."* It is still not clear whether this approach to farm modernization through the provision of subsidies and credit for the establishment of medium scale farms (US $5, 000 per hectare), could be replicated on a wider scale. Modernization strategies based on the establishment of large and medium-sized plantations are bound to have a merely marginal impact on overall output in a peasant environment. A strategy based on the modernization of peasant agriculture may not be in the *short-term* interest of the political elite when one takes into consideration the direct benefits that it may enjoy from promoting large-scale and medium-sized plantations. However, it may well be in their *long-term* interest for several reasons, such as, the need to hold down the wage-costs, expand domestic markets, foreign exchange earnings, and to constrain out-migration from the rural areas.

In 1987 the government announced its intention to 'restructure' state-owned companies and to privatize a number of them. The policy adopted was to close the non-viable ones, sell some of the viable ones to private investors, and to retain only the key companies. A national ad-hoc committee was set up to investigate the public sector along these policy lines. Some parastatals were dissolved, including two agro-industrial parastatals: the Cameroon Banana Organization (CBO) and the Wheat Development Agency. The role of the CBO in the banana sector was then taken over by two multinationals, namely the French *Compagnie Fruitiere* and Del Monte with headquarters in the USA to which the CDC management entrusted in 1987 the development of 1,200 ha of banana plantations in the Tiko Plain (Abina, 1989; CDC, 2005).

In 1991, the Rural Development Poles Programme was launched in three regions of Cameroon with the aim to increase agricultural production, improve living standards, halt rural depopulation and reinforce the organizational capacity of village communities. Inspired by the "growth poles theory" (Perroux, 1971), this programme was meant to put together various economic forces, and provide conditions for development. An experimental phase of the programme started as the Bafut Village Community Project, implemented as a sub-component of the North West Development Authority, in the 1980s. This resulted to the decision to replicate the strategy in Saa and Ntui, in the Centre Region, Sangmelima in the South Region, plus a new phase of Bafut in the North West Region. Placing agriculture as the basis of rural development, the project sought to increase productivity and achieve food self-sufficiency. Road infrastructure, education and health facilities were expanded to trigger a chain reaction in associated services with the ultimate goal of improving the quality of rural life. For 4 years (1991-1997) these development poles were continually provided with investment funds from the European Union to achieve the aims of self-sustained growth and development. When foreign assistance for the project ended, the experience was never replicated elsewhere, perhaps because the theory fosters autonomy and decentralization in decision-making which does not augur well with the Cameroon government's entrenched practice of centralization.

**New orientations in agricultural policy**

Beginning in 2008, the government launched a programme Supporting Family Farming Competitiveness, aimed at implementing an advisory support approach to Family-Owned Agro-pastoral Businesses and to Agricultural Professional Organizations coupled with financing of projects headed by these organizations. The pilot phase of this programme which was rolled out in ten divisions across five regions (Adamawa, North, West, South-West and South), provided the opportunity to fine-tune methods and tools, and finance a number of projects. The projected amount for Phase 1, which ended on July 31, 2012, was FCFA14.16 billion (US \$25.7 million). Phase 2 of the programme, launched on August 1, 2013 for a period of four years, extended the programme to all ten regions of the country (MINADER, 2014).

Despite the continental increased emphasis on small-scale agriculture, Cameroon has not regained food sovereignty because the government gives low priority to investing in rural infrastructure and services that are essential for reducing transaction costs in farming (Fantu & Modi, 2013). In principle, Cameroon is committed to developing its agricultural sector. The terms of Cameroon's agricultural development strategy were given a boost by the New Partnership for Africa's Development's Comprehensive Africa Agricultural Development Programme (CAADP). The government signed and ratified the CAADP on July 17th 2013, an act that committed it to spending 10% of national expenditures on agriculture. The CAADP 10% expenditure target is yet to be met as Cameroon's agricultural spending in 2013 only stood at 6.8%. Cameroon has also not been able to meet the CAADP annual increase of agricultural productivity by 6%. CAADP is Africa's policy framework for agricultural transformation, wealth creation, food security and nutrition, economic growth and prosperity (Diao et al., 2012).

In April 2014, Cameroon adopted a seven year (2014-2020) National Agricultural Investment Plan with the aim of investing about FCFA 3.35 trillion (US $6.09 billion) in four priority areas, which include: (i) the agricultural sector (plants, livestock, fisheries and forestry); (ii) production infrastructure in rural areas and improved mechanisms for access to finance; (iii) sustainable management of natural resources; and (iv) Capacity building and promotion of collaboration among stakeholders (MINEPAT, 2009). Formulated for long-term development, the country's Vision 2035, has the overall objective to make Cameroon an emerging country within the next generation (25-30 years).

## Conclusions and Policy Implications

This study has tried to evaluate the Cameroon government's support of agricultural transformation, with the help of modernization and dependency theories. The evidence shows that the optimistic view of modernization theory on agro-industrial expansion has not met with success. The government's investments in this sector have not led to the expected increase in agricultural output and capital accumulation. On the contrary, its performance and profit-earning capacity has been in doubt leading to the decision to privatize some companies. Few analysts accept either modernization or dependency theories in their entirety. In fact, the very idea of a single development path for a multi-cultural world is untenable. Firstly, because it is now apparent that developing nations are too diverse to be encompassed by a single development theory. Secondly, because the socioeconomic development processes, even in a particular region or nation, are far too complex to be explained by a single theory. However, this does not mean that the insights offered by modernization and dependency theories have not been useful. The government's agricultural policies have never been rigid because it has promoted agro-industrial expansion while also providing support to smallholder agriculture through extension services. Moreover, it has embarked upon a new strategy of agricultural modernization which aims at establishing private, medium-sized plantations and also supporting family-owned agro-pastoral businesses. It has also aligned its agricultural development policy with orientations of the Comprehensive Africa Agriculture Development Programme. In recent years, policy has shifted from an emphasis on "development strategies" promoting agro-industrial expansion towards smaller-scale project interventions, to fix market failures and address problems of poverty relying more on various agricultural extension services. For agricultural growth and development to be sustained, there must be continuous increase in farm output, downstream linkages with industry, upstream linkages in demand for farm inputs, and transfers of labour and capital to other sectors, as labour productivity rises in agriculture. These things do not happen in a plantation economy, largely because most of the linkages are with an external economy.

This study has noted that the underdevelopment of Cameroon is indeed a result of cultural collusion between the development trajectories of the Western powers and those of Cameroon. The former, because of their strategic and technological advantage over Cameroon, has choked and subdued Cameroon's indigenous development path. The journey to genuine emancipation from this dependency syndrome requires a radical approach, which takes Cameroonians to be part of the development problem as well as being part of the solution to its underdevelopment. The Cameroonian experience with agricultural transformation proves to some extent that the promotion of capital-intensive agricultural development projects is unlikely to be successful unless continuous government support and protection, judicious planning, qualified staff, and favourable market prices are provided. Interrogating Cameroon's underdevelopment paradox should bother scholars and development planners who are genuinely concerned about the situation of this resource rich-poor country.

The Cameroon underdevelopment paradox, however, is that this is a country with strong agricultural potentials that engender hope, but whose resources have been plundered and badly exploited. An understanding of development paths is critical to our evaluation of economies in sharp decline amidst efforts to reduce poverty and the vast "inequalities" between rich and poor nations and between rich and poor people within African countries.

# References

Abina, F. (1989). 'De l'Independence a la dépendance: Etude de l'évolution des relations sociales de production dans le secteur agricole camerounais de 1960 à 1987. In: P. Geschiere and P. Konings (Eds.), *Proceedings/contribution of the conference on the political economy of Cameroon-Historical perspectives* (249-277). Leiden: African Studies Centre.

Agbor, M. (1982). *Foreign participation in the agro-industrial sector in Cameroon: The case of SOCAPALM 1968-1981.* (M.A. Thesis). University of Yaoundé, International Relations Institute of Cameroon.

Amin, A. (2008). *Developing a sustainable economy in Cameroon.* Council for the Development of Social Science Research in Africa [CODESRIA], Dakar.

Amin, S. (1976). *Unequal development: An essay on the social formations of peripheral Capitalism.* New York: Monthly Review Press.

Amungwa, A. (2017). Revisiting Chayanov's theory of the peasant household economy:

Relevance to smallholder agriculture, *University of Buea Journal of Applied Social Sciences,* 10 (1), 130-142.

Amungwa, A. (2015). A sociological appraisal of state-driven rural development programmes and economic self-reliance in Cameroon. *Global Journal of Agricultural Economics, Extension and Rural Development,* 3 (9), 308-316.

Amungwa, A. (2013). *Rural sociology: An African perspective.* Yaoundé, Grassroots Publishers Ltd.

Baran, P. (1967). *The political economy of growth,* New York, Monthly Review Press.

Barker, J. (Ed.). (1984). *The politics of agriculture in tropical Africa.* Beverly Hills, SAGE.

Bates, H. (1981). *Markets and states in tropical Africa: The political basis of agricultural Policies.* Berkeley, LA: University of California Press.

Beckford, L. (1972). *Persistent poverty: Underdevelopment in plantation economies of the third world.* New York: Oxford University Press.

Bernstein, H. and Campbell, B. K. (Eds.). (1985). *Contradictions of accumulation in Africa: studies in economy and state*, Beverley Hills: SAGE.

Binsbergen, W. and Geschiere, P. (Eds.). (1985). *Old modes of production and capitalist encroachment: Anthropological Explorations in Africa.* London: Kegan Paul.

Cameroon Development Corporation. (CDC) (2005). An agro-industrial company, *CDC Cameroon Private policy.*

Chilver, M. and Kabbery, M. (1967). *Traditional Bamenda: The precolonial history and ethnography of the Bamenda grassfields.* Buea.

Chumbow, S. (2005). The language question and national development in Africa. In: T. Mkandawire (Ed.), *African intellectuals: Rethinking politics, language, gender and development.* Dakar: CODESRIA.

Courade, G. (1984). Des complexes qui coûtent cher: La priorité agro-industrielle dans l'agriculture Camerounaise. *Politique Africaine,* 14: 75-91.

Dessouane, P. and Verre, P. (1986). Cameroun: du dévelopement autocentré au national-Liberalism. *Politique Africaine,* 22: 111-119.

Diao, X, Thulow, J., Benin, S. & Fan, S. (Eds.). (2012). *Strategies and priorities for African agriculture.* International Food Policy Research Institute, Washington, DC.

Dinham, B. and Hines, C. (1983). *Agribusiness in Africa: A study of the impact of big business in Africa's food and agricultural production.* London: Earth Resources Research Ltd.

Ellis, F. and Biggs, S. (2001). Development Policy Review, 19(4): 437-448.

Epale, S. J. (1985). *Plantations and development in West Cameroon.* New York: Vantage.

Fanso, G. (1989). *Cameroon History.* London: MacMillan.

Fantu, C. and Modi, R. (2013). *Agricultural development and food security in Africa: The impact of Chinese, Indian & Brazilian Investments.* London: Zed.

FAO. (2014). *The state of food insecurity in the world 2014.* Rome: FAO, WFP, IFAD.

Flick, U. (2011). *Introducing research Methodology.* Los Angeles: Sage.

Fomin, D. (2005). Traumas, memories and modern politics in Central Africa. In: E. Fomin, & W. Forje (Eds.). *Central Africa: Crises, reform and reconstruction* (pp. 157-174). Dakar: CODESRIA.

Fonchingong, and Fonjong, L. (2003). The concept of self-reliance in community development initiatives in the Cameroon grassfields. *Nordic Journal of African Studies 12(2): 196–219.*

Fossung, W. (2001). The role of plantation agriculture in regional development: The case of the Cameroon Development Corporation. In: C. Lambi, & B. Eze (Eds.). *Readings in Geography.* Unique Printers: Bamenda.

Frank, G. (1967). *Capitalism and underdevelopment in Latin America.* New York/London: Monthly Review Press.

Gagne-Gervais, C. (1984). *Cameroon-The cash crop sector: Its performance and future development possibilities.* Yaoundé: USAID.

Graham, E. & Floering, I. (1984). *The modern plantation in the third world.* London/Sydney: Croom Helm.

Geschiere, P. (1986). *Hegemonic regimes and popular protest – Bayart, Gramsci, and the state in Cameroon.* Cahiers du CEDAF 2/3/4: 309-347.

Golthorpe, E. (1985). *The sociology of the third world: Disparity and development.* Cambridge: Cambridge University Press.

Handelman, H. (2000). *The challenge of third world development.* 2nd Edition. New Jersey: Prentice Hall.

Henn, K. (1989). Food policy, food production, and the family farm in Cameroon', Geschiere and P. Konings (Eds.), *Proceedings/contribution of the conference on the political economy of Cameroon-Historical perspectives* (531-555). Leiden: African Studies Centre.

Hoogvelt, M. (1985). *The Third World in Global Development.* Basingstoke: MacMillan Publishers.

International Fund for Agricultural Development. (IFAD). (2007). The Republic of Cameroon: country strategic opportunities programme. Executive Board, Rome.

Jeffry, E. (2013). Dependency theory and Africa's underdevelopment: a paradigm shift from pseudo-intellectualism: the Nigerian Perspective. *International Journal of African and Asian Studies*, Vol.1.

Joseph, A. (1983). Class, state and prebendal politics in Nigeria. *The Journal of Commonwealth and Comparative Politics,* 21 (3), 21-38.

Jua, N. (1986). *Economic management in resource-rich countries: A case study of the post-imperial state in Cameroon.* Yaoundé: MESRES/ISH.

Kahn, H. (1979). *World economic development, 1979 and beyond.* Boulder, Col.: Westview Press.

Kamgnia, D. and Timnou, P. (1999). *Poverty in Cameroon: Evolution in an economic adjustment environment.* Interim Report to the African Economic Research Consortium, May, 1999.

Kamndem, E. (2015). Reviving cooperatives: International and regional instruments for promoting cooperatives in the XXIst century. In: E. Kamndem (Ed.), *Pan-Africanism, research, peace and concerted development in Africa* (pp. 215-241) Geneva/Yaoundé: Presses de l'Institut Panafricain pour le Developpement.

Kimengsi, N., Lambi, M. & Gwan, A. (2016). Reflections on the role of plantations in development: Lessons from the Cameroon Development Corporation. *Sustainability in Environment, 1 (1).*

Kimengsi, N., & Lambi, M. (2015). Pamol plantations Plc: Prelude to a looming

Population problem in Ekondo Titi Sub-Division, South West Region of Cameroon. *Journal of Sustainable Development in Africa, 17*(3), 79-94.

Konings, P. (2011). *Crisis and neoliberal reforms in Africa: Civil society and agro-industry in Anglophone Cameroon's plantation economy.* Bamenda: Langaa Research Publishers.

Konings, P. (1993). *Labour resistance in Cameroon.* African Studies Centre: Leiden.

Konings, P. (1986). L'état, l'agro-industrie et la paysannerie au Cameroun. *Politique Africaine,* 22, 120-137.

Long, N. (1977). *An introduction to the sociology of rural development.* London: Tavistock Publications Ltd.

Matunhu, J. (2011). A critique of modernization and dependency theories in Africa: Critical assessment. *African Journal of History and Culture,* 3 (5), 65-72.

Mentan, T. (1996). The political economy of regional imbalances and national "Unintegration" in Cameroon. In: P. Nkwi and F.

Nyamnjoh (Eds.), *Regional balance and national Integration in Cameroon* (pp. 17-28). Leiden: African Studies Centre

Mkandawire, T. (Ed.). (2005). African Intellectuals and Nationalism. In T. Mkandawire (Ed.), *African intellectuals: Rethinking politics, language, gender and development* (pp. 10-55). Dakar: CODESRIA.

MINADER- Ministry of Agriculture and Rural Development (2014). *Basic agricultural public expenditure diagnostic review (2003–12)*. Republic of Cameroon.

MINADER- Ministry of Agriculture and Rural Development (2010). *Rural development strategy document.* Yaoundé: MINADER.

MINEPAT - Ministry of Economy, Planning and Regional Development (2009*). The Cameroon growth and employment strategy paper (2010-20 GESP).* Yaoundé: MINEPAT.

Molua, N. (1985). *The Bakweri land problem 1884-1961: A Case Study.* (M.A. Thesis). University of Ibadan.

Ndzana, O. (1987). *Agriculture, pétrole et politique au Cameroun: Sortir de la crise?* Paris: Ed L'Harmattan.

NIS (National Institute of Statistics). (2001). *Cameroon statistical yearbook 2000.* Ministry of the Economy and Finance, Yaoundé.

Nkamleu, B. (2004). Productivity, growth and technical progress and efficiency in African agriculture. *African Development Review*, 1 (16), 203-222.

Perroux, F. (1971). Notes on the concept of growth poles. In: I. Livingstone (Ed.), *Economic policy for Development* (pp. 279-89). Harmondsworth: Penguin,

Potter, B., Binns, T., Elliot, J., & Smith, D. (2004). *Geographies of development* (2nd ed.). Harlow, Pearson Prentice Hall.

Professors World Food Academy (1988). *Food production and agriculture in Africa*, Athens: Foundation Publishing Company.

Ritzer, G. (2007). *Contemporary sociological theory and its classical roots.* 2nd Edition. Boston: McGraw-Hill.

Rogers, M. (2003). *Diffusion of innovations* (5th ed.), New York: Free Press.

Selwyn, B. (2011). Liberty limited? A sympathetic re-engagement with Amartya Sen's development as freedom. Economic and Political Weekly. VXLVI: 37.

Sen, A. (1999). *Development as freedom*. New York. Oxford University Press.

Silver, B. (1982). *The Political economy of underdevelopment*. London: Routledge & Kegan Paul.

Taylor, J. (1979). *From modernization to modes of production*. London: Macmillan.

Udemezue, C. & Osegbue, G. (2018). Theories and models of agricultural development. *Annals of Reviews and Research*, 1(5).

Wallerstein, I. (1980). *The capitalist world economy*. Cambridge: Cambridge University Press.

Willame, C. (1986). The practices of liberal political economy: Import and export substitution in Cameroon (1975-1981). In: Schartzberg and Zartman (111-132).

World Bank (2015). *Africa's pulse: An analysis of issues shaping Africa's economic future*. Vol 11. Washington DC: The World Bank.

World Bank (2007). *World development report 2008: Agriculture for development.*

Washington, DC: The World Bank.

Yenshu, E. (2018). In Memoriam: Samir Amin 1931-2018. *University of Buea Journal of Applied Social Sciences*, 11(2), 4-5.

Yenshu, E. (1997). Balanced rural development in Cameroon within a democratic context. In: P. Nkwi and F. Nyamnjoh (Eds.), *Regional balance and national integration in Cameroon: Lessons learned and the uncertain future* (pp.129-137). Leiden: African Studies Centre.

# Chapter 4

## Evaluating Extractive Sector Corporate Social Investments in Cameroon: The Front and Backend Activities Methodological Proposition

*Yungong, Theophilus Jong*

**Abstract**

This study sets out to exemplify the front and backend activities framework for evaluating effective Corporate Social Investments (CSI) in Cameroon. It questions the circumstances under which CSI will be expected to effectively contribute to development in the country. CSI are voluntary programs aimed at enhancing the welfare of host countries and communities to extractive firms. The underlying premise of this paper is that the potential for CSI to do this depends on the extent to which it is effectively integrated into the business operations of extractive firms and monitored for results. By building on some methods used in project evaluation, this paper develops and advances the suggested approach using the novel concepts of CSI applicability and CSI effectiveness.

**Keywords**: Extractive Sector, CSI, CSR, Results-based evaluation

## Introduction

This paper sets out to advance the front and the back-end activities approach to evaluating effective extractive sector Corporate Social Investments (CSI) in Cameroon. The relevance of this proposition is being considered at a time when previous research suggests that CSI is only amateurishly and passively integrated in the business operations of extractive firms working in the country. CSI is designated here as voluntary programs within the wider area of Corporate Social Responsibility (CSR) aimed at maximizing

85

development opportunities and value retention for host countries and communities to extractive firms. While it has become a popular claim among extractive firms in Cameroon, there is very weak evidence to show that CSI are effectively conceived and implemented as to contribute to more effective development outcomes. The bone of contention, therefore, is: under what circumstances can extractive sector CSI effectively contribute to development in Cameroon? How can it be evaluated?

This study premises that the potential for CSI to contribute to effective development outcomes depends on the extent to which it is effectively integrated into the business operations of extractive firms and monitored for results. Some methods of CSI integration have been suggested in the literature. This study does not discard them. It builds on these ideas using the novel concepts of CSI applicability and CSI effectiveness and incorporates the notion of results-based, as opposed to activity-based CSI, to develop and to advance the front and back-end activities CSI evaluation framework. By using this approach, multinational companies and development stakeholders in Cameroon, will be able to standardize, determine and reward effective CSI efforts. This is not only in terms of inputs and activities, but most importantly, in terms of outcomes and impact of social investments. This paper is divided into four main sections.

The first section presents an overview of the idea of CSI as retained in this study. This includes a justification and critique of extractive sector CSI. The second section develops and advances the concept of CSI applicability and CSI effectiveness as the main building block to the front and backend activities approach. It covers the main pathways and principles of CSI effectiveness. The third section advances the front and back-end activities proposition based on the preliminary ideas indicated above. The three phases of this approach, its results-based component and its application are covered. The fourth section attempts to compare the front and back-end approach to other approaches in the literature.

## The idea of CSI and CSR

The concept of CSI as used in this study is drawn from CSR. The definitions of both concepts are contestable thereby making it hard to arrive at a definition that satisfies everyone. Nonetheless, the working definition of CSI/CSR in this paper relates to the concepts of charity and philanthropy. They are inspired by Bowen (1953) who maintained that the idea of business cannot be justified by profits alone but also by how much it responds to societal needs – helping it attain more fully, the economic goals society seeks to achieve. While the idea of profit-driven business has achieved this through the market system, its unprecedented riches and opportunities coexist with untold poverty and deprivation (Sachs, 2015; Maddison, 2006). They are disproportionately shared among 'the haves' and 'the haves not' with the majority of resource-rich African countries being the hardest hit (Collier, 2007). While the responsibility of making resources work for development remains the main responsibility of the state and other mainstream development actors, the CSR/CSI debate in this study maintains that development has become a shared responsibility by all societal actors who either are part of the solution or part of the problem to the development challenge in sub-Saharan Africa.

Based on a review of varied definitions of CSR this study designates CSR a range of activities by the modern business corporation to articulate wider societal good and to contribute to mainstream development work in ways that are considered socially, economically and environmentally sustainable (Dahlsrud, 2008; Watts and Holme, 2000). Key issues in the wider area of CSR include engaging in corporate community development programmes, implementing sound environmental practices, respecting national laws, instituting good labour practices and workplace safety measures and providing quality products to customers. CSI in this study follows from the notion of corporate community development (IFC, 2010). It covers activities intended to enhance inclusive development outcomes for target groups and communities. These should ensure or show a strong potential for ensuring considerable qualitative and quantitative improvements in their welfare. For CSI to be considered effective it has to move beyond an activity-based venture to build community relations (CSI applicability), to a process that significantly addresses community development needs to the satisfaction of all development stakeholders (CSI effectiveness).

## Cameroon's resource-development paradox

Cameroon is home to mineral resources that are indispensable to everyday life in a modern economy. With just 40 percent of the land explored, Cameroon has a significant abundance of gold, diamonds, bauxite, iron ore, marble, crude oil, natural gas, cobalt and nickel (MINMITD, 2013; NHC, 2016). However, Cameroon, like other African countries, is faced with the challenge of having its vast stores of natural resource wealth deliver adequate sustainable economic opportunities to its citizens. These failures lend greater credence to the natural resource curse theory: a situation where resource-rich countries are said to be falling behind in their development process compared to less resource-dependent countries. (Barma et al., 2012)

Cameroon still relies heavily on development assistance and foreign loans to support basic development needs. It comes at the bottom place of global competitiveness, with significant underperformance in the provision of social services and infrastructure (Schwab, 2014). Extreme poverty figures have barely improved from the 39 percent prevalence rate recorded in 2007 (MINEPAT and UN, 2013). These figures are higher for the rural areas and for resource-rich regions such as the East and South – ranging from 45 to above 50 percent (ibid). In the same way, the oil-rich Rio Del Rey basin which provides more than 90 percent of Cameroon's petroleum lacks basic social infrastructure and good road networks (Nting, 2010). Child malnutrition and mortality rates are high - respectively reaching as high as 25 percent and 163 per thousand in the northern regions (MINEPAT and UN, 2013). Overall maternal mortality stands at 590 per thousand compared to the world average of 210 per thousand (WBG, 2015).

In fact, Cameroon significantly underperforms in international development indices. This situation has been aggravated by acute shortage of sustainable economic opportunities and critical assets required to overcome the challenges of fairly distributing the fruits of growth. This makes it a typical "bottom billion country" – one that is not only "falling behind" in its development process but is also caught in a development trap (Collier, 2007). It highlights a mismatch between resources and development and leaves development stakeholder with the important question of how to transform CSI into a viable development contributor in the country.

## Cameroon's CSI landscape: key actors and recent contributions[2]

As of 2012, Cameroon counts 22 major extractive companies of which 5 are involved in mining and mining-related activities. Of all these companies, two are nationally owned - the National Hydrocarbons Corporation (NHC) which manages state interests in upstream oil and gas operations, the CAPAM, a Ministry of Mines, Industries and Technological Development project charged with the coordination and promotion of artisanal mining activities in the country. Another unlisted exceptions are the Cameroon Oil Refining Company (SONARA) and Société Camerounaise des Dépôts Pétroliers (SCDP) which manage mid-stream state interest in petroleum refining. Major Private Multinationals include Bowleven Oil & Gas, Addax Petroleum and LAFARGE-CIMENCAM, Sundance Resource Limited, Kosmos Energy, Perenco Oil & Gas, Noble Energy, Glencore Geovic, Mining Corp and Dana Petroleum.

In line with modern business practices, these companies show some level of adherence to the discretionary idea of CSI (Boubakary, 2016; Foumena, 2013). Some of them have committed considerable material and financial resources to the pursuit of CSI. For example, in 2012, social contributions stood at 269.7 Million FCFA (close to 540 000 USD) - 70 percent of which were reckoned to be voluntary and 30 percent obligatory (Moore Stephens, 2014). These contributions rose to 343.14 Million FCFA (about 686 282 USD) in 2013; 65 percent of which was voluntary and 35 percent obligatory.

---

[2] Findings from study, Yungong, T.J., (2017). Evaluating the Development Potential of Extractive Sector Corporate Social Investments in Cameroon: Case of the Oil and Gas & Mining Sub Sectors, (Thesis, NMMU –PE SA)

This represented an increase of 73.40 Million (146 282 USD) during that period (Yungong, 2017). This shows some considerable level of generosity. Companies also tend to have clearly focused areas of CSI intervention - predominantly in education, health and provision of basic infrastructure. This matches observations by Frynas (2008) that these CSI focus areas are common with extractive sector firms (Frynas, 2008; Foumena, 2013).

**Key trends and practices in extractive sector CSI in Cameroon**

A critical review of company reports shows several weaknesses in the way companies integrate CSI in their business operations. The majority of extractive companies show no clear proof of effective CSI strategic frameworks to guide CSI interventions (Yungong, 2017). In some instances, these strategic frameworks are completely lacking. Where these strategies exist, there is no evidence to show that they were conceived to be results-oriented – relying on results-based monitoring and evaluation systems (Imas and Rist, 2009). Hence, CSI is only carried out as discrete and haphazard initiatives and programs in the wider area of CSR (Bradley and Steven, 2006). It lacks carefully thought exit strategies that guarantee continuity or sustainability after company support is withdrawn (IFC, 2010). This lack of clearly articulated strategic approach to CSI supports the observation that companies in Cameroon do not have written CSR policies (Ndzi, 2016). Company approaches to CSI are more inward-looking; that is with the business case for integrating CSI outweighing the need to effectively deliver development opportunities. Needs assessments and baselines studies, target setting and development of indicators to measure CSI efforts are almost absent in Cameroon's CSI landscape. CSI interventions are largely a solo adventure void of partnerships with members of the mainstream development community (Yungong, 2017).

Not all CSI strategic interventions were found to be of development value - focusing more of license to operate and with development seemingly only a second thought. Nonetheless, findings show that there is some significant level of CSI awareness among extractive companies operating in Cameroon (Foumena, 2013).

Although CSI focus covers areas of pressing development needs, it is still only weakly aligned with national and international development goals to which Cameroon is a signatory. This is not only in terms of the lack of accountable and results-oriented CSI systems but also in term of the external environment where major development organizations have programs areas which are only peripheral to enhancing and promoting the effectiveness of CSI in contributing to development. This matches observations by Oyewole and Adewale (2016), that there is no concrete evidence that industries promote sustainable development via CSR in Cameroon. The above weaknesses are a call for continuous quest for meaningful ways of implementing corporate social responsibilities in the business operations of firms as emphasized by Tita and Enoh, (2016). This paper aims to suggest how this can be effectively attained.

## CSI development link – the critique

The analyses above confirm the notion that the adoption of CSR/CSI often follows other imperatives other than the pursuit of developmental objectives (Bond, 2006). It is still hampered by intra-organizational obstacles – business as usual (Halme et al., 2012). This diminishes the positive links CSI ought to have with development (Frynas, 2008). Contributions have been limited to only micro-level development activities often cited in company documents. The business case for CSI dominates the development case. Despite high CSI/CSR awareness and the good intentions that come with it, interventions have only remained amateurish and sketchy (Jamali and Mirshak, 2006). There is a lack of cooperative links between mainstream development planning and investment with CSI (UNECA and AU (2011). These weaknesses leave this study with one critical question - what will make good CSI? How can it be determined to the satisfaction of all extractive sector stakeholders in Cameroon? The main idea in this study is that the notion of CSI applicability and CSI effectiveness combined with the notion of results-based as opposed to activity-based CSI can provide a framework (the front-and-backend activities approach) for measuring CSI performance and optimizing its role as a potential development contributor in Cameroon.

## The Notion of CSI Applicability and CSI Effectiveness

### Defining the issue

The main building block of the front and backend activities approach is the notion of CSI applicability and CSI effectiveness. CSI applicability refers to the extent to which CSI has become an important issue as per corporate policies and activities of extractive firms working in Cameroon. In basic terms, it refers to CSI awareness through CSI programmes. It is evident in company CSI awareness and CSI claims noted earlier. Globally, this is evident in the proliferation of voluntary extractive sector CSR initiatives in natural resource governance - "fourth generation natural resource codes' like the Global Compact and Extractive Industries Transparency Initiative (Besada and Martin, 2014).

CSI effectiveness looks beyond the mere presence of activities, to include the quality of such activities in terms of how they are efficiently integrated into the business operations of companies and the results they produce - outcomes and impacts of CSI projects. CSI effectiveness should also demonstrate strong alignment with pressing local development needs and broader national/international sustainable development goals/plans. They should typically be inspired to contribute to national and international development goals. The strategic orientation of effective CSI should be results-based - integrating evaluation for results with traditional monitoring systems (Imas and Rist, 2009), to determine the success or failure of CSI efforts.

### The main premises of CSI applicability and CSI effectiveness

It is often taken for granted that the profession and practice of CSR/CSI in Cameroon will necessarily amount to effective development outcomes for host countries and communities. The accuracy of this expectation is conditioned to a greater extent by the strategic orientation of CSI and the nature and quality of CSI integration activities.

Development is always in the explicit staged as the central pursuit of CSI activities, but in the implicit, these activities are only secondary or subordinate to company interests. This usually leads to a gap between profession and practice in the conception and implementation of CSI activities and for CSI to naturally trade-off more for 'doing good' for 'the wellness of business than 'doing good' for the 'wellness' of the wider society. Hence the CSI integration process is often governed by competitive and sometimes conflicting stakeholder interests.

To ensure that CSI moves from applicability towards effectiveness in Cameroon, it is required that the quality of CSI integration outcomes match the sustainable development expectations of all development stakeholders in the extractive sector and that it is results-oriented. For CSI in natural resource extraction to be effective, it should be achieved on a win-win basis for all stakeholders. It assumes that CSI applicability is more of a win-lose orientation for all development stakeholders although it tends to favour one stakeholder only for the short term.

**Table 1: Levels of CSI evaluation activities**

| Type of evaluation | Objective |
|---|---|
| **1. Higher Level Evaluation** <br> *(Summative in nature)* | **Results of CSI intervention** <br> *(Outcomes and impact of CSI)* |
| **2. Lower Level Evaluation** <br> *(Formative in nature)* | **CSI integration activities** <br> *(Quality of CSI implementation)* |

(Source: Author, 2015)

CSI applicability and CSI effectiveness can be evaluated at two major levels indicated in Table 1. The first is a lower level formative evaluation. This level of evaluation deals with the quality of CSI integration activities. Its focus is on the quality of the strategic approach or activities to ensure that CSI interventions align with intended development outcomes and impacts.

The second is a higher-level summative evaluation process. It is based on the quality of the CSI results produced: that is, CSI effectiveness from a results-based standpoint. The focus of the higher-level evaluation is to determine the results of CSI interventions on host communities at the impact levels of the results chain.

**The main pathways to CSI applicability and effectiveness**

The determination of CSI applicability and effectiveness follows three distinct and sometimes overlapping pathways or CSI orientations which define the purpose behind CSI (Figure 1). These are the business-oriented, the development-oriented and the hybrid or the mixed pathways.

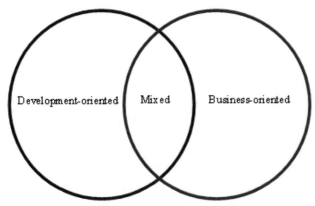

**Figure 1: CSI pathways/orientation** *(Source: Author, 2015)*

The business-oriented pathway to CSI is inward-looking. It focuses on core business objectives, especially profit maximization. This CSI path can be enacted as inclusive business or strategic community investments. It resounds with the thoughts of Friedman (1970); the stakeholder CSR school of thought (Freeman et al., 2010); the shared value proposition of Porter and Kramer (2011) and strategic community investment principles (IFC, 2010). These ideas advocate CSI in ways that sustain and support business objectives under prevailing market circumstances.

The development-oriented CSI pathway follows the purist's notion of CSI. It is more outward-looking and includes development benefits with little or no financial returns on such investments. Benefits are reckoned in terms of the impact and value such an investment makes on recipient communities. It does not suggest total disconnection from core businesses, neither does it under-value business nor the company. What it suggests is that profit maximization is not the sole intent of development-oriented CSI initiatives. It can be enacted through corporate philanthropy and social entrepreneurship.

The mixed or hybrid CSI narrative balances both the altruistic and strategic notion of CSR. It is based on the achievement of both development-oriented and the business-oriented CSI pathways. It is an ideal situation which accords equal concerns for development and for business. On this pathway, profit maximization and development welfare are mutually inclusive. It is to be achieved on a conceptually win-win basis - following the "win-win" game theory principle.

## The principles/criteria for CSI effectiveness

The potential of each of the CSI pathways above to contribute to development outcomes is guided and influenced by the principles of CSI effectiveness.

*i.* Effective CSI integration should build on a clearly elaborated CSI strategy. This strategy should elaborate on how the company sets out to implement the theory of change behind its CSI and the standards against which it holds itself to account

*ii.* CSI strategies ought to be sufficiently communicated to both internal and external stakeholders. This affords them the opportunity to evaluate CSI efforts and activities. This helps build public trust

*iii.* Effective CSI should be results-driven. Its activities should be set against well-defined performance targets and indicators so as to permit effective evaluation of CSI initiatives

*iv.* Effective CSI initiatives should be multi stakeholder-driven and participatory. They should be conducted on the basis of partnerships and collaboration with other stakeholders – CSI self-regulation and CSI co-regulation

*v.* Effective CSI initiatives should be economically, socially and environmentally sustainable as reflected in multiple stakeholder views. There should be a clear strategy to ensure that its benefits become long-lasting and self-sustaining

*vi.* Effective CSI communication/reporting should consider both successes and shortcomings of CSI efforts. Such successes and failures should reflect multi-stakeholder perspectives based on self and co-evaluation of current practices

*vii.* Effective CSI reporting should focus on results: not only lower-level results but also higher-level results at the outcome and impact levels of the results chain

*viii.* In the same light, CSI should not only be measured in terms of financial inputs (volume of spend) and activities, but most importantly, in terms of the results that a company has produced or can produce at the outcome and impact level of the result chain.

*ix.* The benefits of CSI activities should be widespread and inclusive. They should foster the principles of shared prosperity for all and demonstrate a strong potential to improve the welfare of individuals and groups - irrespective of gender or societal status

These principles are not final. They can be reviewed and updated time after time with the intention of ensuring that CSI effectively responds to the aspirations and expectations of all development stakeholders in Cameroon. They make room for the front and back-end activities proposition for evaluating CSI integration activities.

**The Front and Back-End Activities Proposition**

**The three phases of CSI implementation**

The front and back-end proposition suggest that CSI project implementation and evaluation activities have three phases, each having context-specific issues and activities that fit into it. These are the front-end and the back-end phases in between which is the middle phase (Figure 2).

The front-end deals with CSI project planning activities as may be required by the company involved and as determined by the context. Its purpose is to help organizations have an upfront understanding of the context in which CSI activities are being implemented so as to proceed to the proper conception and implementation of CSI interventions. These activities include needs assessment, baseline study and stakeholder engagement activities. It also includes the identification of CSI areas of intervention by the company and communities.

**Figure 2: The front and Back-end activities approach**

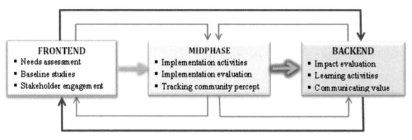

(Source: Author's conception, 2016)

The middle phase is characterized by CSI project implementation activities - including implementation evaluation to track the extent to which commitments are being adhered to as well as community perceptions to gain insights for measuring and improving performance. Evaluation methods should be participatory.

The back-end is characterized by an outcome, impact evaluation and learning activities. CSI activities are reviewed in this phase with an objective to find out if the results of a CSI intervention were achieved at the outcome and impact levels and if they are effective and sustainable. It provides a feedback loop into the system to improve performance. Hence, the three phases are interrelated and mutually reinforcing. Success or failure in CSI is determined based on a shared understanding by stakeholders.

This proposition builds on existing systems and approaches in the literature but suggests that evaluation of CSI applicability and CSI effectiveness can be approached from different vantage points, depending on the purpose of the evaluation. It could be to evaluate the quality of the strategic approach to CSI integration. This is mainly at the front-end and middle phases.

The second vantage point to evaluate CSI applicability and CSI effectiveness is in the quality of CSI results. From this vantage point, the purpose is to determine CSI effectiveness judged from a results-based evaluation perspective. The intended objective is to determine whether the goals and objectives of integrating CSI activities were reached in terms of outcomes and impacts on beneficiaries. For CSI activities to be effective from either standpoint, they should match the development expectations of key development stakeholders.

## The results-based component

The Front and Back-end approach use the results-based evaluation system to determine CSI applicability and CSI effectiveness. This is the second component of the approach (Figure 3). The results-based monitoring and evaluation system combine traditional monitoring and evaluation systems together with an assessment for results (Imas and Rist, 2009). It is based on a theory of change and uses the results chain - how a CSI intervention is expected to lead to desired results (Kusek and Rist, 2004). The chain is a sequence of inputs, activities, and outputs that are expected to improve the outcomes and impacts of a CSI intervention (Gertler, et al., 2011).

## Figure 3: The results chain in the front and the backend

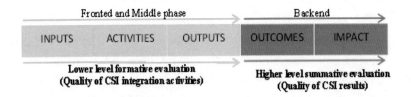

(Source: Author's conception, 2016)

Inputs are resources used in a CSI intervention; activities are things done with the inputs; outputs are the products and services derived from activities; outcomes are short-term higher-level results and should lead to impact - long-term higher-level results (Watkins,

2012). Results are measured against indicators - variables for tracking progress; and targets-the amount of change expected to occur during and after CSI activities (Imas and Rist, 2009). The inputs, activities and outputs section of the results chain constitute the front-end and middle phase in this suggested approach, while the outcomes and the impact sections constitute the back-end section of the approach.

CSI applicability and CSI effectiveness are determined along the results chain as per CSI integration activities/strategies, the theory of change and as reflected in the expectation and aspirations of CSI stakeholders.

**Application of the Front and Back-end Activities Approach**

In the application of the front and back-end activities approach as discussed above, the process should be guided by key elements each applicable to one of the three phases on this approach. These are the elements of context (at the front-end), the element of compliance (in the mid-phase) and the element of result (at the back-end) as illustrated in Figure 4. These together complete the evaluation strategy based on the front and back-end activities approach to CSI.

**Figure 4: Alignment of evaluation elements with the proposed CSI approach**

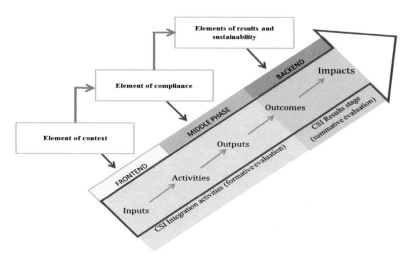

(Source: Author's conception, 2015)

The front-end is a preliminary stage and companies should engage in planning activities for the implementation phase as exemplified in the Likert-scale table below (Table 2). This phase is guided by the element of context: activities should reflect contextual concerns. For example, it could entail setting up targets and indicators to measure outcomes and impacts. Indicators are a "measure tracked systematically over time" while targets are "quantifiable amount of change to be achieved over a specified time" (Imas and Rist, 2009). Other typical concerns are conducting needs assessments, setting up CSI goals and defining areas of intervention.

For CSI activities to be effective, or applicable at the least, companies should be able to state clearly the extent to which they engage in these activities and to show proof that they do so.

**Table 2: Example of front-end, mid-phase and Back-end concerns**

| FRONTEND | Very weak | Weak | Neutral | Strong | Very strong |
|---|---|---|---|---|---|
| CSI based on performance targets and indicators | | | | | |
| Reflects stakeholder concerns | | | | | |
| CSI is based on objective goal setting | | | | | |
| CSI reflects local needs and priorities | | | | | |
| Needs /baselines assessment often conducted | | | | | |
| **MIDPHASE** | | | | | |
| CSI is externally regulated for better results | | | | | |
| Implementation evaluation considered | | | | | |
| Sustainability strategies incorporated in CSI | | | | | |
| CSI should be redressed for greater sustainability | | | | | |
| Effective partnerships to tackle CSI issues are available | | | | | |
| CSI aligns with national/international goals | | | | | |
| **BACKEND** | | | | | |
| Sufficient CSI reporting functions available | | | | | |
| CSI targets and indicators are often met | | | | | |
| Business doing enough to address CSI concerns | | | | | |
| CSI important for the future success of business | | | | | |
| Cameroon on track toward sustainable development | | | | | |

(Source: Author's conception, 2016)

The mid phase (table 2) of integrating CSI concerns deals mainly with CSI implementation activities. It is guided by the element of compliance - level of faithfulness/adherence to things planned to ensure that targets are met. This means indicating the extent to which things stated/ expected are effectively carried out - the gap between profession and practice. Key activities here include implementation of the planned CSI agenda as conceived at the frontend.

The back-end (Table 2) examines the extent to which CSI expectations are met as depicted by the CSI evaluation function. It deals with the desired CSI results at outcome and impact levels. This stage is guided by the elements of results and of sustainability. Here, company claims are to be checked with other stakeholder perspectives on whether CSI activities are actually achieving intended outcomes and generating the desired impact. For CSI to be effective at this stage, it must reflect the development expectations of all stakeholders in the natural resources sector. The extent of match or mismatch in views depicts the extent of CSI applicability and effectiveness.

## Contributions of the Front and Back-End Approach: Some applicable approaches to integrating CSI activities

CSI applicability and effectiveness often will be defined largely by strategic elements guiding the CSI integration process. The front and back-end approach do not create an entirely new system but builds on the weaknesses of existing ones. This includes the seven steps to approaching CSI integration activities by the IFC (2010) as indicated on table 3. It requires that companies assess the business and the local contexts through measuring and communicating results.

**Table 3: IFC steps for developing a community investment strategy**

| Step 1 | Step 2 | Step 3 | Step 4 | Step 5 | Step 6 | Step 7 |
|--------|--------|--------|--------|--------|--------|--------|
| Assess the Business Context | Assess the Local Context | Engage Communities | Invest in Capacity Building | Set the Parameters | Select Implementation Models | Measure and Communicate Results |

Source: Adapted from IFC, 2010 data - 2015

Porter et al., (2011) suggest another step by step approach based on the ideas of shared value. Companies identify the issues to target, make the business case for targeting them (step 2), track progress (step 3), measure results and use insights to unlock new value (step 4). Gradl and Knobloch (2010) suggest the three-phased approach including: the development phase, the implementation phase and the growth phase. Other approaches in inclusive business market development have been proposed by the UNDP Private Sector Division. These include approaches in Inclusive Market Development (UNDP, 2010a) and Brokering Inclusive Business Models (UNDP, 2010b).

These step by step approaches provide clear-cut instructions and activities that can be followed both by extractive sector CSI stakeholders. They cover a plethora of CSI applicability and effectiveness concerns. Users usually will find them adaptable on the ground as they can be easily referred to for supportive information at any stage of the CSI implementation process. However, they concentrate on CSI integration and implementation activities, (strategy), with very limited attention on how to evaluate the applicability and effectiveness of the CSI interventions. They look overly prescriptive and ignore issues of differential user needs. Their strongest motivation is not to tackle development concerns but rather to overemphasize the business case for tackling such concerns. Hence, CSI interventions to them are only necessary when they coincide with business objectives. While profitability is central to every business endeavour, focusing more on the business case undermines the dynamics that drive CSI in the first place (Campbell, 2012).

Besides, these step by step processes carry the suggestion that every other CSI implementation and evaluation process is the same. However, in some contexts, some key steps may not be relevant based on previous company experience. Even when all the steps are relevant, successful CSI implementation may not necessarily follow a sequence. These approaches suggest a system with a loopback mechanism to the initial phase of the system. This weakens their potential for implementation evaluations during the life of a single intervention.

## How the front and Back-end differ

The core question now is how the proposed approach here differs, overlaps or complements existing approaches and how its activities can be evaluated. This approach is called the front and back-end activities approach, (front and Back-end approach for short). It advances the novel concepts of CSI applicability and effectiveness and integrates CSI implementation and CSI evaluation components. Most approaches only suggest that an evaluation is necessary for CSI implementation but don't specify what type of evaluation is required; how and where this could be done and on what basis and using what parameters in the entire process. This is one weakness which the front and back-end approach in this study sought to address. It is less prescriptive and allows room for more context-specific CSI activities. Moreover, it focuses on the developmental case as the most important motivation for CSI efforts. It does not suggest that the business case for CSI should be ignored but rather that every CSI effort, when effectively conceived and implemented, has the potential to benefit all stakeholders - businesses and communities alike. These benefits may not be on company bottom line but could as well be reputational.

## Conclusion

The purpose of this paper was to suggest the front and back-end activities approach to evaluating effective extractive sector CSI taking into account the Cameroonian experience. The novel concepts of

CSI applicability and CSI effectiveness are advanced as major building blocks to the front and back-end activities approach. Since there are no guarantees that CSI can effectively contribute to resolving development problems, this study attempts to develop a framework that can guide extractive companies and other sector stakeholders in ensuring that CSI becomes a viable development contributor. It serves as a recommendation that can be further modified and expanded upon for adoption by extractive sector stakeholders. At a moment when private sector contributions to development have been highlighted as a critical requirement to attaining the Sustainable Development Goals, this framework should serve as a critical input into developing and implementing results-oriented CSI policies, based on a clear theory of change and approach to measuring and evaluating CSI performance. It should serve as a tool for developing and promoting national CSI/CSR policy guidelines/codes of best practices. This will help to improve the effectiveness of CSI/CSR and public disclosure activities.

## References

Barma, N., Kaiser, K., Minh Le, T., & Vinuela, L. (2012). *Rents to riches? The political economy of natural resource–led development.* Washington: IBRD/IDA.

Besada, H., and Martin, P. (2014). Mining codes in Africa: emergence of a 'fourth' generation? *Cambridge Review of International Affairs, 28* (2), pp. 263-282.

Bond, P. (2006). Resource extraction and African underdevelopment. *Capitalism Nature Socialism,* 17(2), pp. 5-25.

Boubakary, and Moskolai, D. (2016). The influence of the implementation of CSR on business strategy: An empirical approach based on Cameroonian enterprises. Arab Economic and Business Journal Volume 11 (2), pp. 162-171.

Bowen, R. (1953). *Social responsibilities of the businessman.* New York: Harper.

Campbell, B. (2012). Corporate social responsibility and development in Africa: redefining the roles and responsibilities of public and private actors in the mining sector. *Resources Policy*, 37 (2), pp. 138-143.

Collier, P. (2007). *The bottom billion: Why the poorest countries are failing and what can be done about It.* Oxford: Oxford University Press.

Dahlsrud, A. (2008). How corporate social responsibility is defined: An analysis of 37 definitions. *Corporate Social Responsibility and Environmental Management,* 15 (2008), pp. 1–13.

Foumena, C. (2013). Corporate social responsibility in the extractive industries in Cameroon: retrospectives and Prospects. *In: Extractive Industries Program.* May edition 2, (1). May 2013, Yaoundé: RELUFA, pp. 6 – 8.

Freeman, D., Harrison, S., Wicks, C., Parmar, B., & De Colle, S. (2010). *Stakeholder theory: the state of the art.* Cambridge: Cambridge University Press.

Friedman, M. (1970, September 13). The Social responsibility of business is to increase its profits. *New York Times Magazine.*

Frynas, G. (2008). CSR and international development: Critical assessment. *Corporate Governance, An International Review,* 16 (4), July 2008.

Gertler, J., Martinez, S., Premand, P., Rawlings, B., & Vermeersc, J. (2011). *Impact evaluation in practice.* Washington, D.C.: World Bank.

Gradl, C, and Knobloch, C. (2010). *Inclusive business guide: How to develop business and fight poverty.* Berlin: Endeva.

Halme, M., Lindeman, S., and Linna, P. (2012). Innovation for inclusive business: Intrapreneurial bricolage in multinational corporations. *Journal of Management Studies.* Retrieved from DOI 10.1111/j.1467-6486.2012.01045.x

Hulme, D. (2009). *The millennium development goals (MDGs): A short history of the world's biggest promise.* Manchester: Brooks World Poverty Institute.

IFC (International Finance Corporation). (2010). *Strategic community investment: A good practice handbook for companies doing business in emerging markets.* Washington, D.C: IFC.

Imas, G., and Rist, C. (2009). *Designing and conducting effective development evaluations.* Washington D.C: World Bank.

Ismail, M. (2009). Corporate social responsibility and its role in community development: An International Perspective. *Journal of International Social Research*, 2 (9), pp. 1999 – 2009.

Jamali, D., and Mirshak, R. (2006). Corporate social responsibility: Theory and Practice in a Developing World Context. *Journal of Business Ethics*, 72, pp. 243 – 262.

Kakabadse, K., Rozuel, C., and Lee-Davies L. (2005). Corporate social responsibility and stakeholder approach: A conceptual review. *International Journal, Business Governance and Ethics*, 1 (4).

KPMG Africa Limited (2013). *Monitoring African sovereign risk: Cameroon snapshot*, 2013 Quarter 1. Douala: KPMG Central Africa.

Kusek, L., and Rist, C. (2004). *Ten steps to a results-based monitoring and evaluation system*. Washington DC: World Bank.

Maddison, A. (2006). *The world economy: Volume 1, A Millennial Perspective & Volume 2, Historical Statistics*. Paris: OECD Publications.

MINEPAT (Ministry of Economy Planning and Territorial Management) and United Nations System in Cameroon. (2013). *The future we want: Report on national consultations for the post-2015 agenda in Cameroon*. Yaoundé: MINEPAT & UN.

MINMIDT (Ministry of Mines, Industry and Technological Development). (2013). *Mining Register*. Retrieved from http://www.minmidt.net/index.php/en/target-sectors/mining-sector/mining-registry

Murphy, D. (2005). Taking multinational corporate codes of conduct to the next level. *The Columbia Journal of Transnational Law*. 43 (2), pp. 1 – 55.

Ndzi. E. (2016). Corporate social responsibility in Cameroon: The hydro electricity sector. *African Journal of Business Management*, 10(7), pp. 151-161.

NHC (National Hydrocarbons Corporation, Cameroon). (2016). *Partner of oil companies in Cameroon at the heart of the Gulf of Guinea*. Yaoundé: SNH.

Nting, T. (2010). *The scramble for mineral resources in Cameroon: How can the government learn from previous conflicts and social responsibility failures?* African Security Review, Volume 18 (2), pp. 107-115.

Oyewole, S., and Adewale, D.O., 2016. Sustainable development and corporate social responsibility in sub-Saharan Africa: Evidence from industries in Cameroon. *Economies* 4(2), 10. Retrieved from https://doi.org/10.3390/economies4020010

Porter, E., and Kramer, R. (2011). *The big Idea: Creating shared value: Rethinking capitalism.* Retrieved from http://hbr.org/2011/01/the-big-idea-creating-shared-value/ar/pr

Sachs, D. (2015). *The age of sustainable development.* New York: Columbia University Press.

Schwab, K. (Ed.). (2014). *The global competitiveness report 2014–2015.* Geneva: World Economic Forum.

Smith, A. (2008). An Introduction to corporate social responsibility in the extractive industries. *Yale Human Rights and Development Journal*, 11(1), pp. 1-7.

UNDP (United Nations Development Programme). (2010a). *Inclusive markets development handbook.* New York: UNDP.

UNDP (United Nations Development Programme). (2010b). *Brokering inclusive business models.* New York: UNDP.

UNECA (United Nations Economic Commission for Africa and AU- African Union). (2011). *Minerals and Africa's development: The international Study Group Report on Africa's Mineral Regimes.* Addis Ababa: ECA Publishing Unit.

Watkins, R., Meiers, M., and Visser, L. (2012). *A guide to assessing needs: essential tools for collecting information, making decisions, and achieving development results.* Washington D.C.: World Bank.

Watts, P., and Holme, L. (2000). *Meeting changing expectations: Corporate social responsibility.* Geneva-Switzerland: WBCSD.

WBG (World Bank Group). (2015). *World development indicators 2015.* Washington DC: IBRD.

Wise, H., and Shytlla, S. (2007). *The role of the business sector in expanding economic opportunity.* Cambridge: Harvard Kennedy School of Government.

Yungong, J. (2017). *Evaluating the development potential of extractive sector corporate social investments in Cameroon: Case of the oil & gas and mining sub sectors.* Retrieved from http://hdl.handle.net/10948/13368.

# Land Rights and Land Conflicts

# Chapter 5

## Land Grabbing in South-western Cameroon: Deconstructing the Complexity of Local Responses

*James Emmanuel Wanki and Frankline Anum Ndi*

### Abstract

In Cameroon, the insatiable urge by foreign agribusinesses to both acquire and exponentially expand landholdings for the purposes of plantation-based monoculture is unfortunately leaving a trail of development reversals behind. This is worsening the vulnerability status of an already marginalized cohort of rural agrarian peoples leading to varied forms of grassroots reactions and visceral oppositional resistance. Building on the scaffold of ethnographic primary data elicited in the Nguti area of South-western Cameroon as well as published scholarly works on land-grabbing, this chapter offers a more granular insight into the diverse, multifaceted and complex universe of grassroots responses to land-grabbing within an African context. It questions the *a priori* bedrock assumption that grassroots reactions to LSLAs have mainly been characterized by a unitary oppositional mobilization in the form of active resistance. It argues that besides episodes of vigorous protests and visceral resistance, segments of affected populations have equally demonstrated their predisposition towards subtle collaborations and compromises as a function of strategic interest-based calculations that rather reflect the complexity of rational human behaviour than anything else. Nonetheless, segments of this grassroots populations are for instance struggling within the ambits of such deals by organizing for better compensation, clamouring for improved development dividends, advocating for better job opportunities within established plantations, and sometimes coalescing in opposition to other grassroots segments opposed to LSLA deals. This encompassing diversity of grassroots responses must lead the baseline of collective reflections, inform research, policy and development thinking on local reactions to LSLAs in Africa, going forward.

**Keywords:** Large-scale land acquisitions, Resistance, Compromise, Local responses, Cameroon

## Introduction

Land grabbing[1] is beginning to exert such a confounding pressure on existing land configurations, land tenure systems and access to forest and water resources especially across Africa that it merits more than just a cursory scholarly glance. Over the last few decades, the mad rush for land in the South has been largely incentivized by accelerating global demand for biofuel, food, fibre and growing interests over water supplies (Vermeulen and Cotula 2010; White et al. 2012; Peluso and Lund, 2011). These interests have combined with increasing investment and trade transnationalization to stimulate commercial pressures on cheap land (Deininger and Byerlee, 2011; Cotula et al., 2009; Zoomers; 2010; Kandel, 2015; Ndi, 2017). Rich industrialized countries and agribusinesses, including some from emerging economies like South Africa, Brazil and India have thus embarked on securing purchase or lease agreements over thousands of hectares of arable land in Southern countries, often through shoddy and hurriedly conducted Large Scale Land Acquisition (LSLAs) deals (Polack et al, 2013; IFAD, 2011; Hall, et al, 2012).

Unfortunately, such deals have tended to violate laid down ethical standards, bypass due process and infringe on globally acceptable social and environmental impact conditionalities. Particularly targeted are those countries emerging from protracted instability and endowed with suitable physical conditions (Millar, 2015; Cotula et al. 2014; Verma 2014) such as Liberia, Sierra Leone, and the Democratic

---

[1] According to Batterbury and Ndi (2018) "land grabbing in Africa refers to the purchase or acquisition of use rights to produce food, biofuels or animal feed" (Batterbury S. and Ndi, F. 2018. Land grabbing in Africa. In Binns J.A., K. Lynch and E. Nel (eds.) The Routledge Handbook of African Development. London: Routledge. We use the phrases 'land grabbing' and "Large Scale Land Acquisitions (LSLAs)" interchangeably throughout this chapter to refer to the same thing.

Republic of Congo (DRC) or those grappling with serious budgetary and financial constraints or reeling from weak governance and institutional deficits (Zoomers, 2013; Borras et al. 2011).

In Africa, the widening footprints of land grabs have already begun upending the human geography of especially rural agrarian communities in affected countries, fanning new debates and controversies that span the agricultural, ecological, economic, political and socio-cultural spectrums. Some estimates indicate that about 70 per cent of land recently transacted in transnational LSLA deals have been in Africa, a continent generally considered to be an ecological haven (Hall et al. 2012) and possibly the world's last surviving reserve of both under-utilized and unused arable farmland (World Bank, 2009; Deininger et al. 2011). Focused predominantly on export-driven monoculture, foreign investors have secured large swathes of fertile lands and water resources for the establishment of vast plantations (Anseeuw, 2013; Ndi and Batterbury 2017), often acting in complacency with local and national political and administrative elite who are motivated by pecuniary gains (Wolford et al. 2013; Fonjong, 2017) to exploit poor land governance laws, feeble enforcement regimes and legal grey areas (Fonjong, Sama-Lang and Fon, 2015; Goldman, Davis, and Little 2016) to coercively dispossess indigenous communities. Harvey (2004) has aptly described this trend as "accumulation by dispossession".

Compounding the irreparable ecological disruptions that accompany land grabs (Balehegn, 2015), the profit-driven production systems underpinning the neoliberal export-based model of existing foreign-owned agribusinesses in Africa have exacerbated an unfolding process of social differentiation that has intensified the social reproduction of an increasingly vulnerable rural agrarian proletariat, unfortunately trapped at the margins of the ongoing process of vast, predominantly extractive, wealth accumulation. Hall et al. (2015) and Wolford (2010) concur, further arguing that even though foreign land acquisitions generally occur through different trajectories that are driven by different purposes and expected varied outcomes (Hall et al., 2015; Wolford, 2010), the asymmetrical power relations underpinning transactions between foreign capitalist investors and national African governments often lead to land deals that are seriously skewed in favour of such investors (Cotula et al., 2014). In fact, as Anseeuw (2013) and O'Brien (2011) have averred, local gains do not even materialize most of the times, and the assumption that such gains will eventually 'trickle down' to local peoples through opportunities such as sustainable employment on plantations, support for out-grower schemes, and through land access royalties, have generally turned out to be colourful pipe dreams (Ndi, and Batterbury, 2017; Anseeuw 2013; O'Brien 2011). Much of the global spotlight remains cast on Africa where the international media continues to produce sensational headlines on the mistreatment endured by local peasants (Borras, Fig, and Suarez, 2011; Li, 2011; Toulmin, 2009).

Albeit belatedly, Cameroon has recently experienced a burgeoning profile of scholarly reflections about LSLAs that have mostly cast critical light on the negative externalities associated with land-grabbing. These have helped gradually galvanize national and international attention on the plethoric ways in which affected agrarian communities at the grassroots are beginning to experience severe reversals in their livelihood and development fortunes. Ndi (2018) and Fonjong (2017) for instance, delved into the disproportionate gendered impact of land grabs amongst affected communities in various degrees, arguing how the loss of land to agro-commercial interests have constrained women's access to land and intensified stresses on livelihood patterns. Fonjong, Sama-Lang and Fombe (2015) and Ndi and Batterbury (2017) examined in minutiae, the processes through which LSLAs occur in Cameroon, mapping out the institutions and actors involved, while Feintrenie et al (2014) widened the analytical prism to more broadly capture the wider impacts of land grabbing on affected communities. Fernando (2013) forayed into the legal issues surrounding LSLAs, interrogating the grey areas around which legal contestations to land grabbing have emerged in the country, laying the building blocks upon which Cotula et al. (2016) later appraise the ways in which the law, as a regulatory constellation, either constrains or enables transparency and accountability in the often-murky process of land-related deal making.

Focusing on Cameroon's Anglophone region which has recently been a hotbed of political agitations, Ndi and Batterbury (2017) have also more recently unpacked the different axis of political conflicts instigated by the exploitative comportment of an American agribusiness, Herakles Farms (Sithe Global Sustainable Oil Cameroon, SGSOC) in the Manyemen, Ebanga and Talangaye localities. What can be conclusively deduced from all of the abovementioned Cameroon-based analyses is that the insatiable urges by foreign agribusinesses to both acquire and exponentially expand landholdings for the purposes of plantation-based monoculture. Ndi and Batterbury, 2017 have precipitated a litany of undesirable consequences that are as diverse in scope as they are far-reaching and differential in impact. As a matter of fact, current scholarship on Cameroon collectively underscore that by appropriating communal lands that serve as breadbasket for dietary and subsistence needs of rural agrarian populations (often without adequate compensation), polluting communal water sources (Vermeulen and Cotula, 2010; De Schutter, 2012; Cotula 2014; Fonjong 2017), establishing enclosures that restrict local peoples' access to valuable water and non-timber forest resources (NTFR), (Fairhead, Leach, and Scoones 2012; Li 2014; Goldman, Davis, and Little 2016). There is also the failure to fulfil corporate social responsibility obligations (Ndi and Batterbury, 2017), and through pseudo-consultation processes that demonstrate sheer disregard for the opinions and active participation of affected communities. LSLAs are unfortunately leaving a trail of disenchantment behind, reversing development gains and worsening the vulnerability status of an already marginalized cohort of people. It is precisely this dismantling of development at the grassroots and the marginalization of rural people's voice that has mostly triggered the groundswell of vocal and sometimes militant resistance from below in affected communities. Yet, as Hall et al. (2015) have prudently cautioned, emerging evidence has strongly emphasized that "political reactions 'from below' to global land grabbing have been vastly more varied and complex than is usually assumed". Overt resistance is not always the sole norm.

It is this urge to offer a more granular insight into the diverse, multifaceted and complex universe of grassroots responses to land-grabbing within a geographical context in Cameroon that most informs our focus in this chapter. It builds on the scaffold of primary data elicited during ethnographic research in the Nguti area of Southwestern Cameroon, as well as literature on land-grabbing in the country. We attempt to deconstruct the *a priori* bedrock assumption that grassroots reactions to LSLAs have mainly been unidirectional (Mamonova, 2015), characterized by a unitary oppositional mobilization that takes the form of active resistances. Far from this default assumption of perpetual visceral resistance to foreign agribusinesses, we build on Scott, (1987)'s views that segments of affected populations have equally shown their predisposition towards subtle collaborations and compromises as a function of "strategic interest-based calculations" that rather reflect the complexity of rational human behaviour than anything else. For instance, affected populations are known to have often also engaged in "mobilizations [that] seek to improve compensations for people's expulsion from their land, to demands to be inserted into land deals as workers or contract farmers, to [even engaging in]...counter-mobilizations against land deal resisters" (Hall et al. 2015; Wolford et al. 2013; Edelman, Oya, and Borras 2013; White et al. 2012). It is thus the limited emphasis on reflecting this complexity in grassroots responses to current land-grabbing scholarship on Cameroon that constitutes the missing link this chapter attempts to repair.

This chapter structurally unfolds as follows: first, it briefly presents the relevant theoretical perspectives explaining local responses to LSLAs before transitioning to an exploration of the physical and socio-environmental attributes of the area of study. Secondly, it succinctly problematizes land-grabbing within the context of the LSLA operations conducted by Sithe Global Sustainable Oil Cameroon (SGSOC), a subsidiary of Herakles Farms in the Nguti area of South-western Cameroon. Thirdly, it undertakes a deconstructive analysis of the multiple facets of local responses to the encroachment of Herakles Farms in the Nguti area and the underlying considerations that inform the choices of dispossessed and disenchanted local populations to either resist, collaborate, compromise or stay in-between, in the face of growing vulnerability and grievances. Finally, it then weighs this complexity against current discussions animating local peoples' reaction to land-grabbing to draw conclusions and recommendations going forward.

## Theoretical underpinnings of local responses to LSLAs

Broadly speaking, theorization around grassroots responses to land grabbing have tended to generally congregate around three main theoretical clusters. The first, dominated by perspectives from the classical collective action paradigms, construe the notion of peasant resistance as an anomaly to the rule, in a dispensation where inaction is the main ethos (Hall et al., 2015). The undercurrent logic informing these perspectives is derived from the central tenet of rational choice theory and neo-classical economics which promote the notion that humans are inherently strategic in their thinking, imbued with a natural propensity to weigh the potential benefits against the perceived risks associated with a given course of action, before proceeding accordingly in ways that advance individual or collective self-interests (Hall et al., 2015). Nevertheless, given that risks imposed by the recourse to collective action tend to be particularly significant (assassinations, beatings, prolonged arrests etc.) especially in undemocratic societies (like Cameroon where the State displays an enthusiastic readiness to deploy coercive force to quell organised protests), rational individuals tend to "sit on the side-lines as free riders, hoping to reap the gains of others' risk-taking and sacrifices" (Hall et al., 2015).

Deductively, the absence of commensurate individual economic incentives for indulgence in class action (Olson, 1965) only further diminishes the rational appeal for individuals to resort to collective mobilisation and active resistance. It is this "pain versus gain" analysis that is seen here to embed the calculus of peasant responses to the exogenous and endogenous threats presented by land-grabbing. Passivity, collaboration, and sometimes complacency to the encroachment of LSLAs are therefore understood as an extension of a rational judgement emanating from an astute appraisal of the contextual forces restraining the pursuit of alternative and potentially more oppositional courses of action.

The second cluster populated principally by Marxist theorists have habitually sought to analytically establish a direct causal, albeit, dialectic link between the fomentation of collective grievances and collective action (Hall et al., 2015). A key assumption here is that collective oppression inexorably precipitates the formation of a class politics of resistance (Barker, 2014). Per Marxist analysis, the increasing proletarianization of peasants through displacements and the aggressive accumulation of profit by LSLA endeavours is the lynchpin behind the current spate of resistances to land-grabbing evident across much of Africa today. Nevertheless, the unlikelihood that the sort of apocalyptic peasant uprising promulgated actively by Marxism and its theoretical permutations would eventually materialize have rightfully attracted scathing scholarly criticism, especially from the neo-liberal economic school which points at ingenious forms of accommodations provided by capitalism to temper and mitigate the grievances of the labour class.

Finally, a third theoretical strand, perhaps most dominated by Natalia Mamonova's works on LSLAs in Ukraine, unveils a compelling facet to the dynamics of local reaction to the establishment of large farms in the former Soviet country that is worthy of close scholarly attention. Mamonova lambasts the default presumption that collective grassroots resistance represents rural peoples' instinctive impulse towards the encroachment of LSLAs in their localities, arguing that such a view flattens their agentic capacity of either "adapting to, or coexisting alongside large-scale industrial farms" (Mamonova, 2015). Advocating a case by case assessment instead of the broad-brush characterisation that is so replete in current scholarship, she argues for example that rural Ukrainian people perceive LSLAs not as a new problematic intrusion into their way of life, historically speaking, but as a modern extension of the Soviet era State farms which they referred to as *kolkhozy* and *sovkhozy* (Hall et al., 2015). Here, large farms provide fruitful employment opportunities with comparatively better wages and social dividends (Hall et al., 2015), making the possibility that rural Ukrainian people will embark on some form of resistance somewhat illusory. Context is consequently crucial to any balanced analysis of grassroots responses to LSLAs.

## The Case of Nguti sub-division

Nguti is in the South West which is one of Cameroon's ten administrative regions. The region has an estimated population of about 1.5 million people, a majority of whom are based in the mostly enclaved rural areas (Cameroon Data Portal, 2015). The region is further demarcated administratively into the Fako, Kupe Manenguba, Manyu, Lebialem, Ndian and Meme divisional units. Nguti, is located in Ndian division (see figure. 1), and peopled by an estimated 17,000 inhabitants, (Nguti Council, 2009While agriculture remains the mainstay of the local economy with over 80 percent of the local population dependent on it for survival (Nguti Council, 2009), artisanal fishing is also conducted alongside animal husbandry by predominantly poor rural inhabitants across sparsely populated villages to supplement household dietary and income needs (Fonjong, 2017). Villagers also take advantage of the very dense tropical rainforest coverage that dominates the area to engage in the harvesting and commercialization of non-timber forest products (Ndi, 2017).

A confluence of natural factors, including abundant fertile volcanic soil (Nguti Rural Council, 2009; Belderman, 1966), rich forest reserves, abundant fisheries, precious wildlife and water resources, high rainfall and conducive climatic conditions, combine to make the Nguti community a veritable ecological paradise (Ndi, 2017). The same combination of factors has for better or for worse also compelled large scale agricultural holdings to gravitate towards the area, and to open large-scale plantations (Ndi, 2017; Fonjong, 2017). Communal division of productive labour is highly gendered (Fonjong, 2017) with subsistence agriculture significantly feminized. For instance, women traditionally cultivate food-based crops like cocoyam, beans, maize, in addition to harvesting non-timber forest products, while men hunt, tap palm wine, and focus on the small-scale cultivation of cash-based products like palms, cocoa and coffee (Ndi, 2017; Fonjong, 2017). Nevertheless, it has been argued that the

119

extensive pressures induced by the economic crises of the 1980s, and the development reversals triggered by the Structural Adjustment Programmes of the 1990s (Fonchingong 1999) have coupled with the relatively recent intensification of emphasis on commercialized agriculture to gradually alter traditional gendered agricultural production patterns. It is thus somewhat difficult for conclusive determinations to be made about crop cultivation based solely on gender considerations (Ndi, 2017).

**Figure 1. Maps of South West Region of Cameroon depicting selected villages in the Nguti sub-division, and the area coverage of the original Herakles Farms project**

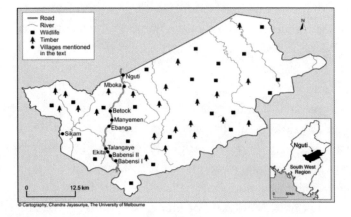

Source: *Adapted from Ndi (2017)*

## Methodology

Qualitative data reflected in this chapter were elicited in 2015 and 2017, during a process of ethnographic research conducted in the Nguti, Ebanga, Manyemen, Babensi II and Talangaye villages affected by Herakles Farms operations in Nguti sub-division (see Figure .1 above). Guided by literature review, both the selected villages and the study respondents were purposively sampled to capture and represent subjects impacted by the Herakles Project. Semi-structured interviews were conducted with about 100 respondents from the grassroots, deliberately chosen to reflect gender parity. They were drawn from a representative demographic and occupational cluster, which generally included Herakles Farms employees, farmers, hunters and gatherers. Additionally, two separate gender-specific focused group discussions were organized in each village – one with women and the other with men - to enable a conducive environment where women had the liberty of expressing their views unconstrained by the domineering presence of men, in a context where patriarchy and hegemonic masculinity remain deeply entrenched.

To consolidate methodological depth, widen latitude for triangulation and supply a top-down counter-narrative, ten key respondent interviews were equally conducted with significant community leaders and representatives such as village chiefs, the committee of village elders, local elites and local government officials, and representatives of local Non-Governmental Organisations (NGOs) based in the areas of study. Representatives of Herakles farms declined to participate in the study. Interviews were mainly conducted in an informal manner in *Pidgin English* which is the *lingua franca* of the areas of study. The informed consent of all respondents was secured, and confidentiality guarantees were requested by and offered to all research subjects due to the very sensitive nature of LSLA discussions across the study areas. Data were recorded both by hand in notebooks since most study participants declined to have their voices recorded. The main thrust of interviews and discussions was an exploration of respondent's views of and reactions to the LSLA process and the engagement of

Herakles Farms in their localities. Data was transcribed, treated, processed and analysed with major themes emerging in line with grounded theory. Technical reports and situation notes on the unfolding process of LSLAs on the area of study kept by government sources and NGOs, also provided a rich basin of secondary data which both complemented and reinforced the primary data elicited, strengthening this chapter's potential to make valid generalizations.

## The unfolding process of LSLAs in Cameroon

A plethora of factors account for the susceptibility of African States like Cameroon to tempting propositions by "big agro-capital interests" as they court their way to large-scale land deals. Of note perhaps, are the profound repercussions of a prolonged crisis in African agriculture, and the dismal failure by most African States to initiate or complete agrarian transitions (Hall et al, 2012; Ndi, 2015; Cotula and Vermeulen, 2011). These have in turn fuelled and exacerbated food insecurity, triggered a flurry of rural-urban exodus, imposed significant food import bills on the States, and deepened rural unemployment and poverty (Hall et al., 2012). Within the Cameroonian context, Fonchingong (1999) has also inputted the nefarious consequences derived from the imposition of draconian Structural Adjustment conditionalities by the World Bank /IMF on the country in the 1990s (which effectively prioritized the country`s debt-servicing obligations over its development needs) as contributory to the steep decline in State revenues, pushing the Cameroonian State to "abdicate its *prima facie* responsibilities in the areas of social and infrastructural provisioning"(Fonchingong, 1999). The Cameroonian agricultural sector, once a booming pride in the sub-region was amongst the hardest hit, nearly imploding under significant stresses. Through subsequent neglect, erstwhile impressive State agriculture promotion schemes, irrigation and mechanisation initiatives, and farm road network extension projects have simply crumbled into a state of disrepair.

That most African States enter LSLA negotiations with well-resourced foreign partners, cap in hand, and poised to welcome prospects of badly needed foreign direct investments (De Shutter

2009; Lisk 2013; Neville and Dauvergne, 2012; see also Fana, 2016) should therefore be understood against a contextual backdrop of mounting developmental needs on the one hand, and limited financial wherewithal to meet such needs on the other. What often ensues thence are sweetheart arrangements between African States and foreign agro-interests in which vast swathes of arable land are sometimes ceded for free or under extremely generous preferential conditions hinged on the presumption that commercialised agriculture will invariably lead to favourable trickle-down outcomes (Nalepa and Bauer 2012). It is this manifest desperation on the part of African States to please foreign partners, in most cases at the precarious mercy of their dispossessed and maligned rural populations that Harvey (2003) aptly refers to when he expounds on the notion of State-capital alliance; a sort of interest-based alignment between foreign commercial investors and national holders of political power (Cotula and Vermeulen, 2011; Vermeulen and Cotula, 2010). Instances of these abound and are well-documented in literature. Hall et al (2012) for instance, report how against the backdrop of chronic under-investment in the agricultural sector, government officials in Ethiopia tend to either summarily eschew local peoples` concerns or simply intimidate them into compliance with the unfavourable wishes of foreign agribusinesses. In Kenya and Tanzania, they further illustrate how government agents brazenly favoured foreign agro-investors over the wailings and lamentations of their own local communities in a series of large-scale land related disputes (Hall et al. 2012). In Cameroon, SGSOC has also benefitted hugely from the activist support of agents of the Cameroonian State (Fonjong, 2017; Ndi, 2017), working in tandem with a large, widening and convoluted network of proxy enablers comprised of local authorities, prominent local businessmen, cultural elites and sometimes local traditional leaders, to foster what Peters (2013) has termed "the accelerating process of appropriation ... [through] national agents"

At the centre of discourse is the role of the Cameroon State in the unfolding process of LSLAs Pursuant to the Cameroon Constitution, the State wields sweeping powers in the arena of land ownership where it has been empowered to control and manage so-

123

called `untitled lands` since the early 1970s (Fonbad 2009; Fonjong et al. 2010; Feintrenie et al. 2014). In short, all untitled land belongs to the State (Ndi, 2017 & 2019). It is this power that government officials often leverage to facilitate LSLAs in the country in ways that bypass due process, dispossessing agrarian and forest-based communities often without appropriate compensation or alternative means of livelihood (Greenpeace 2014; WWF 2012). Decree No. 76-166 of 27th April 1976 lays out the procedures and conditions around which national lands and land concessions are managed and ceded to secondary parties. First, vying parties must tender complete applications for the attention of the national Ministry of Lands and State Property, bearing requests for a delimited parcel of land, including associated maps and cadastral outlines of the proposed area, nature of proposed business and a development plan (Achobang et al., 2009). Second, the conduct of a ministerial assessment is prescribed, and based on project feasibility, land rights are ceded to applicants, first for a maximum provisional period of five years, which is then later extended, conditioned upon satisfactory performance (ibid). The complete absence of the voices and consent of affected population thus constitute a critical missing link in this process.

As a matter of fact, so uninvolved were affected populations in the SGSOC LSLA deal with the government of Cameroon that Fonjong et al. (2015) have described it as a "worst case" project. The company simply met with government officials in the national capital, flagrantly bypassing the local populations concerned, and with the help of a select coterie of traditional leaders and local elites, negotiated away 73,086 hectares of land spanning three administrative sub-divisions – Mundemba, Toko, and Nguti, for a period of 99 years in (Fonjong et al. 2015). No participatory vent was created in the process for local consultations to permit local concerns, expectations and interests. On September 17th, 2009, a deal was simply signed with the Government of Cameroon, after which local villagers and communities were "merely informed of their forthcoming collaboration with a project that had been approved by the national government in the capital city of Yaoundé[2]" (Ndi, 2018). All other discussions and agreements with locals were done *sub obtentu*. What is known of the SGSOC project is contained in the company's Social and Environmental Impact Assessments (SEIA) where it stipulates that about 60,000 hectares of land would be used for nursing, developing and planting palm plantations and establishing palm oil refining plants (Fonjong et al. 2015). The remainder of the approved land, it stated, would be dedicated towards serving as protected zones for socially and environmentally sensitive resources, and for communal livelihood initiatives in favour of implicated villages (Achobang et al., 2009). On the ground, the reality appeared somewhat different, as local populations especially women reported being completely side-lined (Ndi, 2018; Fonjong et al., 2016). Where pseudo-consultation processes were subsequently carried out, they tended to mostly target segments of the population favoured by complacent elites who would not dare oppose the project (Fonjong et al., 2016).

## SGSOC`s footprint of controversy in the Nguti

The pro-developmental contributions of SGSOC's palm plantations in the Nguti area were overpromised but dismally under-delivered. The project appropriated communal lands that served both as breadbasket for the dietary needs of the Nguti populations, and as religious sanctuary (often without adequate compensation), polluted communal water sources (Vermeulen and Cotula, 2010; De Schutter, 2012; Cotula 2014; Fonjong 2017), and failed to fulfil corporate social responsibility obligations (Ndi and Batterbury, 2017). Promises of sustainable local employment went generally unmet, compelling local communities to seek the advocacy of both national and international NGOs to attract global attention to their plight, especially regarding the social, environmental, and economic consequences of SGSOC's operations (Fonjong et al. 2015; Greenpeace 2012, 2013, 2014; CED

---

[2] Cross-section of concerns expressed by research informants are relayed in Ndi (2018), Land grabbing, gender and access to land: implications for local food production and rural livelihoods in Nguti sub-division, South West Cameroon, *Canadian Journal of African Studies*, (1-24).

2012; Nature Cameroon 2011; Oakland Institute 2012; Nguiffo and Schwartz 2012). An official petition was tabled against the project at the Roundtable for Sustainable Oil Production (RSPO)[3] in September 2011(Linder, 2013), with SGSOC reacting by withdrawing its membership from the body by August 2012, protesting that RSPO's grievance enquiry procedures were bound to negatively affect its productivity and financial bottom line (Achobang et al., 2009; Linder 2013).

The culmination of the intensifying pressure against SGSOC's practices was the issuance of an executive fiat by the Government of Cameroon in November 2013 ceding a 3 years temporary lease to the company and drastically downsizing its initially allotted land concessions to 19,843 hectares, a sliver of its original size (Ndi, 2017; Fonjong et al. 2015; WWF 2012; CED, 2012). Nevertheless, the grievances of affected populations remain unaddressed. For instance, certain community segments whose farmlands were affected by SGSOC's revised demarcations continue to harbour premonitions that their lands will eventually be co-opted into the plantation's operations (Ndi, 2018). Without land titles, affected communities in the Talangaye, Manyemen and Ebanga villages face serious difficulties filing acceptable claims for the destruction of their farmlands and forest resources. Many still remain trapped in a limbo. As Ndi and Batterbury (2017) have concluded, ongoing contestations pitting local communities, Herakles Farms and the State over access to entitlements and crucial forest resources reflect a failure of process; and combine with entrenched issues of accountability and lack of transparency in a state of normalised corruption (Nature Cameroon, 2011; Fonjong et al., 2015; Ndi, 2017; Cotula and Vermeulen, 2011).

---

[3] RSPO requires that its members or applicants implement a robust free, prior and informed consent (FPIC) process with local communities, refrain from clearing or pressurizing high conservation value (HCV) areas, comply with all national laws in their countries of operation, and publish a new planting procedure informational document at least thirty days prior to planting oil palm. SGSOC failed to meet up to many of these standards leading to the company's withdrawal (Achobang et al. 2009).

## Facets of grassroots responses to land grabbing

The local arena as a site of human social interactions is not a homogenous bloc characterized by a uniformity of interests, realities and postures (Hall et al., 2015). Local responses to land grabbing too, cannot consequently be expected to be the same. Indeed, they have tended to be far more complex than usually sensationalized by the media (White et al., 2012; Wolford et al., 2013). The core demands of the majority of the Nguti population are developmental dividends such as social facilities (such as hospitals, piped water, electricity, roads, scholarship schemes), even though their personal interests and proclivities differ. Hall et al. (2015) have advanced a wider array of popular responses to dispossession – which can either be covert, realized in the form of subtle everyday resistances, or more overtly, demonstrated in the form of organized or disorganised fiery protests. Those who resist often have varying objectives and goals that tend to be complex as they are transient and evolving. Acknowledging these is thus crucial (Schneider 2011; Scott, 1985) to an encompassing comprehension of local mobilization and response.

## Active oppositional mobilization and resistance towards SGSOC

The choice of strategies deployed in the conduct of peasant resistance vary and are largely dependent on the strengths, specific social structures, and defensive capabilities of resisters (Scott, 1987). Benedict Kerkvliet defines resistance as '…what people do that shows disgust, anger, indignation or opposition to what they regard as unjust, unfair, illegal claims on them by people in higher, more powerful class and status positions or institutions…' (Kerkvliet, 2009: 233). Adding that in positions of subordination, the subjugated often struggle to affirm 'what they believe they are entitled to, based on values and rights recognized by a significant proportion of other people similar to them' (ibid: 233). Scholarship on peasant mobilization against exploitation in the developing world is replete with a variety of shapes and forms of peasant resistance, ranging from the individualised to collectivised, organised to disorganised, and sometimes localised frontal confrontations or dispersed insurgencies that do not often make for juicy media headlines (Moreda 2015: 525). As Scott (1985) has underscored, the overarching '… goal, after all, of the bulk of peasant resistance is not to overthrow or transform a system of domination but rather to survive…within it'. In South-western Cameroon just like Ethiopia (Moreda, 2015), disaffected peasant communities engage in 'everyday forms of resistance', regularly blending overt and covert strategies that can both be structured and unstructured. Scott (1985) points out that everyday resistances could range from the feet dragging of peasant labourers working in large agricultural farms, to false compliance, sabotage, pilfering, feigned ignorance, and arson, to name a few—the principal aim being to illustrate that 'subaltern' people can belittle dominance and will not remain passive browbeaten victims. If existing historical analysis on peasant and agrarian revolts and resistances are to be taken seriously, '…to ignore the weapons of the weak, is to ignore the peasants' principal arsenal…' (Isaacman 1990: 33).

Adnan (2007) and Schneider (2011) have noted with thoughtful vigilance that when peasants can no longer withstand perceived injustices perpetrated by those considered as oppressors, everyday forms of resistance can quickly morph into more violent and direct forms of confrontations. This was the case in Nguti between 2010 and 2013 where the more pacific forms of everyday resistances employed by the Nguti population against SGSOC gave way to visceral and reactionary mobilization which saw mass protests turn physical, necessitating the deployment of the police and government forces. One of such instances occurred on April 4th 2014, when villagers from Babensi II staged a street protest against the illegal occupation of their land, blocking roads and key access points to the SGSOC nursery, demanding amongst other things, SGSOC`s immediate departure and the prompt payment of adequate compensations for villagers` crops destroyed. Agitated protesters also directed their ire at government officials for turning a deaf ear to their wailings. They also deplored the many previous instances when SGSOC company officials had intimidated them (Fonjong et al., 2015), corroborating Borras and Franco`s (2010: 23) assessment that 'the ground for exercising everyday politics is not smooth and is

128

played out under various constraining structures that make such activities difficult…'.

Many factors precipitated such simmering outbursts, topmost of which was mounting anger over SGSOC`s refusal to fulfil compensation promises to villagers whose farms had been appropriated or crops destroyed by the company. Farmers from the Manyemen village interviewed during the study for instance, were quick to express their anger, with the views of one farmer particularly telling:

> '…SGSOC struggled to seize our farms. When they failed, they try to buy the land from us but we refused… then they went ahead to destroy our crops claiming the land was empty… We have asked them to compensate us… (6th June 2015).

The failure to compensate villagers for their loss constituted a modal trend throughout the research, with participants from other villages such as Talangaye and Ebanga quite disenchanted about the perceived ill-treatment endured from SGSOC. Most respondents reported rising communal exasperation at the company's flagrant unwillingness to stick to the terms of a pre-establishment meeting held between the local administration (the Divisional Officer), SGSOC officials and the villagers on September 25th 2009. The company had expressively undertaken to provide prompt and adequate compensations to "persons concerned in case of any destruction of crops cause by the company…" (excerpts of the minutes of the report). To compound the prevailing sense of discontent, affected villagers took exceptions at the general arbitrariness and the top-down manner in which they had lost their farmlands (Fonjong et al., 2015, Ndi, 2018). An embittered Manyemen farmer held that:

> 'When SGSOC came into our village, they invited some elders who agreed to give out our forest without our consent… The elders forced us to accept certain conditions, which were later reflected in the MoU. These promises made in the MoU have unfortunately never been respected...' (8th June 2015).

In fact, villagers also reported that provisions of a follow-up Memorandum of Understanding (MoU) entered between SGSOC and community representatives on the 27th July 2010 had also been breached. For example, the company had promised to provide electricity, pipe-borne water, as well as community health facilities as a *quid pro quo* condition for gaining access to communal lands. None of the above corporate social responsibility obligations were ever met, as SGSOC continued to expand its plantation sizes. Field observations and key respondent discussions with local government officials confirmed the veracity of such grievances, even though these officials believed t such promises were still to be fulfilled in the future. It is this systematic violation of the agreements between SGSOC, government officials and villagers that pushed a particularly reactionary segment of the local Nguti population to call for the company's departure, citing bad faith. A village chief in Manyemen perhaps aptly captured the prevalent communal sentiment this way:

'… There is no MoU between Manyemen and SGSOC because, the company has failed to provide basic social amenities as promised, like piped water, electricity, etc. This means we need to call for their attention to clarify us why they are not keeping to terms, and to establish new contracts…' (13th May 2015).

A surprisingly frank assessment of the prevailing disorder was also rendered by a local representative of the government's forestry department who argued that the company's resort to strong-arming local villagers by employing top-down tactics instead of a participatory bottom-up approach to acquiring land was bound to backfire. It was just a matter of time, he reiterated, further underscoring that "...the process to acquire the land by SGSOC was poor because they started from above (the political headquarters) rather than from the people before informing hierarchy... Furthermore, the convention and meetings did not consider the views of the population. Consultations if any, were generally without the consent of the youths, women and other groups...", the people who matter the most, he concluded[4] This approach amounts to a breach of the principle of free, prior and informed consent (FPIC[5]), considered to be the cornerstone of ethical large-scale land acquisition engagements (see H and B Consulting, 2011).

The question pertaining to who actually owns and controls land in the Nguti area remains an unsettled one. For the Nguti local communities, and perhaps ostensibly so, customary law which in their opinion predates the formal existence of the modern Cameroon State, justify their inherent usufruct or ownership right over their land. Which is why local village representatives interviewed were particularly adamant, even militant, in their insistence that any land agreements completed without their consent did 'not hold water' and had to be renegotiated since it violated a key part of their individual and collective sense of belonging. This posture is nevertheless contradicted with vehemence by government administrators in Nguti who emphasized that while the indigenous population might wield usufructuary rights over their land, any attempts to exercise full ownership rights was a rude contravention of the statutory rights conferred on the Cameroonian State over all untitled land, including the Nguti land. In fact, as the D.O in Nguti sub-division was quick to reiterate during interviews "communities have the right to use the topsoil, but they cannot claim ownership unless they have a land certificate..." He added that "even with a land certificate, individuals might not have rights to subsurface mineral resources, a situation shared with many other nations" (11th May 2015). Another government official was somewhat more sympathetic of the plight of the Nguti people. He averred:

---

[4] See Fonjong, et al., (2015) Disenchanting Voices from Within: Interrogating women's resistance to Large-Scale Agro-investment in Cameroon. Paper prepared for presentation to "2015 World Bank conference on land and poverty" Washington DC, March 23-27.

[5] FPIC is concretized by Article 32 of the UN Declaration on the Rights of Indigenous Peoples (2007) which stipulate that indigenous peoples have the right to approve proposed development engagements on their lands, based on their full information, representative institutions, and iterative, culturally sensitive negotiation, backed up by effective systems of grievance, redress, and mitigation

'The agriculture company came poorly into the communities that almost made them not to operate…. They came with a plan and map from Yaoundé, indicating the areas to be acquired… having those maps does not guarantee them access … the people resisted and complained. We had some initial agreements with them although many people were not involved or consulted …' (11th May 2015).

Another key cause of communal opposition to the SGSOC project in Nguti sub-division is the company`s inability to recognize and respect the sanctity of culturally symbolic sites such as traditional religious shrines, sacred groves, and ancestral burial places which occupy a venerated place at the centre of local worship systems and socio-cultural well-being. Respondents in Benbensi II and Talangaye villages reported for instance that SGSOC workers disrespect and destroyed local shrines and religious worship sites in their villages during the initial surveying and cadastral phase of their work. They also destroyed pristine forest groves that held priceless ecological and cultural value to the local population, to create an extraction corridor for the transportation of lumbered timber and facilitate the movement of their employees. Vowing to resist the SGSOC with his life, an elderly gentleman who happens to be a fervent custodian of the Talangaye culture explained the population`s anger thus:

'…Our lives also depend on those shrines. When we have problems in the village, our kinsmen go into the shrines to consult with our forefathers…. Shrines are places to communicate with our ancestors in case of crises such as poor harvest… or when someone commits a taboo like murder… tampering with the grave of an ancestor, especially by an 'outsider' or a 'foreigner' is an act of violence against the entire village' (27th October 2015).

A youth representative was perhaps much more blunt: '… The company should not dare to enter into our sacred areas, else they will be playing with fire…' (Manyemen 22nd May 2015).

Farmers also decried the fact that they could not peacefully vent their grievances against the excesses of the company without being treated as pariahs. One farmer noted that:

'… SGSOC is trying to make us criminals in our own land. They have encroached into my farm… mapped out some sections. …. How can a foreign company intrude into our village and instead of them acting peacefully, they rather want us to be victims of their plantation…?' (27 October 2015).

In general, the overwhelming perception amongst respondents was that the cost of SGSOC's agricultural intervention in their communities far exceeded the benefits in ways that do not justify the company's continuous existence in the Nguti land. Field observations also revealed a string of unfulfilled promises, underscoring the perceptible sense of profound disillusionment and anger amongst the local population. At the time of the research, there were little traces that the SGSOC was even attempting to fulfil some of its promises. Where the company had fulfilled part of its promise was in the provision of general labour employment to some male villagers, although those fortunate enough to be employed nevertheless reported that their wages were mere pittance, compared to what they gained from their cocoa or coffee farms prior to the company's arrival. Explaining their unresolved plight and the reason why they had resorted to physical resistance against SGSOC's presence in the Ebanga village. Some employees declared that they go for months without salaries and SGSOC needs to leave so that they can return to their land and inheritance to survive.

The resentment echoed by women was particularly palpable, with most accusing the company of either not employing enough women or for their arbitrary dismissal shortly after recruitment. Others faulted the company for the rising food prices since its operations commenced in their villages, blaming SGSOC for women's collective inability to access and cultivate their lands due to rising pressure over fertile lands induced by the plantation's continuous expansion. This has forced women to the fringes where they are compelled to cultivate unfertile marginal lands. As two women leaders observed during focus group discussions in Manyemen and Nguti villages respectively:

> "Our applications to do general labour were rejected. They employ mostly men…they think men are stronger…' (22 May 2015). '… Most of us did not go to school; we cannot apply for office jobs…' (24 April 2015).

The above assessments corroborate Li`s (2011) observation of LSLAs that when land and not labour is mostly needed, current occupants of such lands get undervalued and consequently expelled. Over 70% of the interviewed female cluster of the sample size expressed deep anxiety over current shortages in arable land, a significant concern widely reflected within the ambits of current LSLA literature in political ecology (Rocheleau et al., 1996). As female respondents from Ebanga village further expressed 'We use land to grow food crops. This company took it to grow palms; other parts have been marked… we no longer have access' (6th June 2015).

From the above discussions, the communal anger against SGSOC is deeply entrenched and widespread. The fomentation of these grievances, which began in the form of everyday resistances, evolved into more physical forms of resistance in which community members from affected communities either threatened the use of violence or used violence to disrupt the operations of the company in their localities and to arouse Cameroon government`s attention to their plight.

In a letter addressed to Mr. Paul Biya, President of the Republic of Cameroon dated 1st August 2011 and signed by the Bassosi Cultural and Development Association (MBUOM-NSUASE, 2011), and in another dated 19th August 2011, the villagers seriously admonished that "… anybody dealing with whosoever with regards to Bassosi ancestral land is doing so at his own risk" reiterating that "…we are therefore appealing for the government's intervention…" (MBUOM-NSUASE, 2011) to remedy this situation in a timely fashion before it escalates beyond control. On August 1st 2011, the Directors SGSOC were put on notice, and warned against further encroachment in the Nguti native land or face dire consequences

(MBUOM-NSUASE, 2011). As one village councillor who is privy to the drafting process commented, we drafted the letters to let the government and SGSOC know that we are not spineless, and to try to "...acquire peoples' farmland without their consent is a manifestation of bad faith..." Yet, as Hall et al, (2015) have posited, local responses to LSLAs are always varied. There are equally certain segments of the local Nguti population who have either been co-opted into compliance with entrenched interests or have simply opted for a more 'tempered' approach to the LSLA to avoid being targeted by government forces or simply in to support their welfare and livelihood chances.

## Co-optation, collaboration and compromise

Multiple axes of interests often crisscross in Nguti. While most of the population is opposed to the SGSOC project, others have found grounds for collaboration with the company. Nguti has a diversity of farmers, migrants; local elites; unemployed; politicians; retired government functionaries, each with varying interests. For example, the uneducated and unemployed landless class badly needs jobs, and are often willing to overlook the marginalization they endure at the hands of SGSOC, to provide for their families. For the educated and unemployed, the company's presence has given them an opportunity which they could never gain from the government of Cameroon which has been accused of being extremely corrupt. Some have for instance secured jobs with the company as Community Liaison or Development Officers, a notable example being the Chief of Ayong village. Their loyalties are quite understandable. Yet, others who have been significantly ill-treated by the company such as farmers still believe that a Nguti community-SGSOC deal could be renegotiated to give better concessions to affected villages and to provide space for greater participation and voices of local community members, for more positive developmental outcomes and dividends for communities. For these group of people, their fight is not for the company to be dislodged but for it to be a better and more conscientious partner invested for their development.

135

A cluster of the women interviewed for instance, worry less about land ownership concerns, since they really do not have these in the first place due to patriarchal and local cultural ethos. What they have is usufructuary rights over the Nguti land (Fonjong et al., 2016). It has been widely argued that in such societies, the presence of foreign actors can further exacerbate gendered tensions over land use, and promote intra-family conflicts within households (Carney's, 2004 and Peters, 2002). For Nguti women consequently, SGSOC is welcome to stay, if the company goes further into the Mbo-hinterlands to secure land, an area which has no road access, and which would require significant industrial capacity to disenclave. They also advocate for unlimited access to productive forests reserves, often blocked by SGSOC plantations, to enable the continued harvesting of NTFPs which help supplement their meagre household incomes.

Mounting allegations regarding local elites and chiefs bribed into compliance by local government officials and SGSOC representatives were uncovered which perhaps deserve further attention here. In Manyemen for example, many villagers were persistent in their allegations that the company had paid some chiefs and local personalities to serve as spies and identify purveyors of anti-SGSOC sentiments for further retaliatory action. In Talangaye, Etahoben (2014) reports that the village head had received pecuniary rewards to mastermind the hitch-free arrival of SGSOC in the area, working to expand his network of accomplices to include other local chiefs. In agrarian African societies like elsewhere, elites are expected to protect the interest of their communities, advocate their course and press for their holistic development. Allegations of elite capture such as those underscored above served to weaken a united communal front against the excesses of SGSOC in the Nguti area. As one community member was quick to underscore: "...our so-called elites represent their own interests over the interest of communities" (Manyemen, 22nd May 2015). Others lamented that if their chiefs had been won over, what other choices did they have but to "toe the line" and collaborate with SGSOC to salvage what is left to be gained for the community. In fact, as one villager pointed that "...We know of some chiefs who transformed their lifestyles overnight…some poor chiefs began driving expensive cars" (23rd May, 2015).

What is crystal clear is that the local elites in the area, comprised principally of retired government functionaries and politicians, are not just vying for profitable employment in SGSOC; they are willing to serve as fervent enablers to win managerial positions with greater financial rewards within the company, what has been described as "adverse incorporation (Hall et al., 2015; Hickey and du Toit, 2007). As one local elite underscored: "… We cannot derive maximum benefit from this company without joining the management team… ordinary employment is not enough…" (10 October 2015).

Nguti local community members are not oblivious to the intriguing politics of land grabbing in their area. Some have awoken to the realisation that gains could be maximised within the context of SGSOC's presence in the area and not through its ouster, perhaps corroborating Scott's observation that "… the bulk of peasant resistance is not to overthrow or transform a system of domination but rather to survive…. within it…" (Scott, 1987: 424). Hobsbawm (1973), puts it best, when he further contends that "… the non-utopian aim of peasants is working the system to their minimum disadvantage…" (cited in Scott, 1987: 424). It is this inclination towards compromise that is perhaps vividly revealed in the summation made by a key local figure, when he asserts that:

> "We can only give to Herakles what we have and what we can…. Either the company takes it or leaves it…. They cannot claim they are developmental, and at the same time they want to concentrate their activities only around where there are already developed road networks…" (22nd April 2015).

Cotula and Vermeulen (2009); and Vermeulen and (Cotula, 2010) have accordingly observed that foreign agro-investors often naturally focus on lands that have greater market proximity, access to irrigation systems, experience higher rainfalls or those in areas with fertile soils. In Mali, for instance, they illustrate the high concentration of LSLA deals in areas with significant agro-productivity and long-term potential.

Beyond economic considerations, other cultural, social and even spiritual obligations have compelled certain segments of the disaffected Nguti population to compromise their stance, and move towards collaboration with SGSOC, instead of simply hardening their posture in a long-term fight with the company during which a sure victory remains significantly uncertain. As one traditional elite underlined while impressing other villagers on the need for a more pragmatic and conciliatory stance with SGSOC: "... Apart from the economic benefits derived from our forest, culture is also important...if we fail to negotiate, we might lose connections with our ancestors. We need to ensure they don't go into those sacred places and burials sites... In some villages, graves have been levelled out ... we cannot let that happen in Nguti... we must show them where to establish...if they trespass, they will battle not just with us but also with our ancestors..." (1st September 2015).

In the same vein, others have also called for a communal realisation of the potential benefits that are accruable to the Nguti people, if a more fruitful deal were to be hammered out with SGSOC. For this somewhat minority segment of the population, the choleric approach of blunt visceral resistance championed by the Nguti hardliners is counterproductive to the collective interest of local people. This demonstrates that some villagers are still open to compromise and collaboration with SGSOC, pushing for renegotiation of land deals with affected communities in ways that advance sustainable environmental, social, cultural and developmental outcomes. This is because, ".... development is a game of give and take... you cannot eat your cake and have it back...". (retired civil servant 9th May 2015).

**Trapped in the middle**

A significant minority of the Nguti people appeared somewhat trapped in the middle, between a hard-line stance against SGSOC, and open compromise because of other very pragmatic concerns. As one woman from Babensi II opined '...My husband is hot-tempered; I try to calm him down. We are not happy with SGSOC, but if he is not careful the government can jail him. Sometimes, we (women) stay silent when we are not happy… A woman's silence is dangerous!' (10 May 2015). Another local elite who doubles as government representative, castigated SGSOC's practises in Nguti, while also stressing that he had been trapped in the middle of the struggle for purely political reasons:

> "…I sympathize with my people… I have told them what to write in their letters and have guided them how to do it…. Now, I am representing the interest of the government and obliged to execute its missions without questioning…so the most I can do is to advise my people how to approach the government and the company…" (12th May 2015).

Yet, at the more substantive level, there are villagers who remain confused as to the real motive of SGSOC's presence in Nguti land. Some who were initially willing to support the company's presence in their area, remain overtly suspicious about its real intentions. An incident on 14th May 2015 perhaps best illustrates this prevalent sense of doubt. At the behest of the Senior Divisional Officer (SDO), the highest-ranking government official in the division, a meeting was convened with local chiefs and development stakeholders to address local grievances. After making a presentation behalf of his company, the SGSOC representative also stood up to make a statement on behalf of a logging company in the area called Uniprovince. To the utter dismay of many, the visibly irritated SDO was compelled to harshly intervene, ordering the SGSOC representative to immediately halt his remarks, as he could not possibly both be representing the interests of an agro-plantation company and a timber logging company at the same time.

This incident gave juicy fodder to prevalent allegations that SGSOC had created a shell company - Uniprovince, which was then awarded a *vente de coupe* (sale of standing volume) to harvest and transport valuable timber from the concession zone under question (Potter, 2015). As one farmer remarked: "… SGSOC is certainly not revealing its plans to the local population…. When they first came, they said they want to invest in plantation agriculture, which will create many employments for us… while we were still to go into negotiation, we realized that they were also into timber extraction…. We now wonder what their real intentions are... what happens if we give them land and they discover that it is rich in minerals? We want to know their real intention before we can go into agreement on clearly defined terms…" (1ˢᵗ November 2015).

Summing up his indifference to the current situation, one local farmer who proclaimed his impulses against violence (referring to the hardliners) and in favour of development in his community, also underscored that SGSOC could not ever be trusted. As he poignantly remarked: "…. The problem with agro-companies is that when you give them 1 hectare, they will take 5 hectares. When you give them 3 hectares, they will take 10…" (20ᵗʰ April 2015).

## Conclusions

This chapter has revealed that a lot needs to change in the conduct of LSLA deals in Africa. Granted, while some deals have heralded propitious developmental watersheds for impoverished host communities long abandoned by their own governments – transforming their fortunes for the better, – others, a significant majority unfortunately, have augured pretty much ominous prospects for affected local peoples. It is tragically within the latter category of development "losers" that the Nguti people of South-western Cameroon fall, at the hands of SGSOC.

Going forward, some pertinent lessons need to be learnt. First, there is need for a complete overhaul of the Cameroon government's shady and top-down approach to negotiating LSLAs deals, giving way to a more democratised and transparent process that allows space for the prior, informed and participatory consent of communities affected by prospective interventions, through proper consultations processes. Secondly, better and stronger grassroots-driven social and environmental impact assessments must be conducted that clearly identify risks, measures of mitigation, benchmarks and adequate resources earmarked to manage the risks of local people being tied down in a rotten deal; thirdly better community 'stakeholdership' and incorporation at the managerial and decision-making level within LSLA projects should create space for locally-driven course-correcting measures to be implemented once issues are identified (see Ndi, 2018, and Ndi and Batterbury, 2018). Fourthly, the development of production value chains that capitalise on the local resources and local socio-economic and environmental wellbeing of affected areas should be instituted and leveraged. Furthermore, given the myriad problems that local politicians, local elites and traditional leaders present in the process of LSLAs, there is need to delink this segment from the entire process to forestall their corrupt and corrosive role, engendering an inclusive process that favours stronger community-wide consultations and involvement. Finally, and perhaps most importantly, LSLAs have a gendered impact on affected communities. Preliminary assessments that are gender-sensitive and demographically disaggregated must be conducted to predict the potentially differential impact on men, women, youth and other disadvantaged groups, and corrective measures planned and integrated into the concept blueprint of the endeavour, from the very start.

# References

Achobang, C. A; Nguiffo, S; and Schwartz, B. 2009. Chapter 15: SG Sustainable Oils Cameroon PLC (SGSOC) in South West Cameroon. Forest Peoples Programme http://www.forestpeoples.org/taxonomy/term/696/gallery (10/02/2016)

Anseeuw, W. (2013). The Rush for Land in Africa: Resource Grabbing or Green Revolution? *South African Journal of International Affairs, 20*(1), 159-177.

Batterbury S.P.J. and F. Ndi. (2018). Land grabbing in Africa. In Binns J.A., K. Lynch and E. Nel (eds.) The Routledge Handbook of African Development. London: Routledge. PP 573-582.

Balehegn, M., (2015) Unintended Consequences: The Ecological Repercussions of Land Grabbing in Sub-Saharan Africa, Environment: Science and Policy for Sustainable Development, 57:2, 4-21.

Bassosi Cultural and Development Association -MBOUM-NSUASE - 2011. Memorandum Submitted to the Director, SGSOC on Land Acquisition by SGSOC in Nguti Sub-Division, 10th August 2011.

Bird, K., & Pratt, N. (2004). Fracture Points in Social Policies for Chronic Poverty Reduction. *Chronic Poverty Research Centre Working Paper* (47).

Borras, Jr. S.M., and J.C. Franco. 2010. Towards a Broader View of the Politics of Global Land Grabs: Rethinking Land Issues, Reframing Resistance. ICAS Working Paper Series No, 001.

Borras Jr, S. M., Fig, D., & Suárez, S. M. (2011). The Politics of Agrofuels and Mega Land and Water Deals: Insights from the ProCana case, Mozambique. *Review of African Political Economy, 38*(128), 215-234.

Cameroon Data Portal. 2015. Effective Population by Regions. http://cameroon.opendataforafrica.org/

Carney, J. (2004). Gender Conflict in Gambian wetlands. *Liberation Ecologies: Environment, Development, Social Movements*, 316-335.

Centre for Environment and Development -CED. 2012. Herakles' 13th labour? A Study of SGSOC's Land Concession in South-West Cameroon. http://www.forestpeoples.org/topics/palm-oil-rspo/publication/2012/ced-publication-herakles-13th-labour-study-sgsoc-s-land-conces (08/03/ 2016).

Chu, J. (2011). Gender and 'Land Grabbing' in Sub-Saharan Africa: Women's Land rights and customary land tenure. *Development, 54*(1), 35-39.

Cotula, L., & Vermeulen, S. (2011). Contexts and Procedures for Farmland Acquisitions in Africa: What Outcomes for Local People? *Development, 54*(1), 40-48.

Cotula, L., Vermeulen, S., Leonard, R., & Keeley, J. (2009). Land Grab or Development Opportunity. *Agricultural Investment and International Land Deals in Africa*, 130.

Deininger, K. and D. Byerlee (2011). Rising Global Interest in Farmland: Can it Yield Sustainable and Equitable Benefits? Washington DC. The Word Bank.

142

De Schutter, O. (2009). Large-scale Land Acquisitions and Leases: A Set of Core Principles and Measures to Address the Human Rights Challenge. United Nations.

De Schutter, O (2012). Report of the Special Rapporteur on the Right to Food: Mission to Cameroon. Addendum. UN Human Right Council/22/20/Add2.

Edelman, M. (2013). Messy Hectares: Questions about the Epistemology of Land Grabbing Data. *Journal of Peasant Studies, 40*(3), 485-501.

Feintrenie, et al. (2014). Are Agribusiness Companies Responsible for Land Grabbing in Central Africa? Paper Presented at the 2014 Annual World Bank Conference on Land and Poverty, Washington DC, March 23-27.

Fonchingong, C. (1999). Structural Adjustment, Women, and Agriculture in Cameroon. *Gender & Development, 7*(3), 73-79.

Fonjong, L. (2017) Left out but not backing down: exploring women's voices against large-scale agro-plantations in Cameroon, *Development in Practice*, 27:8, 1114-1125.

Fonjong, L., Sama-Lang, I., Fombe, L., & Abonge, C. (2016). Land Governance and Women's Rights in Large-Scale Land Acquisitions in Cameroon. *Development in Practice, 26*(4), 420-430.

Fonjong, L., Sama-Lang, I., Fombe, L., & Abonge, C. (2015). Disenchanting Voices from Within: Interrogating Women's Resistance to Large-Scale Agro-Investments in Cameroon. Paper presented at the Annual World Bank Conference on land and poverty, Washington DC, March 23-27.

Fombe, L., I. Sama-Lang., L. Fonjong., and A. Mbah-Fongkimeh (2013). Securing Tenure for Sustainable Livelihoods: A Case of Women Land Ownership in Anglophone Cameroon. *Ethics and Economics, 10*(2).

Greenpeace (2014). Herakles Farms: Champions of Illegal Deforestation. http://www.greenpeace.org/usa/herakles-farms-champions-illegal-deforestation/ (08/03 /2016).

Greenpeace (2013). Herakles Farms in Cameroon: A Showcase in Bad Palm Oil Production. *Greenpeace.*

Goldman, M. J., Davis, A., & Little, J. (2016). Controlling Land They Call Their Own: Access and Women's Empowerment in Northern Tanzania. *The Journal of Peasant Studies, 43*(4), 777-797.

Hall, R et al. (2015). Resistance, Acquiescence or Incorporation? An Introduction to Land Grabbing and Political Reactions 'from Below'. *Journal of Peasant Studies, 42*(3-4), 467-488.

Jacobs, S. (2010) *Gender and Agrarian Reforms*. London: Routledge.

Li, T. M. (2011). Centring Labour in the Land Grab Debate. *The Journal of Peasant Studies, 38*(2), 281-298.

Millar, G. (2015). "We Have No Voice for That": Land Rights, Power, and Gender in Rural Sierra Leone. *Journal of Human Rights, 14*(4), 445-462.

Moreda, T. (2015). Listening to Their Silence? The Political Reaction of Affected Communities to Large-Scale Land Acquisitions: Insights from Ethiopia. *Journal of Peasant Studies, 42*(3-4), 517-539.

Nature Cameroon (2011). A letter Addressed to the Minister of Environment and Nature Protection titled 'Critical Observations of the SGSOC ESIA in South West Cameroon' Unpublished.

Ndi, F. A. (*2017*). Land grabbing, Local Contestation and the Struggle for Economic Gain: Insights from Nguti village, South West Cameroon. SAGE Open, 1-4.

Ndi, F.A. (2018) Land grabbing, gender and access to land: implications for local food production and rural livelihoods in Ngutisub-division, South West Cameroon, *Canadian Journal of African Studies/Revue canadienne des études africaines*, 53:1, 131-154.

Ndi, F. A. and Batterbury, S., (2017), Land Grabbing and the Axis of Political Conflicts: Insights from Southwest Cameroon. *Africa Spectrum*, 52(1): 33–63.

Nguiffo, S., and B. Schwartz (2012) Herakles' 13th labour? A study of SGSOC's land concession in South West Cameroon. CED.

Nguti Rural Council. (2009). Monographic Study. Nguti Council.

Oakland Institute (2012). Understanding Land Investment Deals in Africa: Massive Deforestation Portrayed as Unsustainable Development. The Deceit of Herakles Farms in Cameroon. The Oakland Institute.

Ordinance No. 74-1 of 5th July 1974 to establish land tenure in Cameroon

Oya, C. (2013). The Land Rush and Classic Agrarian Questions of Capital and Labour: A Systematic Scoping Review of the Socio-economic Impact of Land Grabs in Africa. *Third World Quarterly, 34*(9), 1532-1557.

Peluso, N. L., & Lund, C. (2011). New Frontiers of Land Control: Introduction. *Journal of Peasant Studies, 38*(4), 667-681.

Peters, P. E. (2002). Bewitching Land: The Role of Land Disputes in Converting Kin to Strangers and in Class Formation in Malawi. *Journal of Southern African Studies, 28*(1), 155-178.

Peters, P. E. (2004). Inequality and Social Conflict Over Land in Africa. *Journal of Agrarian Change, 4*(3), 269-314.

Peters, P. E. (2009). Challenges in Land Tenure and Land Reform in Africa: Anthropological contributions. *World Development, 37*(8), 1317-1325.

Rob Rocheleau, D.E., B. Thomas-Slayter and E. Wangari (eds.) (1996) Feminist Political Ecology: Global Issues and Local Experiences. London: Routledge

Scoones, I., Hall, R., Borras Jr, S. M., White, B., & Wolford, W. (2013). The Politics of Evidence: Methodologies for Understanding the Global Land Rush. *Journal of Peasant Studies, 40*(3), 469-483.

Scott, J. C. (2008). *Weapons of the weak: Everyday forms of peasant resistance*: Yale University Press.

Scott, J. C. (1998). *Seeing Like a State: How Certain Schemes to Improve the Human Condition Have Failed*: Yale University Press.

Toulmin, C. (2009). Securing Land and Property Rights in sub-Saharan Africa: The Role of Local Institutions. *Land Use Policy, 26*(1), 10-19.

Tsikata, D., & Golah, P. (2010). *Land Tenure, Gender and Globalisation: Research and Analysis from Africa, Asia and Latin America*: IDRC.

Verma, R. (2014). Land Grabs, Power, and Gender in East and Southern Africa: So, What's New? *Feminist economics, 20*(1), 52-75.

Vermeulen, S., & Cotula, L. (2010). Over the Heads of Local People: Consultation, Consent, and Recompense in Large-Scale Land Deals for Biofuel Projects in Africa. *The Journal of Peasant Studies, 37*(4), 899-916.

Von Braun, J., & Webb, P. J. (1989). The Impact of New Crop Technology on the Agricultural Division of Labour in a West African Setting. *Economic Development and Cultural Change*, 513-534.

White, B., Borras Jr, S. M., Hall, R., Scoones, I., & Wolford, W. (2012). The New Enclosures: Critical Perspectives on Corporate Land Deals. *Journal of Peasant Studies, 39*(3-4), 619-647.

White, J., & White, B. (2012). Gendered Experiences of Dispossession: Oil Palm Expansion in a Dayak Hibun community in West Kalimantan. *Journal of Peasant Studies, 39*(3-4), 995-1016.

Whitehead, A., & Tsikata, D. (2003). Policy Discourses on Women's Land Rights in Sub–Saharan Africa: The Implications of the Return to the Customary. *Journal of Agrarian Change, 3*(1-2), 67-112.

# Chapter 6

## Understanding the Nature, Challenges, and Implications of Land Conflicts on Local Development in Ndu sub-Division of Cameroon

*Ngeh Roland Nformi, Balgah Sounders N., Lotsmart Fonjong, and Nformi Solange Chewe,*

### Abstract

With growing diversification in land uses, land ownership is increasingly becoming a source of conflicts in Ndu Sub-division. Moreover, because of poor land use planning, land scarcity, competition for suitable arable land between farmers and graziers, and the ineffective implementation of land statues, many more land conflicts are bound to arise in the Sub-division. This chapter highlights some of these conflicts and the extent to which their non-resolution has contributed to stagnated local development. The study is based on a survey conducted among 200 victims of land conflicts using stratified random sampling technique. Data is analysed qualitatively, and the findings suggest that proper land management and development in Ndu Sub-division cannot be separated.

**Key Words**: Land conflict, land resolutions, local development and Ndu Sub-division.

## Introduction

Ndu Sub-division which is on the Nkambe plateau is typically inhabited by agrarian populations. This population has a low purchasing power which prevents them from breaking-even and affording the cost of land litigation. Because of their need for land for production and inability to afford justice, the numbers of unresolved land conflicts in the division continue to be on the rise. Cotula, Toulmin, & Hesse, (2004) observe that population pressure, commercial agriculture, and urbanization, have contributed to the increasing number of land conflicts, particularly where existing land tenure systems may not be well-equipped to resolve such conflicts. Land conflicts could result to displacements and migration of especially the youthful population which is the future of local development (Fonjong et al., 2010).

As the population of Ndu continues to increase exponentially over the years, the reoccurrence of land conflicts remains a fundamental problem to be handled both by the traditional and administrative authorities. Land conflicts and their resolution are associated with significant economic losses and an increasingly serious social problem that undermines both the faith of people in current institutions and their ability to achieve sustainable livelihoods (Sovannarith et al., 2001; Wehrmann, 2017). It is against this background that this study identifies the types and drivers of land conflicts and investigates their resolution process in Ndu Sub-division. The *raison d'etre* is to highlight good practices in the resolution process to mitigate the consequences of land conflicts.

**Methodology**

Ndu sub-Division is one of the five Sub-divisions of Donga-Mantung in North West Region of Cameroon with Ndu town as its sub-divisional headquarters. It is made up of 32 villages with a population of 73.955 inhabitants. It lies between Longitudes 10°.50′48′′ east of the Greenwich Meridian and Latitudes 6°.20′25′′ north of the Equator and covers a total surface area of 1625km² (United Councils & Cities of Cameroon (Cvuc)-visited, 2019). Its position is central to Nwa, Kumbo and Nkambe Sub-divisions (Figure 1). The principal tribal group in the Sub-division is the Mbum whose ancestors are believed to have hailed from Tikari in the Adamawa Region of Cameroon, with Limbum as their indigenous language. The focus on Ndu Sub-division was deliberate, guided by the following considerations: 1) its complex topographic configurations with highlands, lowlands, deep valleys and steep slopes make it difficult to find suitable land for agriculture and settlement and thus provide fertile grounds for land conflicts. 2) Both

148

farming and grazing are practiced in the area still using poor farming and grazing methods. The practice of slash-and-burn, shifting cultivation, and over grazing lead to soil degradation forcing farmers to invade fertile rangelands to maximize production resulting to conflict with the graziers. 3) Most inhabitants in Ndu Sub-division are poor peasants with land as the lone source of livelihood. Since agriculture in the area is still rudimentary, crop yields remain very sensitive to environmental changes. These changes, in most cases present impediments to livelihoods sustenance and local development.

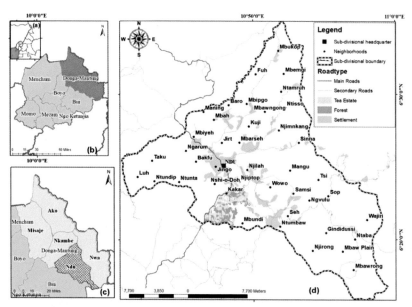

**Figure 1: Location of Ndu Sub-division**

a) North West Region in Cameroon, Donga-Mantung in the North West Region, b) Ndu Sub-division and its Environs, c) A Detailed Layout Map of Ndu Sub-division

**Source: Adapted from the Topographic Map Sheet of Cameroon**

A multi-disciplinary approach for data collection has been employed for this study. The numerous communities in Ndu Sub-division necessitate a stratified random sampling technique. For this reason, the following spots of land conflicts in Ndu Sub-division were considered for this study. These included: Ndu, Fuh, Ngarum, Njimnkang, Wowo, Talla, Sehn, Mbarseh, Mbiyeh, Ngvulu, Mbawrong, Ntumbaw, Kakar, Njilah, Mbipgo, Sinna, Sop, Jirt, and Mbawngong (Figure 1). Field work was carried between November 2015 and March 2017. From these, the sample size was estimated using sample calculation for population using Epi Info 6.04d software (Nana, 2018) to be 200 to achieve the objectives of this study. The sample size of 200 participants was made up of women and men, 51% and 49% respectively. This adequate gender stratification was commendable for diversity and representativeness.

Field surveys constituted the main technique of data collection. It provided a huge amount of raw data source collected with the help of observations, questionnaire and interviews. The thirty key informants included administrative and traditional authorities, religious authorities, NGOs and the affected members of the population in each of the communities. Although the field work was carried out in Ndu Sub-division, reference is made to land conflicts between Nwa Sub-division and Ndu Sub-division over Tudig, Ndu people and Nso people over the area covered by the tea estate. Secondary sources provided useful data and facilitated the understanding of the genesis and the ramifications of land conflicts. Some official documents were consulted from the secretariats of the Senior Divisional Officer (SDO) and the Sub-divisional Officer (DO), Divisional and Sub-divisional delegations, religious institutions, and the secretariats Non-governmental Organisations (NGOs). Population statistics were obtained from the North West Regional Delegation of the Economy and Planning, and some case files from archival materials, the Land Management Authority, State Inspection Office, National Assembly, the Ministry of Justice, and branches of these offices at the Divisional and Sub-divisional levels. Various historical and legal documents were important in verifying and complementing the views of the informants.

## Types of Land Conflicts in Ndu Sub-division

Field investigations revealed that the major types were the Crop farmer-Livestock farmer conflicts (38%), followed by Inter-village conflicts (31%), land inheritance problems (12%), Crop farmer-Crop farmer conflicts (11%), while Livestock farmer-livestock farmer conflicts (5%) and Intra-village conflicts as the least with 3%. These different conflicts constitute discussions in the succeeding paragraphs.

## Crop farmer-Livestock farmer conflict

Farmers just like graziers' livelihoods depend on the same resources, especially land and water, and in times of climactic stress, such as a drought, environmental pressures increase the possibility of conflict between both groups. Findings reveal that the major causes of Crop farmer-Livestock farmer conflict is competition over land, encroachment by crop farmers into areas mapped out for grazing, conflict of culture, struggle for leadership, and corrupt tendencies of some traditional and administrative authorities. Furthermore, the increase in the number of Crop farmer-Livestock farmer conflicts has been caused by the illegal sale and the allocation of grazing land to farmers and non-farmers by some incompetent personalities (Tata et al., 2013).

Insufficient numbers or the near absence of herdsmen to manage free-range grazing in most parts of Ndu Sub-division has also been identified as a cause of Crop farmer-Livestock farmer conflicts (Kaberry, 1959). It was observed that while some herds were without herdsmen, other herds were being controlled by teenagers of age below 14 years. In addition, some herders have developed bad habit of allowing the animals to feed on the crops of the Crop farmers, especially at night or on market days. Some livestock farmers also are not willing to construct paddocks or cultivate improved pastures for their cattle. They instead use bamboos and sticks frequently infested by termites that render the fences fragile and liable to destruction by cattle even with the least force exerted on them; as noticed around Fuh, Mbipgo and Njimnkang (Figure 2).

Crop farmers are often attracted upland by the cattle dung which is relatively cheaper and easy to access compared to the chemical fertilizer. Livestock farmers on the other hand are pulled to farmlands by fresh weeds or water points down slopes. Generally, the quest for pasture rich areas, especially during the dry season, pushes livestock farmers to take their livestock to wetlands, marshes and other riparian areas in the wetlands which are equally densely cultivated by Crop farmers (Tata et al., 2013). Poverty therefore, aggravates land conflicts due to the inability of Crop farmers and Livestock farmers to acquire sustainable inputs for their economic activities in the same neighbourhood (for example, in Sop, Mbawrong and the Kugha hill) without compromising the interest of one another.

**Figure 2: Poor Cattle Fence in Sop**
Source: Field work (2015)

**Crop farmers-crop farmers conflict**

The scarcity of soil resources caused by land degradation (Lambi, 2001) has led to the number of Crop farmer-Crop farmer conflicts. Unlike Crop farmers-Livestock farmers conflicts that are very common during the dry season when pasture is scarce, Crop farmer-Crop farmer conflict are more common during the months of March and August. These months, respectively, correspond to the first and second cycle periods of crop planting. Amungwa (2009) observes that these conflicts are mostly concentrated in the low-lying areas which are rich in soil fertility because of the increasing population of the dominantly migrant crop farmers. The conflict between Ntumbaw and Njirong people on the farmland at Mbawrong, and other conflicts occurring frequently in the valleys, especially during the dry season are glaring examples. This conflict manifest in a series of confrontations (such as fighting, killing and looting) staged on farmland between villages or the boundaries separating Crop farmers. During such clashes, traditional and the administrative authorities sometimes intervene to suspend all activities in the disputed area until the dispute is resolved. These bans are occasionally flouted as recorded in villages of Mbawrong and Boyar, and when this occur, it may result in heavy fines and sanctions.

**Land inheritance problems**

Land inheritance conflict is a common form of land acquisition in Ndu sub-Division. During inheritance, the land is passed down to the family successor at the death of the family head. Most problems occur where the head is a polygamist. At his death inheritance problems could sometimes result to hatred, disunity and even loss of lives. About 98% of the respondents reported that this type of land conflicts is common because most family heads die without leaving wills on how their landed properties should be administered.

**Intra-Village and Inter-Village Conflicts**

**Table 1: Inter-Village Conflict in Ndu Sub-division**

| Village | Characteristics of the Conflicts |
| --- | --- |
| Ntumbaw-Nso (around the Ngar-Buh area) | Land boundary |
| Ntumbaw-Njirong | Fertile land of Mbaw plain |
| Ntumbaw-Sehn | Land boundary |
| Ntumbaw-Ngvulu | Land boundary |
| Mbipgo-Talla | Land boundary |
| Mbipgo-Njimnkang | Water catchment |
| Mbipgo-Ndu (between Fuh and Jirt) | Land boundary |

| Mbipgo-Mbarseh | Water catchment |
| Mbipgo-Mbawngong | Grazing land |
| Ngarum I-Mbiyeh | Land boundary |
| Ngarum I-Ngarum II | Land boundary |

Source: Field work (2015)

It emanates from the nature of human wants and competition for scarce resources. This type of conflict is very common in communities where there are both crop farmers and livestock farmers who need land for their agricultural and grazing activities. Several land boundary differences, water catchment, and forest resources associated with community conflicts have been recorded over the years in Ndu Sub-division (Table 1).

## Livestock Farmer-Livestock Farmer Conflict

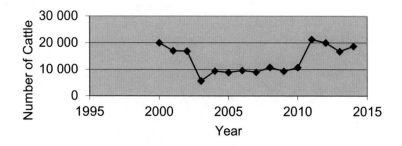

**Figure 3: Cattle Population Growth in Ndu Sub-division from 1998 to 2014**

Source: Ndu Municipal Council Periodic Reports, 2015

Livestock farmer-Livestock Famer conflicts is another type of land conflict recorded. It is not very common compared to the other types of conflicts earlier discussed. It is caused by the increase in the number of animals on an ever-reducing grazing land as a result of encroachment by other land uses. The introduction of Cameroon Development Corporation (CDC) in 1947 in Ardo Gidado's grazing area (Ndu-Ntumbaw area), reduced the size of available grazing area and intensified grazier-grazier conflicts. The CDC introduced plantation agriculture with the cultivation of tea in the area as

154

livestock farmers were pushed to the marginal lands. This resulted to a stiff competition among livestock farmers which in most cases ended up in conflict. Moreover, as the number of cattle increases, there is a scramble for available pastures and water points which occasionally provokes clashes and conflict (Figure 3). These conflicts are more prevalent in villages like Mbawngong, Sop, Njimnkang, and Ngarum.

**Drivers of Land Conflicts in Ndu sub-Division**

Field investigations reveals that the drivers of land conflicts in Ndu sub-Division are: population growth and land scarcity (representing each 30% of respondents), the land tenure system (23%), transhumance (13%), climate variability and limited access to land and its related resources (11%), hydrological change, topography and soils quality (9% each), and the privatization of Ndu Tea Plantation (5%).

## Climate variability and limited access to and its related Resources

Climate vulnerability and limited access to land and its related resources have contributed to land conflicts which have affected food security and development of Ndu Sub-division (Ngeh, 2016). Climate change in the tropical region has begun to show somewhat unexpected trends in the past few decades (IPCC, 2007). In Ndu, drought conditions have become more frequent, severe and protracted, as the rainfall patterns have changed and provoked the migration of pastoralists since the land is unable to sustain these farmers (Sumelong, 2008; Chambah, 2015). Consequently, this resulting change in the ecosystems has caused graziers to move more frequently in search of pastures and water resources. Furthermore, this phenomenon affects land fertility, thus causing crop farmers and the livestock farmers to scramble over the parcel of fertile land left.

The lowest cumulative values (CVs) are observed in January (5.1mm) , December (8.7mm) and February (19.1mm), while the highest CVs are observed in September (321.6mm), August (311.5mm) and October (295.5mm) (Figure 4). The lowest CVs observed imply that rainfall is not dependable during these months. Thus, there is the need for farmers to scramble for available pasture and water points in their struggle to optimize agricultural productivity, which occasionally provokes clashes and conflict leading to retaliatory acts.

Furthermore, the fact that a greater portion of Ndu Sub-division (such as Luh, Ntamru, Ntaye, and Mbaw plain) is located at lower altitude alongside highlands (such as Ndu and Mbiyeh) having different harvesting periods illustrate temperature variability (Figure 5 shows that temperature rises from January to March, fall back from April-August and rises back from September-December) which trigger Crop farmer-Livestock farmer conflicts. The planting of eucalyptus trees on large expanses in areas like Ndu town, Kakar, Ntumbaw and Mbiyeh serves as carbon sink and degrades the water catchments by soaking much water from the ground especially during the dry season.

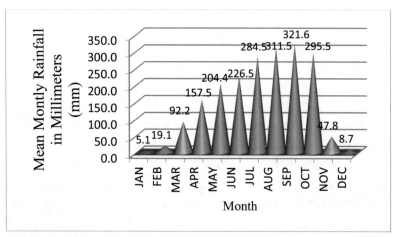

**Figure 4: Mean Monthly Rainfall Conditions in Ndu sub-Division (1981–2014)**

Source: Cameroon Tea Estate, Ndu (2016)

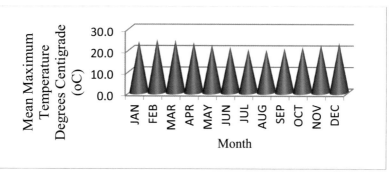

**Figure 5: Mean Monthly Temperature Conditions in Ndu sub-Division (1981–2014)**

Source: Cameroon Tea Estate, Ndu

### Hydrological Change

The geology, relief and drainage networks of Ndu Sub-division show that it is an important watershed in Donga-Mantung Division. But there appear to be significant variations over time in the discharge of springs (Amawa, 2001) (Figure 6). There has been changing patterns and increased water uses by the increasing population.

Watersheds have been systematically converted to eucalyptus plantations since the 1920's. This conversion causes adverse hydrological problems and is responsible for inter-village conflicts over water catchments (Mbipgo-Mbarseh, Mbawngong, Ntisso and Kugha). Other factors responsible for declining water yields are the practice of slash-and-burn, shifting cultivation, and over grazing.

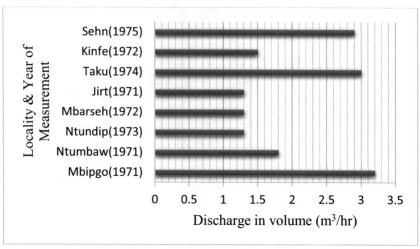

**Figure 6a: Discharge of Streams over the Years in Ndu sub-Division (Year of first measurement)**

Source: Adopted from CAMWATER Nkambe (1997)

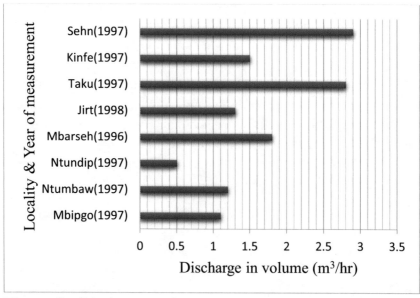

**Figure 6b: Discharge of Streams over the Years in Ndu sub-Division (Year of second measurement)**

Source: Adopted from CAMWATER, Nkambe (1997)

Eucalyptus trees are highly effective water pumps which remove water from the soil and transpire it to the atmosphere. The conversion of indigenous Motane and Sub-Montane forest with deeply-rooted eucalyptus plantations and higher transpiration rates accounts for the fall in water yields (Chomitz and Kumari, 1998). Ndi and Amawa (2014), indicate that eucalyptus planted in catchments lower water tables and render some streams dry during dry season with many becoming intermittent in flow, appearing in the rainy season and disappearing in the dry season.

The rule of hydrological change as a driver to land conflicts is evident in the dry season when the cultivation of legume and spices are limited to the valleys where there is water. Farmers scramble for the limited fertile grounds for cultivation and animal grazing, often destroying crops as they move down the valleys, leading to conflicts.

**Topography and Soils**

The complex topographic configuration of Ndu Sub-division with highlands, lowlands, deep valleys and steep slopes is a major issue in land conflicts, in terms of finding suitable land for agriculture and settlement. On the steep slopes of Sinna, and Ngvulu for instance, soils are thin limiting water storage capacity, deficient in nutrients and do not provide necessary conditions for plant growth, reason why farmers are forced to invade fertile rangelands which triggers conflict.

Settlement and farms have encroached onto pasture land and push the herders deeper into unproductive land (Figure 7). Graziers in their search for ideal grazing space are confronted with serious obstacles from the native cultivators leading to conflict.

**Figure 7: Encroachment of Settlements into Grazing Land at Mbawngong**
Source: Field work, (2015)

### Population Growth and Land Scarcity

The large number of women of childbearing age in Ndu Sub-division, still carries the momentum of past population growth. Even while growth rates fall as a percentage of the existing population, the number of new births each year continues to rise. The annual growth rate is 2.6%. The 1987 and 2005 General Housing and Population censuses recorded 61.717 and 73.955 inhabitants respectively in Ndu Sub-division (Figure 8). An increase in the population figures has increased the pressure on the available land since the demand for more land for agriculture, settlement and other uses are on the rise, while land is fixed in supply (Ndenecho & Balgah 2007). Hence, people scramble for land which results in clashes and conflicts. Amungwa (2009) identifies population pressure on land as the main cause of inter-ethnic conflict.

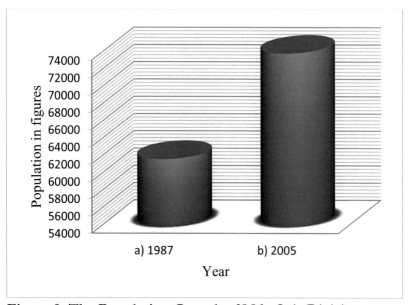

**Figure 8: The Population Growth of Ndu Sub-Division**
Source: The 2005 General Housing and Population Census, Regional Service of Statistics Surveys North West Bamenda

Using the data obtained from questionnaires to test the relationship between population growth and land conflicts, the Pearson's Product Moment Correlation Coefficient was calculated and had a value of 0.72. The coefficient of determination ($r^2$) indicated that with 0.72% increase in population (x) will lead to 0.52% increase in land conflicts. This shows a strong positive correlation and direct relationship between population growth and land conflicts. This implies that as the population continues increase land conflicts are bound in Ndu Sub-division.

## Land Tenure and Land Conflicts

Land tenure system refers to the terms and conditions, under which rights to land are acquired, returned, used, disposed of or transmitted. In the past, land ownership in Ndu Sub-division was quite simple. It required individuals to carry along palm wine, kola nuts and some fowls to the Fon's palace. Once these items were presented, portions of land were attributed to individuals. According to Ngwa (1989), land tenure system range from inherited land, rented

161

land, land acquired by purchase, land acquired as a gift from traditional council or ruler, trust land and pledged land (Figure 9).

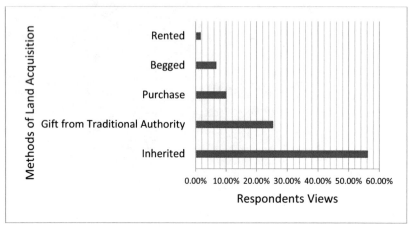

**Figure 9: Methods of Land Acquisition in Ndu sub-Division**
Source: Field work (2015)

Field investigations reveal that land in Ndu Sub-division is acquired from diverse sources and these are drivers to the numerous land conflicts that plague the area with profound consequences. Apart from the appreciation on land value, the love of money by authorities and landlords has marred land dealings with multiple sales of parcels of land which have been a source of land conflict in Ndu Sub-division. In some cases, the situation has been made complex by the successors of some traditional authorities who upon their enthronement began to ask for the return of land their predecessors accorded some individuals or groups. In many cases, farmers have access to ancestral family land but lack control and ownership rights. This prohibits them from using land as a collateral security for loans and this hinders productivity and development.

Furthermore, land tenure in Ndu Sub-division is discriminatory against the marginalized population (women, the poor, orphans and widows). Often, those who claim ownership on land with proof of Land Titles are the well to do in the community, mostly the men folks who sometimes are absentees (Neba, 1999). As a result, vast village land is left to fallow or kept on the pretext that it is inheritance for their offspring which impedes local development.

## Transhumance and Conflicts

According to the herders in Ndu Sub-division, transhumance is one of the ways to sustain livestock, mainly cattle in times of growing environmental threats and stress resulting from droughts and prolonged dry seasons. This is the seasonal movement of animals in search of available fresh pasture and water points.

Following the law on transhumance, Livestock farmers and their herds are expected in the hollow frontiers between late December and late March when the hills are dry but because of the absence of strict implementation of this law, livestock farmers take their animals to these wetlands before the stipulated date which is 25th of December when the crop farmers have not harvested some of their crops like sweet potatoes, cocoyams and cassava that take much longer to be mature and ready for harvest. But herdsmen continue to stay in the transhumance areas even after late March when they are supposed to go back to the hills. These lapses in the transhumance law have intensified the Crop farmers-Livestock farmers' conflict.

## The Privatization of Ndu Tea Plantation

The Fon of Ndu and his people welcomed the cultivation of tea because some Wimbum elites (like Messrs John Takenang Ndze and John Nsame) constituted the negotiating team and land was available; the plantation was to serve as a buffer zone between the Ndu and the Nso territories to put to rest the occasional boundary conflicts that have plagued the two fondoms. It was also intended to create employment and cause development in Ndu Sub-division. However, today, with changes in the management policies of CTE, this has emerged as one of the drivers to land conflicts in Ndu Sub-division. The privatization of the Ndu Tea Plantation rendered over 50% of the working population of the surrounding villages jobless, especially as over 364 labourers were sacked. The privatization of the tea estate in Ndu caused the Wimbum elites to loss their positions in the negotiating team. The construction of worker's camps for those who were strangers facilitated the dismissal of recalcitrant workers (especially those who are indigenes of Ndu Sub-division), replacement of old workers who revolted through strike action from 2002 to 2007 and resulted in the importation of workers from Douala and the Northern parts of the country (who were strangers). Worse of all, there was the conversion of permanent workers to temporary workers, reduction in the categories of workers which affected their allowance thereby depriving them of their retirement benefits and leading to frustration and misery. Consequently, these disgruntled workers who reside around the Tea Estates in villages such as Kakar, Njiptop and Njilah, started demanding for the return of their land from the management of the Tea estate which led to conflict.

## Resolution of Land Conflicts

The study reveals that about 66.4% of the respondents prefer traditional councils to resolve their land conflict cases. They believe that these councils have well-structured institutions, are nearer to the people, easily accessible and justice is rendered promptly. This is in contrast with frequent postponement noted with the judicial system and the Land Consultative Board, institutions which are located far away in Nkambe, the divisional capital and require additional time and transportation. Respondents also raised the issue of loss of trust in these institutions due to injustice emanating from bribery and corruption, promoted by the well to do of the society. However, with the increased level of awareness through education and sensitization on land issues, 17% of the respondents admitted that they settle their land conflicts at a formal institution (the Court of First Instance located at Nkambe town), and 23% admitted that they settle their land crises with the land commission under the coordination of the Divisional Officer (DO) for Ndu Sub-division. Many of the respondents believe that the commission uses conflict situations for money making through the exploitative attitudes of some of its members. According to these respondents it is a very expensive process, and as a result many people have adopted the attitude of "...I do not care..." Some simply endure the pain caused by these conflicts and do not report their case to any institution. The government via the D.O in consultation with the Fons, notables and invited representatives from some lined ministries in the country

164

enforces the resolutions of the Board. Findings equally reveal that 7% of the respondents settle their land conflicts with the police, gendarmerie, and religious institutions. Results further reveal that 50.78% of the respondents prefer peaceful settlement of conflicts through dialogue. This indicates that they found peaceful and amicable resolutions through dialogue or negotiation more lasting because there is genuine understanding once the two parties are satisfied. Some victims noted that they always feel cheated with the intervention of a bias third party in the resolution process.

The church equally has a vital role in the resolution of land conflicts. The church does this in the following ways: restoring societal values that could encourage the making of fair and just decisions by those who have been entrusted with the authority to make decisions, assisting in the implementation of the land laws and land conflicts management systems, and raising public awareness through religious institutions (church, school and media). However, institutions can be more useful in reducing the number of conflicts and sometimes bringing lasting solutions if they are made to function effectively through adequate resourcing and respect to their *raison d'etre.*

On the efficiency of the above institutions, 33.7% admit that these institutions are efficient in land conflict resolution, 66.3% of the respondents think they are not up to their task in the study area. Respondents advance the following reasons for the failures of these institutions in resolving land conflicts: a) administrative bottlenecks (76.8%), b) corruption, and the poor implementation of land laws, ordinances, decisions, decrees and instructions (87.3%) c) population ignorance of the law, d) tribalism, favouritism, land grabbing and greed for benefits, poor documentation and poor working conditions (10.6%). These difficulties sometimes affect the outcome of the resolutions, causing the people not to have trust in their institutions.

Generally, the respondents agree that the inspection fees required to visit the land in conflict are not fixed and victims also provided transport fare, feeding and drinks to the commission. The fee ranges from 5.000 FCFA to 50.000 FCFA depending on the crop type, and the location of the farm as determined by the commission. The existence of a fixed field visit fee across different villages categorized according to their location in the sub division is very important. This can reduce corruption in the whole process (especially with members of the Land Consultative Board). Respondents observed that the penalty levy paid by defaulters who violated the verdict passed of the Land Consultative Board was not fixed. Some 28.57% of the respondents admitted that penalty levy ranges from 200,000 FCFA to 500,000 FCFA and even more while 71.43% of the respondents admitted that the penalty levy paid by defaulters was not fixed but depended on the gravity of the loss recorded.

Historically, colonial and post-colonial governance in Cameroon have remained highly centralized. Despite the much talked about decentralization, the authority of decision-making and execution of projects, have remained in the hands of those away and without sound knowledge of the conditions prevailing in affected communities. In addition, there is no real coordination between the related ministries in the domain as each of them (the Ministry of State Property and Land Survey, Agriculture and Rural Development, Livestock and Fisheries) acts independently of the other.

Government inadequacy in planning and implementing local development projects such as schools, hospitals, commercial farms among others is particularly evident. For example, officials directly involved in a local project may lack the capacity to make better decisions, as most of the well-trained officials prefer to work only in the cities than villages. 2) In most cases, field staff serve only as a source of information but without the power to act and make decisions without referring to hierarchy located far away in the regional or national capitals. During this time the local authorities and general population are bound to bare the stress of waiting for feedbacks or instructions from the centre on a problem they do not really master. As a result of this situation, the inhabitants of Ndu Sub-division feel neglected by the central power, thus the need to promote local governance in the country in the areas of project identification, execution, monitory, conflict resolution, to name just these few.

While 15.4% of respondents admitted that promises made by offenders to victims of land conflicts were respected, 84.6% thought otherwise. Some reasons were identified for the non-respect of these promises which included embezzlement, lack of proper follow up, bribery and corruption (administrative bottlenecks), violation of orders and the law of the powerful.

## Conclusion

Conflicts over land ownership and exploitation are obstructing the efforts of the international community to achieve key development priorities in the domain of the environment, peace, security and democracy. Given that land is a key resource that can offer direct returns to peasants in rural areas, its quantity, quality, nature of exploitation and ownership is important. Therefore, addressing land grievances and conflicts is fundamental to creating an enabling environment for development in Ndu Sub-division. Furthermore, it is important for the stakeholders charged with the resolution of land conflicts to prioritize the early measures of resolving land issues in order to reduce the human, economic, social, and environmental costs of these conflicts. Thus, ignoring these conflicts is unwise because apart from reducing output, impoverishing victims, creating uncertainty and tension, they could escalate into real inter-tribal wars and instabilities.

The types of land conflicts tend to vary with the different villages. However, community members mostly admitted that boundary conflict is the main type of land conflict are: conflicts between individuals and villages who are neighbours on farmland or on the boundary separating them, followed by conflict over land ownership and access rights, and inheritance problems that develop on land. The classification of land conflict according to the social level at which the conflict takes place: interpersonal, intra-societal or inter-societal is relevant in conflict resolution, and illustrates diversity when compared. Although, in most cases interpersonal land conflicts can be addressed by existing resolution bodies, intra-societal conflicts are difficult to tackle because some conflict resolution authorities at the higher level are part of the problem. Need, greed and covetousness easily trigger land conflicts. Scarcity and increase in land value aggravate this situation, even though, the shortcomings in the administration and management of land give rise to conflicts (such as legal pluralism, corruption, information not sufficiently disseminated to the public, insufficient establishment of the rule-of-law-principle and insufficient implementation of legislation to mention a few). Thus, effective land administration and management including relevant policies, laws, procedures, technology and human capacity could result in security of land tenure and sustainable land use.

There are measures which if instituted can serve as effective ways of resolving land conflicts and help move the bar away from the unpleasant consequences of recurrent land conflicts on local development in Ndu. For example, the local administration could carry out strategic land use planning that recognizes the interest of the different groups involved in the conflict. The introduction of agricultural extension workers that can help to improve the productivity of land will compensate for land scarcity. Such a measure should be followed by a good application of the land laws of the country. The local inhabitants of Ndu Sub-division in conjunction with government should be encouraged and assisted to build capacity and skills on non-farm activities (for example transport, health, industries and education) in order to reduce over dependence on land or activities that lend so much land to avoid conflicts.

## Bibliography

Amawa, S. (2001) Variation in Spring Discharge on the Mbum Plateau (N.W. Province of Cameroon) In C Lambi (ed). Readings in Geography. Unique Printers Bamenda. p: 127-141.

Amungwa F. A. (2009). Agrarian Crisis and the Management of Rural Inter-ethnic Conflicts: Some Cases from the North West Region of Cameroon. Proceedings of the 2nd Postgraduate Seminar on Conflict Prevention, Management and Resolution in Buea University, Buea.

Babette W, (2017). Understanding, preventing and solving land conflicts: A practical guide and toolbox, (Revised/Second Edition) Deutsche Gesellschaftfür,

InternationaleZusammenarbeit (GIZ) GmbH, Bonn and Eschborn, Germany

Chambah C. Z. (2015). An Assessment of the Impacts of climate Variability on Agricultural vulnerability in Ndu Sub-division, North West Region of Cameroon, University of Buea, Unpublished

Cotula, L., C. Toulmin, & C. Hesse, (2004). Land Tenure and Administration in Africa: Lessons of Experience and Emerging Issues, International Institute for Environment and Development, London.

United Councils and Cities of Cameroon-National Office (Cvuc.cm/national/index.php/fr/carte-communale/region-du-nord-ouest/90-association/carte-administrative/339-ndu-visited 1/5/2019)

Fonjong, L.F., Sama-Lang, I. and Fombe, L. F., (2010). "An Assessment of the Evolution of Land Tenure System in Cameroon and its Effects on Women's Land Rights and Food Security," in *Perspectives on Development and Technology* No. 9

IPCC (2007b). Climate Change 2007: Synthesis Report. Contribution of Working Groups I, II and III to the Fourth Assessment Report of the Intergovernmental Panel on Climate Change [Core writing team, Pachauri, R.K and Reisinger, A.(eds.)]. Geneva, Switzerland: IPCC.

Kaberry, P. M. (1959). "Report on Farmer-Grazier Relations and the Changing Pattern of Agriculture in Nso, South Eastern Federation Bamenda, Southern Cameroons," London: University College.

Kenneth M. Chomitz & Kanta K. (1998). The Tropical Benefits of Tropical Forest: A Critical Review, The World Bank Research Observer, Vol. 13, Issue 1, p: 13-35

Lambi, C. M (ed). (2001). Environmental Issues: Problems and Prospects. Unique Printers, Bamenda.

Nana. C. (2018). Research Methods and Applied statistics: Beginners and Advanced Learners: Foundation of Applied Statistics and Management (FASTDAM), Buea, Cameroon

Ndenecho, E.N and Balgah S. N (2007). The Population Resource Scarcity and Conflict Trinity, Unique Printers, Bamenda.

Ndi, H. N. and Amawa, S. G., (2014). Environmental Degradation and Emergence of Agricultural Frontiers in North West of Cameroon Journal of Sustainable Development, vol. 7 No. 5, Canadian centre of science and education, Canada

Neba A. S. (1999). Modern Geography of the Republic of Cameroon, (Third Edition) Bamenda: Neba Publishers

Ngeh R. N. (2016). Implications of Land Conflicts on Economic Development in Ndu Sub-Division, North West Cameroon, University of Buea, Unpublished

Ngwa N.E. (1989). Cameroonian Small Farmers and Agro-Pastoral Credit, Speedy print, Yaoundé, Cameroon

Sovannarith, S., Sopheap, R., Utey, U., Rathmony, S., Ballard, B. and Acharya, S. (2001). Social Assessment of Land in Cambodia: A Field Study-Working Paper 20.

Sumelong, E. (2008). How Bush Burning and Deforestation cause Climate Change in the North West of Cameroon.

Tata, E Sunjo, Lambi C, M, & Mirjam De Bruijn (2013). Agro-pastoral Movements and Conflicts in Bui Division, Cameroon: Problems and Prospects, African Journal of Social Sciences, Vol. 4, Number 3, p: 4-19

# The Gender Dimension of Natural Resources and Development

# Chapter 7

## Gender and Household Water Resource Management: Acquisition, and Challenges in Bomaka, Buea

*Ethel N Nangia, Eyongeta N Telma and Nkongho C Ayuk*

### Abstract

The importance of providing a safe and reliable water supply to households in developing countries in general and Cameroon has been a major concern over the years. Water is one of the most valuable natural resources used by men and women to carry out different functions with different outcomes like increased labour and cost for women and increased leisure time for men. However, women play key roles in water matters at the level of acquisition, management, and conservation with varied challenges and constraints which impact on other gender roles and women's social development. Thus, innovations in water resource management and women's capacity building through water discourses may not only improve health and sanitation but sustain this change for the future. The premise of this study is to valorise women's contribution to water management at household level especially during persistent water crisis periods and promote an environment friendly to the enhancement of water welfare. The Sustainable Development Goal 6 which aims at achieving water justice particularly for women and girls by 2030 informed this work which involved a sample of 200 participants, randomly selected in Bomaka through a descriptive design. Data was collected using questionnaires and interview guides and analysed qualitatively and quantitatively. Results show that, women have run out of options for water management and are in dire need of assistance while the water distribution company and community water points need technical support for continuous water availability and effective distribution.

**Keywords**: Gender, Household, Water management, and Challenges

## Introduction

Water is a critical resource for meeting daily household needs and is also a key input for other activities such as agriculture, livestock production and various types of small businesses. Poor management can have adverse impacts on water quality, acquisition and availability and even accessibility and conservation. But an effective sustainable management of water resources and sanitation provide significant benefits to families, society and the economy as a whole (Chee, 1995).

Water is essential not only for drinking and food production and preparation but also for care of domestic animals, personal hygiene, care of the sick, cleaning, washing and waste disposal (Baur, and Woodhouse, 2010). However, because of women's dependence on water resource, which accompanies most of their reproductive roles, women have accumulated considerable knowledge about water resources, including location, quality and storage methods. (Chan & Nitivattananon, 2006c).

Consequently, in many developing countries women have the principal responsibility for management of household water supply, water budget, sanitation and health. They are integrally responsible for domestic water management the irrigation of subsistence (Fonjong, 2012). In this light, Strang (2004) observes that women are typically responsible for collecting, storing and using water (drinking, preparing food, dry cleaning, bathing, and washing clothes and dishes, brushing, watering the yard and garden). This also includes cooking, cleaning, and child care services in a bid to ensure the healthy maintenance of their families. In developing countries an average household consumes about 40-60 litres of water daily for drinking, cooking, sanitation and hygiene (Sultana, 2009). This entails several trips for women and children to water-collection points.

It is important to note that when women save water in the home, they also educate their children and family members about the importance of water conservation. Therefore, it is probable that as teachers who instruct, organize and coordinate household water related activities, most women can contribute immensely towards the education of our young in the ultimate creation of a water saving society in (Chan and Nitivattananon, 2006c).

This notwithstanding, men also have different roles pertaining to the use and management of water. In Uganda, Baur and Woodhouse (2010) point out that men tend to use water primarily for commercial and income generation purposes, including for direct sale as water vendors or for livestock. However, Cardona, et al. (2012) observe that men who collect water for domestic purposes are seen by women as either poor, without children or unstable mentally. Women are often associated with domestic and subsistence production use of water and excluded from commercial use (Peters et al., 2002). This limits women's opportunities for water-based income generation which may bring extra income for household welfare (Van Koppen, 2001).

Thus, these diverse water-related activities of men and women resulting from gender division of labour and gender norms, assign the majority of water-related responsibilities to women while reserving most water-related powers and rights to men. In this light, women are integrally responsible for water fetching, management and conservation while men under the canopy of community or government representatives, make decisions relating to land on which water resources are found and most often ignore the interest of women in these decision-making processes. This goes a long way according to Liu et al (2008) to determine their water consumption rate and the related cost incurred to acquire, manage, and conserve water.

Moreover, the socio-economic status is also a determining factor for access to water. This is evident where, women and girls from poorer, marginalized communities, without secure land rights, are generally more dependent upon open water sources which may expose them to higher risk of disease and increased rates of competition. In the case of Uganda, research (Baur, and Woodhouse, 2010) shows that women can face direct competition with men for communal water resources during droughts.

Studies from 45 developing countries show that women and children bear the primary responsibility for water collection in 76 per cent of households. In 12 percent of household's children carry the main responsibility for collecting water, with girls under 15 years of age twice as likely to carry this responsibility as boys under the same age. Women and girls spend long hours fetching water both for domestic and productive use, while their unpaid work in managing water scarcity is often not adequately recognized and addressed in policies and programmes. The hardship of women and girls associated with primary care of the family, as growers and producers of food and as unpaid water collectors add to their drudgery and deprive them of educational and employment opportunities to break the intergenerational transfer of poverty and lack of empowerment (Blackden & Wodon, 2006). Men are visible on tables at all levels: local, national and international where time is spent on negotiations and decisions for their specific interest, which is then documented as policy. Thus, this diverse water related roles and activities for men and women tend to significantly affect their participation and benefits in water decision-making process where women's water needs are side-lined. In other cases, governments fail to consider women's specific needs and concerns and rather relate women's interest in water to their domestic roles.

The marginalization of women in water justice in terms of participation and benefits are linked to multiple factors including, illiteracy, social norms preventing women in some communities from taking up any public role, limited access to land and also due to women's lack of confidence in speaking up for their rights (IFAD, 2012) . But there is no life without water and consequently no development. This nonchalant and discriminative attitude does not only increase women's burden, but also constrains the formulation and implementation of effective and sustainable water management policies and practices (Thornton et al, 2002). It is for this reason that Kumar (2000) avers that gender and social disparities in terms of equitable access to and control over water resources, benefits, costs, and decision making between women and men is a major concern.

Reliable and convenient access to potable water is important in facilitating women's management of household water supply, health, sanitation and domestic tasks. However, this comes with various challenges at different levels for both genders. Women lose up to 27% of their caloric intake in fetching water in East Africa. This is due to the long distances they cover to fetch water. Most importantly, during the dry season, rural households often collect their water from contaminated sources which when consumed causes water related diseases (Dagdeviren & Robertson, 2009). Moreover, this contaminated water is a threat to women's health. In urbanized areas like in Mombasa more than 60% of slum dwellers lack access to portable water. Hence, they are highly involved in water and land conservation practices and rely on rainwater harvesting during rainy season. Nevertheless, the act of fetching water among women and girls fosters social and group cohesion. As they walk long distances to find and fetch water they enjoy the opportunity to communicate with other women and people outside the household context (ibid, 2009). In the year 2000 The Millennium Development Goal 7, Target 7 C aimed to halve the proportion of people without sustainable access to safe drinking water and basic sanitation. It is regretful that as of 2015, one-third of the world's population was without access to improved sanitation according to a joint WHO/UNICEF Progress Report as a result of inaccessibility to reliable water sources; thereby increasing women's vulnerability to health risks (WHO/UNICEF Report, 2015).

In Cameroon, a continuing lack of access to potable water is still a serious problem in rural areas of Cameroon, where just 44 percent of the population has access to safe water, compared to 86 per cent of urban dwellers (UNICEF 2010). This is still below expectation because gender and water resource management has been a major focus on the development agenda of many developing countries and international conferences since 1977 (United Nations Water Conference). This continued through the 1980s, 90s and 2000s. Nevertheless, governance policies still fail to consider gender-specific needs, concerns and constraints of women and men. This is evident in research (Cleaver, 2002), which suggest that water allocation mechanisms give priority to agricultural, industrial and power production at the expense of household needs.

Chee (1995) holds that, sustainable management of water resources and sanitation provide great benefits to a society and the economy as a whole and Loucks and Van (2017) indicate that the integrated water resource management is the approach that strengthens and supports the sustainable management and development of water resources for the economic and social benefits and wellbeing of the household. Consequently, involving both men and women in water resource management and sanitation policies is critical to the achieving water development and improving household welfare.

## Statement of the Problem

The African culture, governments and donors have traditionally instituted the maintenance of family health through safe water and sanitation as a primary responsibility of the female gender. In this light they carry out most of the unpaid water related activities: acquisition, management and conservation. This entails collecting, storing and using water for drinking, cooking, dry cleaning, bathing, washing, watering the yard and garden and child care services to ensure the healthy maintenance of their families. In sub-Saharan Africa about three quarters of households fetch water from a source away from their home and 50% to 85% of the time, women and girls are involved and walk an average of 3.7miles per day to fetch water (UNICEF/WHO, 2012).

However, in the course of fulfilling this responsibility, especially during the dry season, where water is not only scarce but contaminated, and women trek long distances to fetch water. This exposes them to avoidable risks, violence, water borne diseases and other health complications like strained backs, shoulders and necks, calorie lose and other injuries as well as accidents if they must walk over uneven and steep terrain or on busy roads. The situation is more precarious for pregnant women and others who carry along young children.

These challenges are critical to women's health and substantial participation in the development process. It takes a heavy toll on their budget and time which constrains the performance of other gender roles and productive work which may contribute to the wellbeing of the family. In some parts of Cameroon, the increasing unavailability of safe water has significantly affected girl's schooling with schools recording alarming rate of late coming (Kindzeka, 2017) and up to 70% rate of absenteeism (World Bank, 2017).

Substantial efforts in terms of legal instruments, has been made by both national and international governments to maximize access to water but there are still lapses at the level of the quality, management and cost. Most importantly, even though women are more involved in water related activities in the home than men, they are yet to be a visible part of informed decisions which can transform their challenges in household natural resource management to opportunities and benefits in the process of social development.

The purpose of this study is to examine the key role women play in household water matters at the level of acquisition, management, and conservation. This is in tandem with multiple and diverse challenges which do not only influence women's other gender roles but also affect their social development. Specifically, this study aims to answer three questions: a) what are the various means by which women and men acquire water for household use? b) what are the water management strategies used by women and men? and c) What are the challenges faced by women and men in the acquisition, management and conservation of water?

**Water Situation in Cameroon**

In Sub Saharan Africa, Cameroon is relatively endowed with both surface and ground water resources. Cameroon is the second country in Africa in terms of quantity of available water resources estimated at 322-billion-meter cube (Mafany & Fantong, 2006) of which groundwater constitutes 21% (Sigha-Nkamjou et al.1998). Cameroon is ranked 49th out of 182 countries in the world in terms of abundant water supply. Conversely, these water resources are inequitably distributed due to variations in the topography, rainfall pattern and climatic changes (MINMEE 1997).

According to Ako et al. (2010), in 2006, 70 % of Cameroonians had access to potable water, but this access varied between urban (88 %) and rural areas (47%). Thus, the demand for water surpasses supply in most rural areas. Peri-urban dwellers equally lack access to safe drinking water since infrastructures have become inadequate because of rapid urbanization. Women and girls assume the drudgery in collecting water. Only 15% of urban and 18% rural populations

179

use improved drinking water sources over 30 minutes away (ibid,2010). Only 58% and 42% of the population in urban and rural areas have access to improved sanitation facilities respectively.

Thus, in an era where development efforts are strategically meaningful, it is still common for Cameroonian households to experience drastic water shortages. The phenomenon affects the population of major cities in the country with significant consequences. This includes water related diseases like typhoid and cholera due to improper hygienic methods caused by inadequate or contaminated water. Also, the time girls and women spend finding and fetching water impacts on their productive abilities. In Yaoundé the capital of Cameroon, where the population is over three million, residents need about 300,000 cubic meters of pipe-borne water supply per day but barely 35 percent of it is supplied (Kindzeka 2017). Even though statistics show that Yaoundé enjoys over 185,000 cubic meters of potable water per day (Nfor, 2016), the population is yet to validate this fact as they still experience constant water shortages. To cope, Kindzeka (2017) notes that people have resorted to unsafe sources of water which expose them to health risks and subsequent related expenditures which affect income and living standards in the metropolis. However, Cameroon planned to increase Yaounde's water supply to 500,000 cubic meters in two years by tapping into the Sanaga, one of the country's largest rivers. The move had to increase potable water supply from more than 30 percent to 60 percent of the population (Nfor, 2016) to satisfy household water needs and consequently reduce related constraints.

In Garoua, people rely on the water table, rivers, and rainfall to meet their drinking and agricultural needs. Unfortunately, towards the end of the dry season, these sources often dry up and leave people, particularly in more remote areas, without water. Hence to survive individuals depend on conserved water only which is usually insufficient (Winter, 2015). Nevertheless, an architect with the Cameroonian branch of the U.N. Department of Economic and Social Affairs who also works on water sanitization and collection projects to stabilize people's water supply throughout the North Region of Cameroon, emphasized that one of the strategies to address water supply in the North is to construct and use dams.

In Kumbo the headquarters of Bui Division of the Northwest Region according to Nformi (2018), the population is currently experiencing an unprecedented water shortage. In the administrative headquarters of Tobin, both the young and the old are seen crisscrossing the town during unholy hours in search of water. For over a year, the people have witnessed acute water shortages and are forced to fetch water from doubtful sources.

In Buea, water crisis has a long history marked by water catchments with less than 10 per cent flow. Consequently, Inhabitants go for days, weeks, and months without water and others experience severe rationing. This problem reached its climax during the preparations of the 50th anniversary celebrations. Authorities concerned underestimated the problem and rather concentrated on lengthening the pipes, expanding the reservoir and strengthening the water pumping capacity, which did not produce any expected results, as the inhabitants increasingly walk several kilometres to fetch water even from unsure springs (Guyzo, 2014).

Alternatively, Cameroonians rely heavily on rainfall, wells, and water tables deep underground. Residents in the South have a reliable water source thanks to an annual rainfall of up to 10,000 mm (394 inches) (Winter, 2015). But experts from the environmental non-governmental organization Bio-Resource and Development Centre in Cameroon affirmed that constant changes in weather patterns as a result of climate change impact on water supply (Kindzeka, 2017). Other challenges like population growth and privatization also have an impact on the accessibility and quality of water (Fonjong and Fokum, 2015). Thus, increase in population needs to be commensurate to water supply and privatization of water must take into consideration the welfare of the population in terms of quantity and quality of water supplied.

Most households in the country, especially women and girls largely depend on and trek long distances to fetch water from unsafe sources which come with its own challenges (water borne diseases) to women's development. Narayan (1993) argues that even though women face these challenges, they traditionally play a major role in managing and maintaining communal water supply. They are responsible for the regulation and control of the social use and safe maintenance of water resources. For example, they restrict washing to specific downstream sites on the river. This corroborates Hajar et al. (2002) who purports that women in the older generation used water wisely.

Women's unique activities within the natural environment (collecting water, fuel, and fodder for domestic use, and in generating income), their experience and knowledge (locating of water and protection of the source) are critical for environmental management and household welfare (UNEP, 2004). Hence the integration of women's knowledge in natural resource management is important in shaping environmental sustainability and livelihoods (IFAD, 2007).

**Water Management in Cameroon**

The concept of water resources management according to Savenije and Hoekstra (2002), is a multi-disciplinary domain that combines scientific, technical, institutional, managerial, legal, and operational activities required to plan, develop, operate, and manage water resources. Also, water management refers to a range of different activities among which are: monitoring, modelling, exploration, assessment, design of measures and strategies, implementation of policy, operation and maintenance, and evaluation.

In Cameroon water has been managed by both public and private companies. They used two diverse systems of supplying water to the population: a national network to supply water in urban areas and a system of fixed rural potable water point to supply water in rural areas, managed by the local communities (Totouom and Sikod, 2012). According to Article 2 of the Decree N° 2005/494 of 31st December 2005 creating the Cameroon Water Utilities Corporation, CAMWATER, water management entails, planning, construction and maintenance, production, abstraction, transportation and storage and sale of drinking water. In 1964 there was the establishment of a provisional service of the Waters of Cameroon for a period of 03 years. In May 1967, la Société Nationale des Eaux du Cameroun (SNEC) was created and placed under the Provisional Administration in 2002. Three years later Cameroon Water Utilities

Corporation (CAMWATER) took over and launched its activities in 2008. CAMWATER mainly managed urban stations with more than 100 potable water urban stations while rural water points are managed by users (communities) under the supervision of the authorities (CAMWATER 2005). So far Totouom and Sikod (2012) observe that even though the national coverage rate for improved water services has gradually improved, the Cameroonian water supply system has partially failed since millions of people still get drinking water from unreliable water sources.

The principal objective of CAMWATER is to provide quality water and provide it in sufficient quantities to the people. In a recent presidential decree (February 2018) reorganizing CAMWATER, the public-owned company not only retained the production, abstraction, transportation and storage of drinking water, that were devolved to it, but also inherited distribution and sale of drinking water in urban and peri-urban centres of Cameroon. (CAMWATER, 2018). To achieve its goals and objectives of ensuring the availability of quality water to the population, the human resource capacity of CAMWATER has been increased from 240 to 1700 staff (Nyobia, 2018), with the expected know-how on water management for both short and long-term benefits. However, the major challenge of CAMWATER remains the distribution of water to households (Nfor, 2016).

**Materials and Methods**

This study was carried out in Bomaka located in Fako division for reasons of their long experience in water scarcity. The sample of the study comprised of 200 persons (women -75% and men 25%), randomly selected from the total population of various social classes (marital, educational), with ages ranging between 15 to 55 above, who were also involved in different occupations (entrepreneurs, secretaries, teachers, farmers, students). The research design was mainly descriptive, and data was collected from both primary (questionnaire and in-depth interviews) and secondary sources (published and unpublished). Data was analysed quantitatively with the use of Statistical Package of Social Science and qualitatively, using descriptive statistics and thematic content analysis.

The research was informed by the Sustainable Development Goal 6 "Ensure availability and sustainable management of water and sanitation for all" which is one of the 17 goals of the United Nation's 2030 Agenda for Sustainable Development (2015). These goals aim for transformative steps to shift the world on to a sustainable and resilient path by building on the Millennium Development Goals and completing what they did not achieve from three dimensions: economic, social and environmental, in a balanced and integrated manner. Their vision is a world free of poverty, hunger, disease and want, where all life can thrive (United Nations, 2015).

For the purpose of this study the focus is on Target 6.1: achieving universal and equitable access to safe and affordable drinking water for all, Target 6.2: achieving access to adequate and equitable sanitation for all... paying special attention to the needs of women and girls and Target 6.4: ... Supply of freshwater to address water scarcity and substantially reduce the number of people suffering from water scarcity by 2030.

Fundamentally, equal access to society's goods (such as water) should be guaranteed for all including women. Water is a key resource because it is crucial to all forms of social and economic development (UNICEF 2003). The incidence of water-related diseases such as diarrhoea, typhoid and cholera is directly related to unsafe water consumption from unsure sources which people resort to, due to water rationing, shortages and scarcity. Also, home produced foods such as vegetables, eggs, milk and meat are related to the availability of land and water which may be polluted (WHO/UNICEF 2004). Thus, providing effective and sustainable water supply and sanitation services is relevant for improvements in general health and nutritional situation. It also has an impact on school attendance as girls will not be late or skip classes due to water crisis. This is in terms of time girls spend in water fetching compared to boys and the health risks in case of unsafe sources which may affect their school attendance and social development in general. More importantly improved water supply services will save women's time, both directly in terms of reduced transportation time and costs, and indirectly in terms of time for caring for sick family members and participating in income-generation activities. However, providing effective and sustainable water supply and sanitation services requires good governance (MDG 8) (WHO/UNICEF 2004) which can ensure equal participation, accountability, transparency and equity in the process of water justice.

Inadequate household water supply is a major problem experienced by women and men with differential effects at the level of access, uses, challenges, management and outcomes. While women deal with water related responsibilities including fetching water from more doubtful sources for domestic purposes, men rather enjoy water related rights. Consequently, women suffer health complications, time constraints while men simply face difficulties bringing water into the household. Hence, women need to participate significantly by negotiating water sources and using water wisely to manage the problem while men barely contribute in this process at home. The outcome is evident, increased labour and cost for women which translate into delayed social development. But men gain time. Therefore, women's water needs are problematic and demand urgent attention. Discussion will be informed by the various sources of acquisition of household water supply, uses of water, management strategies and challenges and their relevance to the social development of women and men.

## Results and Discussion

### The Demographic characteristics of respondents

The profile of the 200 participants in this study present the age ranges, marital status, educational level, occupation, household size and the number of children. Majority of respondents (46.7%) are between 46-55 years with women making up (26.7%) and the average age was 43. Also, 40% of participants mostly between the age bracket of 36-45 are married while widows/widowers and single make up 30% and 25% of the sample. Most respondents (74.5%) have formal education of which Postgraduate degree, High School, certificate holders make up 4%, 11% and 32% respectively while Secondary and primary levels make up 9% and 18%. Their occupational status included: entrepreneurs (32%), civil servants (27%) and students (20%) farmers (7%), private sector workers (9%) and unemployed (5%). The household size and number of children vary between1-5 to 16-20 but the modes for both are 6-10 (35.5%) and 1-5 (51%) respectively.

Summarily, most respondents fall within the economically active population age group as they produce goods and services through labour. Despite their varied educational, marital and occupational statuses men and women experience water shortage at different degrees with divergent ramifications on their lives. The relatively large household sizes and number of children which could have served as reserved labour for water fetching is however useless as water has rather become luxury. However, these demographic characteristics are inconsistent with the report by the Federal Democratic Republic of Ethiopia Population Census Commission (CSA, 2008), which also suffered from water shortages but who made a living barely from subsistence agriculture and animal farming since only 1% had attained formal education (Aschalew,2013).

# Fig. 1: Sustainable Development Goal 6 Target 6.1, 6.2 and 6.4

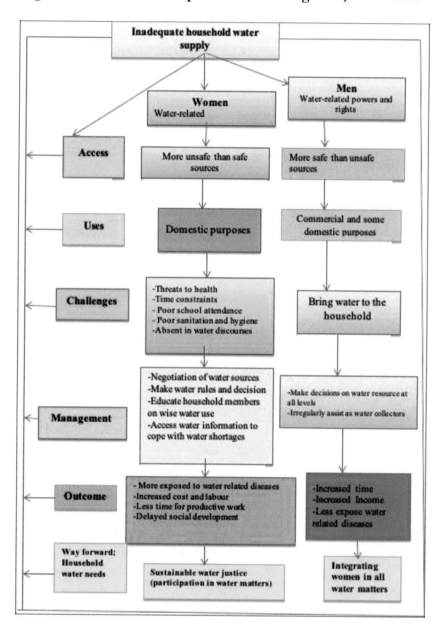

## Water acquisition

The process of bringing portable water into the household during shortage periods is complicated. In this study there are five principal sources of water supply which could be safe (uncontaminated) or unsafe (contaminated) (WHO, 2018). These include: boreholes, public taps, streams, wells and rainwater of which stream and rainwater are more unsafe than the others. The majority of respondents (33%) who use mainly boreholes are mostly small-scale business men/women, farmers, students and 16% of civil servants. They note that since they merely fetch water from boreholes owned by neighbours, they are not very sure of how such water is treated and managed. Some 25% of respondents (made up of married civil servants and private sector workers), use public taps located out of the community and remark that the water develops colour (greenish) when conserved for more than a week and becomes inconsumable. According to a 37years old woman,

> "…We were taught in Primary school that safe drinking water neither have colour, smell nor taste, so when I fetch water from taps, conserve in bottles and notice these characteristics, I take it off the drinking stand…"

However, others use double sources (streams and boreholes, (21.5%) and some (26.5%) use triple sources (wells, streams and boreholes). The last category of respondents (10%) depends on all sources available including rain. They indicate that only bottled water which they cannot afford is safe. Thus, safe drinking water which is a basic human right and imperative for the poverty alleviation and sustainable development and achievement of gender equality (UN, 2015) is still an illusion for the population of Bomaka. This enormously buttresses the opinion of Totouom and Sikod (2012) who observes that Cameroonians still fetch drinking water from unreliable water sources, hence exposing them to avoidable health risks.

Moreover, findings reveal that, 55% of women fetch water from sources (public taps) very far away from home (about 15km) and definitely spend more time (6 hours approximately trekking and queuing) since water closer to home like streams and wells are more unsafe. This tallies with the findings of WHO/UNICEF, (2012) which indicated that in Asia and Africa, women walk several kilometres to fetch water but also portrays the magnitude and nature of underdevelopment in the water sector in the locality which affects the performance of women's gender roles. Nevertheless, a quarter (25%) of respondents spend 3-5 hours over 6-10km while 20% spend less time (1-2hours) to reach unsafe sources of water around the community. In addition, rain water harvesting is one of the common water acquisition tactics used by women. Unfortunately, women complain of less rainfall this year, which has aggravated the search for water.

**Table 1: Distribution of respondents by distance and time spent in fetching water**

| Distance | Time | Description | n | % |
|---|---|---|---|---|
| 1-5km | 1-2hrs | Near | 40 | 20 |
| 6-10km | 3-5hrs | Far | 50 | 25 |
| 15km and above | 6hrs | Very far | 110 | 55 |
| Total | | | 200 | 100 |

**Source: Fieldwork, 2018**

Pertaining to the periods that water was fetched, 45% of the respondents fetch water in the morning hours of the day since they need water for household chores scheduled in the mornings before work, 20% fetch at any time of the day depending on the need and availability while 35% of women fetch water in the evening periods because there is less congestion. However, the difference lies in the containers adult male/female and boys/girls use. Whereas men used medium size drums, big gallons and big buckets (20-40liters), women use smaller gallons and basins (20-25liters) while girls and boys use smaller buckets and gallons (10-18liters). Younger children used plastic bottles (1-2 litres). Household members inconsistently assist in water fetching which insignificantly reduces women's load.

Moreover, water in the Bomaka community is used both for domestic chores and productive work and the different sources of water are used for different purposes. Tap water and boreholes are used for drinking and cooking, streams, wells and rain water for washing and cleaning while water from all sources is used for flushing of toilets. Relating to productive work, a third of the community practice gardening and used wells/streams/boreholes to water their crops. Water usage in households varies between 80 and 100 litres a day. Besides, women use more water in carrying out reproductive roles than other household members. This shows that water is an indispensable need in women's lives.

**Table 2: Sources and Uses of Water in the Bomaka Community**

| Sources of water | Uses of water |
|---|---|
| Tap water and boreholes | Domestic chores: |
| Streams/rain | Drinking/cooking |
| Streams/wells/rain | Laundry/cleaning |
| Streams/wells/boreholes/rain | Washing cars, watering, |
| | Care for domestic |
| Wells/boreholes | animals and flushing toilets |
| | Outdoor chores: Gardening, |
| | watering of plants |

**Source: Fieldwork, 2018**

**Water management strategies**

Pertaining to water management strategies, findings revealed that 86 % of women in the capacity of mothers or wives are the main water managers in the home. These women usually strategize management techniques when taps go dry and water supply is interrupted or during long or successive power cuts which obstruct the smooth functioning of borehole systems. Generally, they conserve water fetched from boreholes and taps in large containers for use during periods of water shortage. There were four key strategies adopted by women which take diverse forms.

The first strategy involves negotiating for sources of water supply with providers in exchange for a fee. Accordingly, both parties agree on amount, how and when to fetch water. Majority of women respect a monthly payment agreement of five to ten thousand FCFA. This falls in line with Fonjong and Ngekwi (2014) where women equally spend money on water related issues (community water catchments or broken public stand taps). In some cases, particular attitudes are requested for like quietness, organization and care during fetching.

The second strategy consists of making rules relating to water collection and conservation in the household. Apparently, women lay down rules on when and how to fetch water. Considering the insecurity rocking the Bomaka community, women together with children fetch water mostly during the day and in groups when children are by themselves. Besides women decided what quantity they fetch and train household members on how to handle water containers, for instance, not filling them to the brim.

**Table 3: Women's Water Management Strategies**

| Women's water management Strategies | Form | Details |
|---|---|---|
| **Negotiation of sources** | Closer to home and in exchange for payment | Require specific attitude: quietness carefulness and a sense of organization |
| **Making rules binding water collection and conservation** | Sourcing, fetching and storing methods and quantity -Teach household members how to handle water containers | Fetching during the day and in groups Cleaning of containers avoid filling to the brim |
| **Educate household members on proper water use** | -Use same water for various purposes -Wise-dishwashing | -laundry, dry cleaning of the floor and watering of the yard -Using two half-full sinks |

| and coordinate water activities | - Use of buckets in watering plants rather a hose -Avoiding preparation of foods requiring much water | -Hose conveys much water. -Adopt cooking with less water like sauces and porridge |
|---|---|---|
| Accessing water information | Informal conversation/discussion | to be informed of available sources of water supply and methods of coping |

**Source: fieldwork, 2018**

Thirdly women educate members of the household on proper water use to avoid wastage and non-coordinated water activities. Here women figure out which source of water to use for which purpose. This captures Chan & Nitivattananon (2006c) who purport that many women are teachers and can contribute towards the education of our young in the ultimate creation of a water saving society. In more critical cases women use same water for various purposes. For instance, the same water used for laundry can be used to dry clean the floor and after that, to water the yard. At other times women measure the quantity of water to be used in litres, most often for dish washing and bathing. A 34-year-old lady practices wise-dishwashing by using two half-full sinks (one sink for washing with dishwashing liquid and the other for rinsing). Others use buckets in watering plants rather than a hose which conveys much water. Besides, cooking meals like vegetables, which require a huge supply of water, is avoided. A 41-year-old woman says, "I cook only sauces and porridge during such periods because of inadequate water…". Such a practice prevents household members from water related diseases like typhoid and cholera and thus enhances sustainable development goal 6.

The last strategy consists of women accessing water information. In this light they make water a topic of discussion in every conversation to possibly find new available sources of water supply and methods of coping with water crisis. A 53-year-old woman observes that:

192

"We talk about water in our women's meetings every month. We even learn about methods of purifying water for safe drinking and about long-lasting containers to store water and their prices…"

Thus, women control and manage water in the household by rationing water for both indoor and outdoor activities and wish to be exposed to more strategies to cope with inadequate water supply. This strongly confirms Hajar et al. (2002) who argue that women use water wisely. More importantly, women and girls are the main collectors of water, and choose water sources according to accessibility, availability, time, quality and use.

It is worth noting that 24 % of men participate in water matters in the household. They do so as independent male students and as fathers, husbands, or eldest male who receive instruction from the mother. This is usually when the women are absent or involved in productive activities which affect their stability at home (women students and small-scale business owners). However, men and boys assist in water collection but are not frequent water collectors or vendors as in the case of Uganda (Gordon et al, 2004). In cases where they collect water, they use more of wheel-barrows or vehicles while women and girls use their heads.

## Challenges in Acquiring and Managing water by Women

The challenges faced by women and girls because of their involvement in water matters at household level are many and varied. These include: health threats, distance, time, cost, fights/quarrels, insecurity and poor sanitation practices which take a heavy toll on their health, availability to fulfil other gender roles and productive activities which may improve their socio-economic development and spare them from the shackles of poverty.

Water sources are not located close to homes, so women and girls cover between 1-15Km to and from water sources on foot. This takes them 1-6hours and above on stony, slippery and muddy terrains. Women confirm that they find the exercise daunting but at the same time they need to fulfil their gender roles. Besides, "who will do it for me if I don't… and what would be my reasons for not carrying out my responsibility?" were the questions asked by a 29 year old married woman. Carrying heavy loads of water over long distances causes women to suffer permanent skeletal damage as experienced by mostly mothers with very young children and without house-helps. Walking long distances equally robbed women of their time to engage in economic activities. This corroborates Fonjong and Fokum, (2015) who note that water scarcity impacts low income women and girls who must walk miles to access clean water compromising other opportunities. Water scarcity equally presents a serious challenge to sanitation and hygiene practices which expose women to health risks.

Another challenge experienced by women is cost. All women affirm that they spend significant amounts money (between 3000francs a day to 10000-50000 francs per year) for buying containers (drums, gallons, buckets, basins) to conserve water. Over the years prices of such containers have doubled as water scarcity persists. However, these changes have not come along with changes in women's water budget which they complain is insignificant. Others rather buy bottled water (Supermont) for about 2000francs a crate of six bottles of 1.5 litres each, which is insufficient for a household per day just for drinking. In some cases, women spend on the transportation of water by taxi, motor-bikes, trucks or wheel barrows. A few women who own cars point out that fetching water using their cars mean additional expenditure on fuel and maintenance. Considering that women in Sub Sahara Africa and Cameroon are still entering the labour market where salaries are dwindling, the expenditure on household water matters is quite alarming. Consequently, women do not only have the allowance to manage household water budget but equally need to strategize to ensure that the objective of water welfare is attained despite the inadequate budget.

Women are also exposed to incidences like fights and quarrels. This often occurs when there were no strict regulations or organization in the order of fetching water. Women tend to disrespect each other with very nasty insults. Young girls get involved in fights and incur bruises and sometimes broken containers while women quarrel but later made up. Insecurity here is in terms of theft. Usually young girls/boys steal each other's gallon covers after they have misplaced theirs which later render water conservation complicated. Furthermore, young girls and boys are exposed to road dangers like accidents during crossing major roads to fetch water.

However, women remark with enthusiasm that water fetching though a tedious exercise, is also an exciting one as it provides the opportunity for gossips which lamely affects their relationships. This also gives room for the creation of useful social ties among women and girls, in line with Dagdeviren & Robertson (2009), who appreciates water fetching among women and girls because it enhances social cohesion.

**Conclusion**

Water increasingly remains irreplaceable and indispensable natural resources for the survival of human beings. Water is used in all sectors of life from the macro to the micro for daily activities. The domestic sphere is salient for water use and is championed by women so much that they are described as closer to water since their daily activities revolve around the use of water. In this light woman serve as collectors, users, conservers and managers of water in households for the wellbeing of family and community. But with continuous water shortages and scarcity partly due to irregular power cuts women are obliged to devise means of mitigating the situation which comes with new challenges. The outcome is that there is low household utility, women are overburdened, incur extra cost to ensure the availability of water for household members, exposed to health complications and experience time constraints which jeopardize their ability to participate in productive activities and function effectively. Thus, bringing women to the centre of water matters and welfare in the community is critical to their social and economic development. Their advantage lies in the water knowledge they already traditionally possess. Consequently, strengthening women's capacity through water discourses may not only improve health and sanitation but also contribute to achieving the sustainable development goal 6 and influencing policies on water resources to the advantage of women and the household as whole. Besides, understanding and recognizing the key role of women in water matters by mainstreaming their water needs through participation in water decisions will be very beneficial to women, the household and community at large.

## References

Ako, A. Shimada, J. & Takem E. (2010). Access to potable water and sanitation in Cameroon within the context of Millennium Development Goals (MDGS). *Water Science & Technology*, 61(5), 1317-39.

Aschalew D. Tigabua, Charles F. Nicholsonb, Amy S. Collickc, Tammo S. (2013). *Determinants of household participation in the management of rural water supply systems: A case from Ethiopia.* Retrieved from http://soilandwater.bee.cornell.edu/publications/aschalew-WPOL-D-12-00160AP

Blackden, M. and Wodon, Q. (Eds.). (2006). *Gender, time use, and poverty in sub-Saharan Africa.* World Bank Publications.

CAMWATER. (2018). *Reorganization of Camwater: What will change.*

CAMWATER. (2005). *Le secteur de l'eau et de l'assainissement au Cameroun.* Fiche de synthèse, Ambassade de France au Cameroun

Cardona, I., Müller, C., Mitchell, B., & Justino, P. (2012). *From the ground up: Women's roles in local peace building in Afghanistan, Liberia, Nepal, Pakistan and Sierra Leone.* Institute of Development Studies: UK.

Cleaver, F. (2002). Men and masculinities: New directions in gender and development. In F. Cleaver (Ed.), *Masculinities matter ! Men, gender and development* (pp. 1-27), London : Zed Books.

Dagdeviren, H., & Robertson, A. (2009). *Access to water in the slums of the developing world.* International Policy Centre for Inclusive Growth Working Papers, No. 57. International Policy Centre for Inclusive Growth.

Davis, G. (2004). A history of the social development network. In the World Bank. Social development papers (pp. 1973 -2002), World Bank.

ECRI. (Environment and Climate Changes Research Institute). (2010). *Study of assessment of environmental impact on the hydroelectric station attached to the new barrage assiut.*

Fonjong, L. (2012). *Issues in women's rights to land in Cameroon.* Langaa Research and publishing Common Initiative Group Mankon Bamenda North West region of Cameroon.

Fonjong, L. and Ngekwi, M. (2014). Challenges of crisis on women's socio-economic activities in Buea municipalities. *Journal of Geography and Geology.* 6(4), 122-131.

Fonjong, L. and Fokum, V. (2015). Rethinking the water dimension of large scale land acquisition in Sub Saharan Africa. *Journal of African Studies and Development,* 7(4), 112-120.

Guyzo. (2015). Eximbank USA Offers FCFA 63 Billion for Buea Water. Cameroon Tribune19 and Education. Canada.

Hargreaves, K. (2012). *What is social development?* Retrieved from http://www.mission.ca/municipal-hall/departments/social-development/

Haskey, J. (1996). Population review: Families and households in Great Britain. *Population Trends,* 85, 7-24.

International Fund for Agricultural Development-IFAD, (2012). *Securing water for improved rural livelihood: The multiple-uses system approach.* IFAD, Beccio.

Kindzeka, E. (2017, March 16). Water shortages plague major Cameroon Cities-Yaoundé. Cameroun Tribune.

Kumar, K. (2000). *Women and women's organization in post-conflict societies: The role of International assistance.* United States Agency for International Development: Washington, D.C.

Loucks, P., and Van Beek, E. (2017). *Water resource systems planning and management: An introduction to methods, models, and applications.* Springer.

Liu, Y., Gupta, H., Springer, E., & Wagener, T. (2008). Linking science with environmental decision making: Experiences from an integrated modelling approach to supporting sustainable water resources management. *Environmental Modelling& Software,* 23(7), 846-858.

Nfor, V. (2016). *Water supply: Akomnyada's additional 35,000 cubic metres available.* Retrieved from https://www.cameroon-tribune.cm/article.html/1505/en.html/water-supply-akomnyadas-additional-35-000-cubic-metres-available

Nyobia, A. (2018*). La fin du contrat d'affermage survenue lundi ouvre une nouvelle page, pleine de défis.* Cameroun Tribune. Retrieved from www.cameroon-tribune.cm

Opio, A. (2014). *CAMWATER: Who sponges all the borrowed billions? Privatisation; la CAMWATER remplace la SNEC sur l'effort Camerounais* (Version Française).

Rathgeber, E. (1996). Women, men, and water-resource management in Africa. In E. Rached, E. Rathgeber, and B. David B. (Eds.), *Water management in Africa and the Middle East: Challenges and opportunities* (pp. 49-69), IDRC, Canada.

Rosen, S and Jeffrey R. (1999). *Household water resource and rural productivity in sub Saharan Africa: A review of the evidence.* Harvard Institute for International Development, Cambridge.

Savenije, H and Hoekstra, A (2002). Water resource management. *Encyclopedia of Life Support Systems, 2,* 155-180.

SNEC. *Nouveaux enjeux pour la privatisation.* Retrieved from http://www.cameroon-info.net/

Strang, V. (2004). *The meaning of water.* Oxford: Berg.

Sultana, F. (2009). Fluid lives: subjectivities, gender and water in rural Bangladesh. *Gender, Place and Culture, 16*(4), 427-444.

Totouom. A and Sikod, F. (2012). Household choice of purifying drinking water in Cameroon. *Environmental Management and Sustainable Development, 1*(2), 1-15.

WHO/UNICEF Report (2015). Retrieved from www. Who.int.

WHO, (2018). Drinking water: Key facts. Retrieved from http://www.who.int/news-room/fact-sheets/detail/drinking-water.

Winter, I (2015). *Northern Cameroon's water shortage.* Cameroon, environment, December 17, 2015

World Bank Report (2017). *Water to break the cycle of poverty.* World Bank.

# Chapter 8

## An Assessment of the Role of Gender Equality in Accessing Agricultural Resources: A Look towards Cameroon's Emergence

*Fabinin N. Akem and Ernest L. Molua*

**Abstract**

The gender gap has a moral and economic imperative central to creating sustainable economies. The study examines challenges to women's agriculture resulting from gender issues, with a view to its negative influence on development prospects for Cameroon. The study made use of the non-neutral/single stage approach of the frontier model: application of the Cobb-Douglas stochastic frontier function to analyse access to production resources and productivity levels for both male and female maize farmers. Findings empirically reveal that out of the explanatory variables identified, the main factors that contribute significantly to technical efficiency are farm size/land ownership/access to land, access to credit, labour, and the use of fertilizers and improved seeds. About 36.7% of the female-managed farms have an efficiency level below 50% with only 28.6% of the male managed farms, while 40% of male managed farms operate at an efficiency level above 76% and only 33.2% of female-managed farms operated in this category. Hence, given the gender gap in accessing agricultural production resources, technical efficiency and productivity for the female folk in agriculture is negatively affected.

**Keywords:** Gender, Agricultural resources, Technical efficiency, Productivity, Cameroon.

## Introduction

The gender gap has economic implications central to creating sustainable economies. According to the Food and Agriculture Organization State of Food and Agriculture Report (2011), if women had the same access to productive resources as men, they could increase yields on their farms by 20–30 percent. This could raise total agricultural output in developing countries by 2.5-4 percent, which could in turn reduce the number of hungry people in the world by 12-17 percent. With limited and inadequate access to land, capital, and labour amongst others for women, there exist non-inclusiveness and diminution in agricultural wage labour and productivity, as well as diminishing national output for tomorrow. Agriculture is underperforming in many developing countries for a number of reasons including the fact that women lack the resources and opportunities they need to make the most productive use of their time (FAO, 2011). The traditional patriarchal gender norms of African societies in general has emphasized such role of women (suppressing female roles outside of reproductive and household management activities) that the potentials of women that could be exploited and trained to maximize economic growth are left unused and exploited. According to a Morgan Stanley Report (2016), more gender diversity, particularly in corporate settings, can translate to increased productivity, greater innovation, better products, better decision-making, and higher employee retention and satisfaction. The agricultural wage labour will be increased and improved to meet up the demand for emergence and the global market with equal female inclusiveness, especially in terms of access to farm production resources.

Traditional land tenure laws make for unequal rights of access to landed property based on gender. This inequality has far-reaching consequences for access to other agricultural development resources for women: they form an important population amongst small-scale farmers and play an indispensable role in food production, hence addressing constraints to their access to food production resources would be a vital step towards sustainably improving food production (Yengoh, 2012). Women are farmers, workers and entrepreneurs, but almost everywhere, they face more severe constraints than men in accessing productive resources, markets and services (Molua, 2007). This gender gap hinders their productivity and reduces their contributions to the agriculture sector and to the achievement of broader economic and social development goals.

Closing the gender gap in agriculture would produce significant gains for society by increasing agricultural productivity, reducing poverty and hunger and promoting economic growth (FAO, 2011). Hence, what are the major problems and challenges to women agricultural entrepreneurship in the Cameroon society? What is the status of women's agriculture? What are the prospects of agricultural entrepreneurship for Cameroonian women? The main focus of this study is to examine the challenges to women's agriculture resulting from gender issues: a view towards Cameroon's emergence. The underlying hypothesis is that, given the same level of production technology, there exist significant differences in productivity levels between male and female farmers. Any significant differences are attributed to differences in access to farm production resources. Fostering entrepreneurship in agriculture and gender sensitivity through gender-neutral legal frameworks is a key policy yet to be effectively enforced by the government which shares the expectation that high rates of entrepreneurial activity will bring sustained job creation and boost the development of new products, processes, and organizational innovation. Tillmar (2006) argues that special programs for women entrepreneurs are needed, in addition to gender-awareness among mainstream business providers, since the male norm and the male gender labelling of entrepreneurship and business ownership unconsciously may influence the selection of clients and exclude women. Whereas Hafizullah et al, (2013) highlighted that male dominance in culture creates problems for female entrepreneurs in terms of limiting their mobility, business participation and market interactions, Tillmar (2006) found that women face additional handicaps due to the prevailing social and cultural gender-based inequalities and biases. A recent study by Staveren (2013) empirically revealed significant effects of gendered institutions on women empowerment with different institutions affecting different dimensions of empowerment. It has been argued that the empowerment of women is more sensitive to variations in gender systems generated by social contexts than to the personal characteristics of women (Mason and Smith, 2003).

**Methodology**

In the model estimation, the single-stage approach by Battese and Coelli (1995) was used. Based on the approach, the frontier model expresses the technical efficiency (TE) effects as a function of the vector of the farm specific variables and the random error term. The assumption of the approach however is that there is interactions between the farm-specific variables and the input variables. Hence, the technical inefficiency (TI) effects are expressed in terms of various farm-specific variables and the estimation procedure entails the estimation of the production frontier and the variance of the output below the frontier (TI) effects simultaneously.

A fundamental problem with deterministic frontiers is that any measurement error, and any other source of stochastic variation in the dependent variable, is embedded in the one-sided component making the resulting TE estimates sensitive to outliers (Greene, 1993): a sensitivity problem addressed by the Stochastic Frontier Production (SFP) model. Although the Cobb-Douglas has a restriction in its unitary elasticity of substitution, it yields satisfactory estimates than the trans log model, evident from the likelihood ratio test at 5% significance level. The Cobb-Douglas model can be specified as follows:

$$Y = \alpha X^\beta \ldots\ldots\ldots\ldots e^\varepsilon$$

... Y is the total output, $\alpha$ is the constant, $\beta$ is the production elasticity with respect to $X$, X is the ith farm input, $\varepsilon$ is the error term, and e is the base of the natural logarithm. Hence, the specific model in this analysis is given as:

$\ln Q = \alpha_0 + \alpha_1 \ln x_1 + \alpha_2 \ln x_2 + \alpha_3 \ln x_3 + \alpha_4 \ln x_4 + \alpha_5 \ln x_5 + \alpha_6 \ln x_6 + \alpha_7 \ln x_7 + \alpha_8 Dc + \alpha_9 De + \varepsilon$

Where In represents the natural logarithm, Y is the total output (in Kg per hectare), ... $\alpha_0$ is a constant, $\alpha_1$... $\alpha_9$ are the production elasticities, $X_1$ is improved seeds (Kg per hectare), $X_2$ is the labour input (expressed in man-hours), $X_3$ is the age of the farmer, $X_4$ is the farm size (in hectares, henceforth Ha), $X_5$ is the quantity of fertilizer use (in Kg/Ha), $X_6$ is the farmer education attainment, $X_7$ is the amount of manure used (in Kg/Ha), Dc is the dummy for access to credit (1 = access to credit, 0 = otherwise), De is the extension services dummy (1 = access to extension; 0 = otherwise), ... $\varepsilon(U - U_i)$ accounts for the random error (U) and technical inefficiency ($U_i$). It is expected that farmer production efficiency increases with age (at least up to some point based on the law of diminishing marginal productivity). Older farmers can be expected to be more efficient than younger farmers due to experience and a stock of accumulated capital over time: controversially younger farmers with better education could be expected to be more efficient. In the same light higher educational levels of farmers are expected to positively influence production efficiency as adoption of best practices and efficiency in resource use are positively correlated with higher educational levels. 'Marinda et al., (2006) carried out a similar estimation, with respect to maize revenue in Kenya for male and female headed households with an unequal distribution of male and females in their sample; a possibility for gender dominance bias. Our findings provide comparable results to their work.

Mburu et al (2014) empirically reveals relatively high levels of technical efficiency among small scale farmers who are the sample points of this study. Hence, it could be expected that the farmer group with the smaller farm size are relatively more technically efficient. It is anticipated that the use of inputs (fertilizer, manure, information/extension services, labour, improved seeds and access to capital/credit), in appropriate quantities will increase the production efficiency of the farms. Non-farm income received could positively affect productivity since the farmer would be capable of purchasing farm inputs and paying for hired labour and machinery (Heidhues, 2004). This analysis will provide diagnosis as to the presence of productivity differences between the two farmer groups: Male-Managed Farms (MMF) and Female-Managed Farms (FMF), for corresponding policy interventions. STATA 8.0 was used to determine the Maximum Likelihood Estimates (MLE) of the parameters of the Stochastic Frontier Production (SFP) function.

According to Quisumbing (1996), if the farms under consideration are producing the same or similar crops, a pooled regression is recommended and has been commonly used to estimate differences in the TE between male and female farm managers. Saito et al. (1994) suggest an approach to estimating sex differences in technical efficiency, involving performing regressions on plot-level observations, either for the pooled sample of male- and female-managed plots, or for male and female plots separately. If production functions are estimated separately to allow for different input coefficients for male and female monocrop farmers, the underlying technologies are identical (Quisumbing, 1996). However, failure to reject the null hypothesis (of two groups having the same technology for a crop farm production) would suggest that the parameters for the production frontiers differ across the two groups of farmers, in which case a pooled estimation of the parameters will be preferred.

**General Description of Study Area and Data**

Cameroon is a country in West Africa predominantly constituted by farm households. Often referred to as "Africa in Miniature" it exhibits major climate and vegetation characteristics that can be found across the entire continent of Africa. It has 2 seasons: the rainy season and the dry season and is home to the highest mountain in Sub-Saharan Africa. Its climate varies across regions from equatorial to tropical (Guinea equatorial, tropical humid, sudano-sahelian and equatorial monsoon), and it has 5 ecological regions (the sudano-sahelian, the high Guinea savannah, the Western Highlands, the humid forest/monomodial rainfall and the humid forest/bimodial rainforest. According to Molua and Lambi (2006), variations in rainfall from year to year, sporadic floods and droughts are significant in the country; with average annual temperatures of about $25^{0}C$ in the Guinea Equatorial, $21^{0}C$ in the equatorial monsoon (up to $25.5^{0}C$ in the Littoral within this region), and $28^{0}C$ in the Sudano-Sahelian. The Southwest region of Cameroon covers an area of $24.910Km^{2}$, representing about 5.2% of Cameroon's surface area. With a population of about 1.2million inhabitants, 70% of the total households are engaged in farming as primary activity. The area has an equatorial and sub-equatorial climate characterized by heavy rainfall (2.000mm on average per year) and a long rainy season of at least 3months. Temperatures are averagely above $22^0$C and a high general humidity of about 85%. Predominant crops are cocoa, corn, potato, plantain, cassava and vegetables. Livestock production is concentrated in the production poultry meat and eggs, and pigs, amongst others. It is worth mentioning that a household can have several farms and different crops and/or livestock products, some combined on the same piece of farmland.

Following from Macauley (2015), considering the low average maize grain yields that are still pervasive in farmers' fields in SSA, meeting the projected increase demand for maize in Africa presents a challenge given that it is a major food crop staple. In view of the possible prospects of Cameroon's emergence in the agricultural sector, this presents an opportunity that could be maximized especially at the level of export revenue: hence the choice of the crop in the study. According to Epulle and Christopher (2015), maize as a staple crop is further important because it is mainly grown by small scale subsistence farmers who constitute more than 35% of the rural population. Given that the value of production shows great variance depending on the various production systems, the empirical analysis takes small scale farmers as a benchmark, particularly households with farm sizes less than or equal to 3 hectares (Ha). One hundred and fifty questionnaires were administered to a representative 75 male and female individuals each, based in the South West Region of Cameroon: 10 each from 15 radomly sampled localities. Corresponding households were visited every two weeks for three months. In total, each household was visited 6 times during the data collection process. Visits over a one-month interval were found to be quite lengthy and not effective for follow-up and recall, while weekly visits could become burdensome to the farmers. Inconsistencies were reviewed in the survey and in adjustment, the total sample was 130: 65 male and 65 females, 13 representing each region of the country.

## Results and Discussion

### Descriptive statistics

It can be observed that women in the study site were disadvantaged in terms of accessing land. T-tests empirically reveal significant differences between male and female managed farms regarding access to fertilizers, improved seeds, years of schooling, and maize yield.

In terms of labour force, male managed farms were at an advantage, having 19% more labour force than the female managed farms. Different farmers will have different access to labour, depending on their gender and status within the household and the community (Dos, 2001). Access and availability of labour depends on the household and local market for labour. According to Dos (2001), female-headed households may have less access to labour because they include fewer men and may have fewer resources for hiring nonfamily labour. Within male-headed households, women who manage agricultural activities may also have difficulty in mobilizing labour.

Male managed farms have higher maize yields in comparison to the female managed farms. This could also be associated to their advantaged land ownership status. Women's relatively less favourable access to land can be a strong deterrent to adopting new techniques or investing in the land (Saito and Weidemann, 1990), hence decreasing their technical efficiency and agricultural productivity.

Female farmers attested to being relatively more needy in accessing formal credit as opposed to male farmers who seemed relatively less resourceful in outsourcing informal credit. However, as noted by Heidhues and Buchenrieder (2004), with improving credit products or offering new credit lines would only slightly improve the credit coverage of poorer households. A more promising approach would be to introduce a specialized pro-poor extension service to widen the scope of their investment ideas, combined with a general improvement in the infrastructure.

# Technical Efficiency

Estimates of the parameters of the stochastic frontier production function and inefficiency effects in maize production in the study area are presented in Table 1. The estimations considered male and female managed farms, respectively.

**Table 1: Parameter estimates for the Stochastic Frontier**

| Variable | MMF | | FMM | |
|---|---|---|---|---|
| | Coefficient | T-value | Coefficient | T-value |
| Labour | 0.577 | 3.560 | 0.141 | 3.600 |
| Farm size | 0.861 | 1.616 | 0.634 | 1.584 |
| Improved seeds | 0.578 | 3.561 | 1.004 | 30.87 |
| Age | 0.372 | 1.831 | 0.031 | 0.122 |
| Credit | 0.423 | 2.525 | 0.575 | 3.560 |
| Fertilizer | 0.995 | 67.92 | 0.014 | 1.289 |
| Education | 1.503 | 0.803 | 1.325 | 3.993 |
| Extension services | 0.105 | 0.133 | -0.018 | -0.964 |
| Manure | -0.599 | 0.491 | -0.028 | -1.5 |
| Constant | -0.482 | -1.201 | -1.538 | -3.025 |
| Log likelihood | −154.3246 | | −133.0100 | |
| $\sigma^2$ (u) $\sigma^2$ (u$_i$) | 0.017 0.213 | | 0.012 0.206 | |

**Source: Survey data (2018)**

The variance parameters (U and U$_i$) support overall technical inefficiencies in both male and female farms, however relatively this is in line with Marinda et al., (2006). The coefficient for manure is surprisingly negative for both the male and female managed farms). A negative coefficient for manure means that farmers tend to be technically inefficient without access to manure. While animal droppings and other such basic inputs do improve crop yields, there are constraints at the farm and household levels that may have to be overcome to optimize the availability and use of these inputs (Yengoh, 2012).

207

The positive coefficient of credit for male managed farms indicates that their access to credit positively contributed to their yields and consequently, their technical efficiency (TE). The estimates for the coefficient associated with education of the farm heads are positive and significant as expected. A farmer's educational attainment increases his ability to understand and evaluate information on and adopt new production technologies which increase productivity. This emphasizes the significant role education plays in influencing the TE of farmers. The result is in line with that of Mburu et al. (2014). Likewise, access to extension services contributed to the improvement of the TE of male farmers in the study area, as indicated by the positive coefficient. A negative coefficient in the case of the females could be explained by their lower abilities to adopt which ties with their lower levels of education. This phenomenon can be attributed to lower human capital for women in the study area relative to men.

The coefficient for labour is significant for both groups implying that labour contributed positively to maize production. However, MMFs have a more significant coefficient. Female labour is remunerated at much lower rates than their male counterparts: while female-headed households may have less access to labour because they include fewer men and have fewer resources for hiring non-family labour, even within male headed households women who manage agricultural activities may also have difficulty in mobilizing labour (Dos, 2001).

The positive signs of the coefficients in age, extension services and education suggest they are associated with increases in the TE levels. The variables are however not significant. The age coefficient indicates that older farmers are more capable to take proper decisions regarding farm input practices associated with their higher years of experience (Begum et al., 2016) and in the case of education suggest considerable variation in scope of the sampled area (Ahmad et al., 1999). The positive and insignificant coefficient of extension contacts is in line with Marinda et al., (2016), however disagrees with Ahmad (1999).

The frontier production function from the Cobb-Douglas production function is estimated with the aim of comparing the technical efficiency of male and female managed farms, as well as the overall combination of both the male –managed farms and the female-managed farms: hence the technical efficiencies are computed at different levels (the ratio of the actual output to the potential output) for the mentioned categories. The potential output is the output from the frontier production function while the actual output is the observed output. Several studies have used this method to determine technical efficiency (Bravo-Ureta and Riegler, 1990; Parikh and Shah, 1994). The average production functions were estimated using the coefficients of the Cobb-Douglas production function and observations with positive error terms were retained: after two iterations against the same explanatory variables, the estimates were stable. The coefficients for fertilizers, improved seeds and education were still significant.

**Table 2: Relative technical efficiency of farm management**

| | Male manager | Female manager | Overall |
|---|---|---|---|
| Level of efficiency (%No. of farms) $\leq 0.49$ | 28.6 | 36.7 | 28.2 |
| $0.50 \leq x \leq 0.75$ | 31.4 | 29.1 | 21.8 |
| $\geq 0.76$ | 39.9 | 33.2 | 42.1 |
| Mean | 0.71 | 0.65 | 0.73 |
| SD | 0.28 | 0.26 | 0.25 |
| Min | 0.21 | 0.27 | 0.21 |
| Max | 0.95 | 0.92 | 0.95 |

Source: Survey data (2018)

When the mean technical efficiency of the different farms is compared based on management using ANOVA, the F-value if found should be significant at $p < 0.05$. Only the technical efficiency of the female managed farms are however significantly different at $p < 0.05$. 36.7% of the female managed farms have an efficiency level below 50% while only 28.6% of the male managed farms and 28.2% of both farm units are in this category. Overall, the mean technical efficiency is 73% with a minimum of 21% and a maximum of 95%. This implies that on average, the respondents are able to obtain 73% of potential output from a given mix of production inputs. This level of technical efficiency is lower than that given by Bravo-Ureta and Riegler (1991) for dairy farms (83%). It is however higher than that given by Bravo-Ureta and Evanson (1994) for cotton and cassava farmers (58-59%). 42.1% of farms have an efficiency level of above 75% while 28.2% operate at an efficiency level of below 50%. About 22% operate at an efficiency level between 51% and 75%. When farms are compared based on farm management, female managed farms have the lowest proportion of farms with technical efficiency above 75% while the overall combination of both male and female managed farms have the highest proportion (33.2% and 42.1% respectively). Mean technical efficiency is 65% and 75% for the female managed and male managed farms respectively.

**Conclusion**

The study examined the challenges to women's agriculture resulting from gender issues, with a view to its negative influence on development prospects for Cameroon. The study made use of the non-neutral/single stage approach of the frontier model: application of the Cobb-Douglas stochastic frontier function to analyse access to production resources and productivity levels for both male and female maize farmers. Findings reveal the major factors significantly influencing TE as farm size/land ownership/access to land, access to credit, labour, fertilizer use and the use of improved seeds. The difference in Technical Efficiency levels were most discernable in fertilizer, labor, and improved seeds across male and female farmers. Credit and farm size most significantly affected the Technical Efficiency levels across males and females, while extension contacts, education and age proved least significant.

Over 36.7% of the female managed farms have an efficiency level below 50% with only 28.6% of the male managed farms while 40% of male managed farms operate at an efficiency level above 76% and only 33.2% of female managed farms operated in this category. Hence, it is recommended that the government policy frameworks should be more gender sensitive and feminine inclusive to ensure that the legal framework allows for gender mainstreaming in accessing agricultural production resources. Addressing the problems in the agricultural sector is imminently a push towards the vision of emergence in Cameroon.

## References

Ahmad, M., M. Rafiq and A. Ali. (1999). An analysis of technical efficiency of rice farmers in Pakistani Punjab. *The Bangladesh Journal of Agricultural Economics*, 22: 79-86Battese, E. and Rao D. (2002). Technology gap, efficiency, and a stochastic metafrontier function. *International Journal of Business Economics*, 1(2), 87-93.

Battese, E., Rao, D. and O'Donnell J. (2004). A metafrontier production function for the estimation of technical efficiencies and technology gaps for firms operating under different technologies. *Journal of Production Analysis*, 1 (2), 91-103.

Begum, M. E. A., Nastis, S. A., Papanagiotou, E. (2016). Determinants of technical efficiency of freshwater prawn farming in southwestern Bangladesh. *Journal of Agriculture and Rural Development in the Tropics and Subtropics*. 117(1):99–112.

Bravo-Ureta, B. and Evanson, E. (1994). Efficiency in agricultural production. The case of peasant farmers in eastern Paraguay. *Agricultural economics*, 10, 27-37.

Bravo-Ureta, B. and Riegler, L. (1991). Dairy farm efficiency measurement using stochastic frontiers and neoclassical duality. *American Journal of Agricultural Economics*, 73, 421-428.

Dos, R. (2001). Designing agricultural technology for African women farmers: Lessons from 25 years of experience. *World Development*, 29(12), 2075-20192.

Epulle, E. and Bryant, R. (2015). Maize production responsiveness to land use change and climate trends in Cameroon. *Journal of Sustainability*, 7(1), 384-397.

FAO, (2011). The state of food and agriculture 2010-2011, Women in Agriculture: Closing the gender gap for development. Rome: Food and Agriculture Organization of the United Nations. Retrieved from http://www.unwomen.org/en/docs/2011/1/state-of-food-and-agriculture-2010-2011

FAO. (2011). State of food and agriculture. Women and agriculture: Closing the gender gap for development. Rome: Food and Agriculture Organization of the United Nations. Retrieved from http://www.fao.org/3/i2050e/i2050e00.htm

Greene, W. (1993). The econometric approach to efficiency analysis. In O. Fried, K. Lovell and S. Schmidt (Eds.), *The measurement of productive efficiency: techniques and applications* (pp. 68–119). Oxford University Press.

Greene, W. (Ed.). (1993). Econometric analysis. (2nd ed.). Englewood Cliffs, NJ: Prentice-Hall.

Hafizullah, H., Naomie, S., Oh, S., Ahmad, O., Alex, S., Aryati, B., Nor, Z., Roliana, I. & Shahir, O. (2013). A New database integration model using an ontology-driven mediated warehousing approach. *Journal of Theoretical and Applied Information Technology*, 56(2), 392-409.

Heidhues, F. (2004, November 8-12). Africa's *food and nutrition security: Where do we stand? Successes, failures, lessons learned.* Paper Presented at the CTA Seminar on The Role of Information Tools in Food and Nutrition Security, Maputo, Mozambique, Retrieved from http://www.cta.int/ctaseminar2004/HeidhuesDraft151004.pdf

Heidhues, F. and Buchenrieder, G. (2004). Rural financial market for food security. In M. Schulz and U. Kracht (Eds.), *Food and nutrition security in the process of globalization.* Münster, Germany: Lit-Verlag.

Luibrand, A. (2002). *Transition in Vietnam: Impact of the rural reform process on an ethnic minority.* Peter Lang Europäischer Verlag Der Wissenschaften; Frankfurt am main, Germany.

Ma, W., Renwick, A., Yuan, P., and Ratna, N., (2018). Agricultural cooperative membership and technical efficiency of apple farmers in China: An analysis accounting for selectivity bias. *Food policy*, 81, 122-132.

Macauley, H. (2015). *Cereal crops: Rice, maize, millet, sorghum, wheat.* Background paper, United Nations Economic Commission for Africa.

Marinda, P., Bangura, A., and Heidhues, F. (2006). Technical efficiency analysis in male and female-managed farms, a study of maize production in West Pokot district, Kenya, *Paper Presented at the International Association of Agricultural Economists Conference.* Gold Coast, Australia, August, 12-18, 2006.

Mason, K. O. and Smith, H. (2003). *Women's empowerment and social context: Results from five Asian countries.* Gender and Development Group, World Bank.

Mburu, S., Ackello-Ogutu, C., and Mulwa, R., (2014). Analysis of economic efficiency and farm size: A case study of wheat farmers in Nakuru District, Kenya. *Economics Reserch International,* 2014, 10.

Molua, E.L. and Lambi, C. (2007). *The economic impact of climate change on agriculture in Cameroon.* The World Bank, Policy Research Working Paper Series.

Molua, E.L. (2007). Women's Productivity and Access to Resources in Peasant Agriculture of Northwest Cameroon. *JENDA: Journal of Culture & African Women Studies,* 11(1), 84 – 101Moock, P. (1976). The efficiency of women as farm managers in Kenya. *American Journal of Agricultural Economics,* 58:559-583.

Morgan Stanley Report (2016). *Why it pays to invest in gender diversity.* New York.

Ogolla, D. and Mugabe, W. (1996). Land tenure system and natural resource management. In C. Juma, and J. Ojwang (Eds), In land we trust: Environment, private property and constitutional changes (pp.79-120). Nairobi, Kenya: Initiatives Publishers.

Quisumbing, A. (1996). Male-female differences in agricultural productivity. Methodological issues and empirical evidence. *World Development,* 24, 1579-1595.

Saito, A., Mekkonen, H. and Spurling, D. (1994). *Raising the productivity of women farmers in Sub Saharan Africa.* World Bank.

Shi, W. and Tao, F. (2014). Vulnerability of African maize yield to climate change and variability during 1961–2010. *Food Security,* 6: 471–481.

Staveren, V. (2013). An exploratory cross-country analysis of gendered institutions. *Journal of International Development, 25*, 108–121.

Tillmar, M. (2006). Swedish Tribalism and Tanzanian entrepreneurship: preconditions for trust formation. *International Journal of Gender Studies*, 18.

# Chapter 9

# Mainstreaming Gender in The Process of Large-scale Land Acquisitions for Agro-Investment in Cameroon[1]

## Lotsmart Fonjong

**Abstract**

Although most land regulatory frameworks neglect women, studies have shown that when women's land rights are improved, overall production and motivation to work on land increase and the fight against poverty in Africa is enhanced. This chapter examines the gender nature of the process of large-scale land acquisitions (LSLAs) and opportunities created by its investments in sub-Sahara Africa. It is based on a primary survey conducted between 2014 and 2015 in some divisions of the Littoral and South West regions. Findings reveal that current legal and cultural contexts of land tenure in Cameroon do not provide an enabling environment for women's effective participation in LSLAs. Some gender-shared opportunities offered by these investments are nonetheless acknowledged but are judged not enough to compensate for the gender differential losses women suffered because of LSLAs. Thus, land-related investments for "rural development" will miss their mark unless stakeholders recognize and address the spate needs of women and men through properly designed and executed gender-inclusive agro-investments. The chapter advocates for gender mainstreaming in the process of consultation, negotiation and compensation, through the creation and enforcement of national gender inclusive guidelines and frameworks for LSLAs. However, these guidelines and frameworks will only deliver where governments, NGOs and the media see themselves as partners of the same struggle.

---

[1] Paper first presented at the World Bank Land and Poverty Conference, March 2016, Washington DC, USA

215

**Key Words:** Women, gender mainstreaming, land rights, large scale land acquisition, accountability.

## Introduction

A wide-ranging body of empirical evidence has demonstrated many ways in which women are essential to improvements in household agricultural productivity, food security, and nutrition. Agarwal (2003) and Ahikire (2011) argue that when women's land rights are improved, overall production efficiency and motivation to put greater efforts and investment into land also increase. The FAO (2011) has also stressed that improving women's access to land is crucial in fighting hunger and poverty, and further estimates that equalizing access to productive resources between female and male farmers could boost agricultural output in developing countries by as much as 2.5% - 4% (FAO, 2012). Similar studies have supported the need for mainstreaming gender equity in land tenure governance as essential to the attainment of Millennium Development Goals 3 on promoting gender equality and women's empowerment (FAO, 2013) and even the realization of sustainable development goals. These positive gender influences at the various levels are no surprise when one considers the fact that about 80% of food providers in the continent are women.

There is a large body of literature, (notable Fonjong, 2015, Fonjong et al. 2014, Borras, and Franco 2012, Cotula, 2012, and De Schutter, 2010) indicating that the acquisition of large-scale land by many local and foreign capitalists for agricultural investments in Africa is a public concern. This is partly because the process is unaccountable to customary communities and unfair to women. Although LSLA has become a generalized phenomenon, the GRAIN (an NGO) has since 2006 identified Africa as a particularly vulnerable target. Over 56.2 million hectares of land deals have taken place in sub-Saharan African alone since 2000 (Anseeuw et al, 2012). Greenpeace International belives an area of more than 2.6 million hectares in ten West and Centr al African countries has either been earmarked for or is already home to large-scale plantation projects by

216

Asian and European-based investors (GRAIN, 2012). The majority of these projects are at least within agricultural land and forested areas, and many have sparked resistance from these communities (The Oakland Institute, 2012).

Most regulatory frameworks governing large-scale land acquisitions and investments, however, only provide some gender checks and balances on paper but which are hardly implemented on the ground. LSLAs in Africa have been associated with dispossession, inadequate compensation, environmental degradation and abuse of human rights which mostly affect women. But the literature on the scale and effect of these land deals has shown little discussion on their gender differential effects on African rural men and women. There are rare references to, and limited discussions of, gender effects (Cotula et al. 2009 and Schutter, 2009) although a few case studies and empirical projects do address gender dimensions of land deals (Daley 2010, Behrman et al, 2011).

Efforts to promote women's participation in LSLAs may yield little fruits because of women limited and insecure rights to land. In Ghana, for example, efforts to promote female participation in Integrated Tamale Fruit Company's out-grower scheme still leaves the participation of women workers at barely 12% (King and Bugri, 2013).The right of women to own land as stated in the legislation and constitution of Cameroon and most sub-Saharan African countries is in itself, not a sufficient measure that can be used to achieve gender equality in land tenure. Implementation of these legislations often lags behind (Cotula and Vermuelen, 2010). Some approaches used so far only integrate rather than institutionalize gender in LSLAs and thus, do not always produce lasting gender-inclusive outcomes. This is because of the pre-existence of socio-cultural norms which give women lesser rights than men to land and other resources or services that are necessary in securing the potential benefits from the investment schemes. Pre-existing socio-cultural attitudes and practices about women's status, rights and roles have a strong influence on gender outcomes, especially in the household where women have weaker bargaining and decision-making power, since those attitudes and norms keep the women in situations where they do not benefit directly from compensation and other advantages of LSLAs (Fairhead et al, 2012).

## Contextualizing LSLA, Gender and Land Governance in Cameroon

Large-scale land acquisitions in Cameroon take place on national land. National land has dual and conflicting claims from the state and customary communities. This is the land on which most rural women depend for survival. *Decree No. 76/166 of 27 April 1976* on LSLAs in Cameroon provides that national lands may be allocated as a temporary grant which may eventually be converted to absolute grant to natural persons for development. The application for grants may be made by any natural persons or corporate bodies to the Divisional Officer (DO)[2] of the area where the land is located and who in turn solicits the opinion of the Land Consultative Board (LCB). The Minister of Land approves allocations for land of less than 50 hectares and the President of the Republic for any land above 50 hectares. Where acquisition is sought on state land, the decision to grant it or not becomes the responsibility of the Senior Divisional Officer (SDO) of the Division concerned, in collaboration with the Side Board Commission (SBC). Whatever the level of transaction, the process is most often not engendered.

Gender-based discrimination on rights to land is sometimes supported by legislation rooted in inherited discriminatory colonial practices, customs and traditions (Fofack, 2014). The enforcement of these socially and legally recognizable claims by traditional and some national institutions in Cameroon and sub-Saharan Africa has already been thoroughly investigated in scholarly works by the likes of Nadasen, 2012; Fonjong, 2010; Fonjong et al., 2013; Fombe, 2013; Harrington and Chopra, 2010; Kimani, 2008; Bigombe and Bikie, 2003, who observe that indigenous African cultures and post-

---

[2] Cameroon administrative setup consist of five units: the state under the control of an elected president, the regions administered by appointed governors. The regions are further divided in to divisions and sub divisions which are controlled by appointed Senior Divisional (SDO) and Divisional officers (DO) respectively.

independence gender biases are obstacles to women's land rights. Customary practices give men inheritance rights but treat women as users without any strategic grantees of rights to land. Women customary land rights are fluid, just as customary rights under statute, particularly with the introduction of private land ownership. Consequently, the government occasionally claims the sole legal authority to sign off transactions with or without the consent of the local communities in which the national land is located. In fact, Cotula (2011) notes that in many reported deals in Africa, local people are not properly consulted.

The effects of land deals are felt more by women than other members of the community because of their (women's) over-reliance on the forest for cultivation, water, exploitation of Non-Timber Forest Products (NTFPs) and medicinal plants, resources which they risk losing. A close review of the process of LSLAs in the two regions under study reveal that women's interests are not considered in the deals both because they are not part of the decision-making concerning land deals, but also because they lack agency. One of the major effects of LSLAs projects is the destruction of water resources and catchment points, and the resulting water scarcity observed in most of the villages. This scarcity only adds to women's workload in ensuring household survival. The disparities in men and women's interest in land, their use of natural resources and their power over resource allocation highlight the need to protect women's land rights, mainly through gender mainstreaming. This paper thus examines some of the efforts and challenges so far in mainstreaming gender into the processes of land acquisition and opportunities created by land investments in sub-Saharan Africa, particularly in Cameroon.

Women farmers make up a greater majority of small-scale food producers in sub-Saharan Africa, and play an important role in the food and livelihood security of their households and communities. Land is an asset to them. Among other things, it enables them to accomplish these household roles and also functions as a source of employment, fuelwood and water. The income they generate from it gives them and their families' access to otherwise inaccessible facilities like hospitals and schools. Through their exploitation of land-based resources, women have become an indispensable force in the evolution of rural settings and constitute an essential stakeholder group in the future of rural socio-economic development in their respective communities (FAO, 2011). Despite this important contribution, women continue to face substantial challenges to their rights and access to land resources in Cameroon, and in having their views factored into the process of allocating land for plantation agriculture. Given the differential impact of land deals on different members of the community, adopting gender mainstreaming by identifying men's and women's concerns, challenges and difficulties arising from LSLAs could translate into actions that can reduce the negative consequences of land deals on women and strengthen their roles in ensuring community survival.

Some strides have been made by the Cameroon Government in local laws and in the signing of several international, regional and national policy instruments and conventions that make provisions for the protection, respect and promotion of women's property and land rights. Such instruments include the Convention on the Elimination of All Forms of Discrimination against Women, the 1995 Beijing Declaration, the Protocol to the African Charter on Human and People's Rights, signed and/or ratified by Cameroon. Even the 1996 constitution, in its preamble, emphasizes the rights of every citizen without exception of race or sex to property. However, the small benefits of such efforts to embrace and promote gender-responsive growth are currently at risk of being further undermined by LSLAs which have the potential to rob rural women of their source of livelihood sustenance and economic and financial independence. Doss et al. (2014) explain that the lack of attention to gender issues in current LSLAs research is due to the chronic gender blindness in mainstream literature, which translates into gender-blind research output and policies on the issue.

The land registration process in Cameroon underpins such chronic gender blindness and results in the exclusion of women from land ownership and participation in land deals. The registration process consolidates patriarchal rules of land ownership to the disadvantage of women. For example, the Land Consultative Board presided by the Divisional Officer, is composed of government officials, the village Chief and two notables from the affected areas, who are usually all men. Given the composition of the LCB, the land titling/lease process inadvertently promotes customary views which often are biased against women. Yanou et al, (2012) also highlight the fact that the LCB relies on the chief and the two notables as reliable village authorities to provide recommendations on the registration or lease process. Peters (2004:277) adds that customary tenure ignores among other things, illegal sales of land by these same traditional leaders.

The stakes are even higher today than in the past. In the current system of political support and clientelism, the state and investors use elites to bring pressure to bear on chiefs as a means of forcing and cajoling them to cooperate in the sale of national land as a sign of their support to the administration and to investors. In return, these elites and chiefs enjoy financial/material remuneration and are appointed into boards of companies by Government and investors (Mope, 2009). Empirical data have shown that most chiefs and elites represent mostly their self-interests and are prepared to sell the future of their communities to investors at the least financial or political motivation. Some of these chiefs will stop at nothing, including threats and intimidation of their subjects, to comply with the terms of the investors; after all, in most cases these chiefs are the ones who do the final negotiations and sign the land deals, if any. It is against this background of gender neglect in the exploitation of a very gender-sensitive resource like land that this paper examines if any efforts by states and investors have been made to mainstream gender in the process LSLAs; and if so, the challenges they have encountered, and the way forward.

**Methodology**

Primary data used is extracted from an ongoing IDRC-sponsored project on women and LSLAs in Cameroon. Cameroon consists of ten political regions which are further divided into administrative divisions. Primary survey was conducted in two of these ten regions covering four administrative divisions. The data was collected through in-depth interviews. Different interview guides were used for the five different target groups of respondents (women, chiefs, state officials, NGOs and investors) implicated in the process of land acquisition or who had made investments on the land. Although we reviewed the general situation of investors in the larger project, data for this paper emphasizes the activities of four investors: Sith Global Sustainable Oil Cameroon (SG-SOC), a subsidiary of the US-based Herakles Farms, PAMOL in the South West Region, *Plantations* du Haut *Penja* (PHP) in the Littoral Region, and the Cameroon Development Corporation operating in both regions.

Issues addressed during the interviews include the role of stakeholders in the process of LSLAs, the fairness of the process vis-à-vis the community, women land rights, the involvement and participation of affected communities and women in the meetings and consultations, and community's response to the seizure of land by investors. Data collected have been analyzed thematically and complemented with secondary data on LSLAs from Cameroon and beyond, including other published sources. This paper is focused on engendering the process of land acquisition which is one of the themes identified in the literature and during thematic analysis.

**Context and Process of LSLAs in Cameroon**

The Millennium Development Goal (MDG) 3 aims at achieving gender equality and empowerment of women in education, wage employment, the non-agricultural sector, and political representation in parliament. Gender equality and women's empowerment are seen as effective strategies in combating poverty, hunger and disease, and in stimulating a truly sustainable development (United Nations, 2000). The strategic role of land in developing economies makes it a key resource in the attainment of the Millennium Development Goals. That is why the UN System Task Team, (2012) believes that gender inequality in securing rights to land and property impedes progress in achieving inclusive economic and social development, environmental sustainability, and peace and security. In other words, secure rights to land and property for women are widely regarded as fundamental to ensuring effective and sustainable human development. MDG 3 thus provides an interesting framework in evaluating the impact of LSLAs on women as it touches on key areas

222

of women's lives such as employment, off-farm income, rights and even representation. Where women failed to fare well in these domains, the process of land takeover can only be a wakeup call for gender inclusive reforms.

To better appreciate the situation of women in the process of LSLAs in Cameroon, it is important to understand the process itself, which is both formal and informal. The formal process occurs where acquisition is done following statutes, and informal process is based on customary norms. In both cases, it is a top-bottom approach. On the one hand, the government imposes its will on affected communities, and the chiefs impose theirs on their subjects. Local public officials[3] confirmed that some of the investors acquired their land (size and sites) directly from the central government in the nation's capital Yaoundé, reducing the local administration to implementing decisions from hierarchy. This was the case with SG-SOC, whose land was negotiated at the level of the central government. These negotiations ended in a signed contract between the company and the Ministry of Economy, Planning and Regional Development. The company appeared one day with their contract to inform the affected community of their palm oil plantation project. Consequently, there was no need for a consultation with the women who depended on the land for their livelihood. This is probably because the conceded land was national land, and as many local public officials claim, the state has the right to dispose of the land wherever need be, without necessarily consulting the communities, much less the women who are often exploiting the land with only users' rights. This argument is not tenable here because the land law requires that communities are consulted through their representatives in the LCB even if these representatives, as is often the case, do not necessarily represent the communities.

The LCB as a structure involved in the process of land consultation in Cameroon does not make any specific provisions for women representation. The DO is the Chairperson of the LCB, the Divisional Chief of Land Tenure its Secretary, and the Divisional

[3] Interview with the Senior Divisional Officer (SDO) of Mundemba, April 4th 2014.

Delegate of Urban Development, Divisional Chief of Service, Sub Divisional Delegate of Agriculture, the Chief of the affected locality and two notables are members. As observed during field work, the notables are men, although women may be considered notables in traditional council and co-opted to represent their villages. The DO of Mbanga[4], however, argues that although the law does not make provision for women to be part of this committee, the Secretary of this committee (the Divisional Chief of land Tenure) is most often a woman. This argument is wilting because studies carried out by both Fonjong et al 2012 and Yanou et al 2011 in the North West and South West Regions with thirteen administrative divisions indicated that there was only one female Divisional Delegate. The DO of Nguti also reinforced the fact that women are not statutorily consulted since the LCB is not technically designed to have a female representative. Besides, this token woman who is not even the chairperson or chief or from the affected community is easily overwhelmed by her male colleagues on the Board. This is obviously gender blindness which continues to be replicated in policies. Doss et al. (2014) attribute the lack of attention to gender issues in current LSLAs to the chronic gender blindness in mainstream literature which often translates into gender-blind research outputs.

**Women Representation without Effective Participation**

Another factor of the limited level of consultation from women in LSLAs deals is culture. It is in most cultural beliefs in Cameroon that women have no say in land matters[5]. In this case, cultural norms do not give women the power to take decisions over land. This was even echoed by some of the women. In Ndian, some of them held that they heed totally to their husbands and the chiefs and had no say in land matters. Such docility is increasingly being challenged as one moves away from closed to open societies, especially where land is becoming scarcer and scarcer, as in Mungo and Fako Divisions.

---

[4] Interview with the Divisional Officer, Mbanga, November 11th 2015.
[5] Interview with the SDO of Ndian, April, 2014

Local administrations are insensitive to gender. As a result, the SDO of Ndian believes that "...women are often left out of the consultation process because in the minds of the administration, there is no need for a special role for women... The administration takes gender equality for granted..." and looks at the problem as a community rather than a gender issue. In this case, as one of our interviewees observes, those considered as stakeholders in land issues are taken to be the state, elites, chiefs and ministries concerned. Even local elected members of some of these communities hold that land deals do not concern women and so they are not to be consulted[6].

Just like the LCB where women are tokenized and without a voice, most of the respondents in Ndian, Nguti, and Fako confirmed that even though women are increasingly part of the traditional council, when it comes to consultations on land matters, they still continue to be silent. As a result, their interests are not taken into consideration as they ought to. Some local officials say that even in the few circumstances where women are part of the consultation process, they do not talk in meetings. Some women, however, refute this allegation. They point to the fact that they are given limited scope to express their opinions. One women's leader in Malende, for example, explained that she is consulted on issues relating to LSLAs in the area only when those concerned want her to take some information or gifts given by the investors to other women in the village. Other women believe that women who are consulted do not highlight the plight of women in the process of LSLAs because they are coerced by frugal gifts to remain silent. Other women believe women are given observer status in consultation meetings because they are invited but never given the chance to speak. "...The administration expects women to be more of passive listeners, so they are often not given the opportunity to talk even if they wish to. As a result, we wait for our men to take decisions and we follow..." one of them observes. Nonetheless, not all women subscribe to this marginalization theory of women by men and push the blames on the women. Some hold that women do not speak out because they

---

[6] Interview with the Deputy Mayor, Mundemba Council

are afraid of intimidations[7]. A male respondent says women are not even available to be consulted. He observes that, "...women are not serious, when meetings are called these women do not show up ... so they are left out..." However, if this is true, it could also be attributed to poor scheduling of meetings during hours when women are supposed be in their farms and so unable to attend. Another possible reason is inadequate information and sensitization surrounding LSLAs among women. Survival is the top priority for rural women and this survival depends on their farms. Where there is no adequate information as to why they should forgo their farms and attend meetings, they are mostly likely to forgo the meetings.

The reasons for women not participating in consultation meetings notwithstanding, they are hardly included in negotiations with investors seeking to acquire land. In the case of Ndian and Kupe Manenguba Divisions, some negotiation meetings were held in Kumba, Buea and Douala with investors to renegotiate the acquisition because of local hostility to the initial deal struck at the top in Yaoundé without involving the community. Field implementation of the deal proved difficult because of community resistance Renegotiation, according to local public officials, was aimed at ensuring that the interest of affected communities was expressed by their representatives in a tripartite between investors, the administration and the community. Community interests have always been left in the hands of the elites, chiefs and elders who are expected to work together on behalf of the people. But this is no longer the case, admitted the SDO for Ndian. He noted the many differences and conflict of interests between the chiefs, elites and villagers, especially concerning needs and dedications. Since the chiefs are the statutory signatories, they end up taking the final decision. The chief is seen to be the right person to be responsible for the wellbeing of his people but very often this role is sacrificed for personal interests[8].They are often cajoled by gifts and throw away community interests for personal aggrandizement[9] and would not include women in their delegations even if advised to do so. Mope

---

[7] Interview president Ndian Women Forum
[8] Interview with SDO Ndian, April 4th 2014
[9] Interview with Deputy Mayor, Mundemba, April 4th 2014

(2009) believes that the elite and chiefs enjoy financial/material remuneration and appointments from investors, with little regard for women who depend on the land for their survival.

There are other views that hold that women's exclusion from land negotiations is partly because the statutes exclude them from such activities, and more fundamentally because of the customary belief and assumption that women do not own land and so cannot negotiate on what they do not own.[10] Even if local administrations do not share these beliefs, it is not easy for them to dismiss the beliefs and impose women, particularly in charged cultural environments such as theirs.

This gender hostile environment has led not only to the exclusion of women who depend on the forest and land for their livelihood, but also to the exclusion of the youth and men who though members of the traditional council are unlikely to align with the self-seeking agenda of the chiefs and the elite. Some chiefs even sideline the traditional council and take along only people who will collaborate with them in land negotiations.[11] In some cases where women take part in the negotiations, chiefs do not allow them to co-sign the agreement but prefer "their men."[12] Some chiefs even insist that land matters are within their sole purview. When asked why the chief leaves women and other smart members of the traditional council out of these negotiations, one of the women from Kupe Manenguba Division answered "...the Chief says he is in control not the traditional council in land issues.... So he takes the decisions..."[13] This behaviour by chiefs was also reported in Ndian Division. Interestingly, women representation in the traditional council in all the localities studied is no longer in question as was the case in the past. However, such representation does not translate into automatic participation in important village businesses such as land negotiation.

One cannot ignore the role of investors in the exclusion of women in land negotiations. These investors are aware of the key demands of women, considering the importance of land to their

---

[10] Interviews with the Divisional Delegate MINEPAT, Ndian, April 4th 2014
[11] Interview with the First Deputy Mayor for Mundemba, April 4th 2014
[12] Interview with native of Bima in Ndian, August 16, 2014
[13] Interview with Nguti Sub Division, December 18th 2014

triple role of reproduction, production and community management. For this and other reasons, investors are happy not to see women around land negotiation tables. Chiefs are greedy and easy to convince because their stakes on the land are low. Fortunately for them, Cameroon land laws are gender neutral, which helps their cause as leaving women out contravenes no law. In fact, there are no clearly stated gender-sensitive laws governing consultations and negotiations in land deals. Investors are given free rein. Where they are minded to hold meetings with communities, they do so mostly with chiefs and traditional male members of the council.[14] Where state land was acquired either from government or through a tender as in the case of PHP in the Mungo, the company had no legal obligation to negotiate with affected communities or women. Moreover, whether on state or national land, the government always tries to facilitate the process for investors because they are regarded as agents of development.

Effective representation is fundamental to successful LSLAs and examples of good practices abound in the continent. The Mozambican 1997 Land Law ensures representativeness by insisting that the outcome of any land deal must include men and women, diverse socio-economic and age groups, neighbours, and must also be signed by three to nine men and women selected in public meetings (Technical Annex, Land and Law Regulations, 2000). Again, the Biofuels Guidelines that require land-use plans to be drawn up prior to land transfer is an important tool to enable villagers to decide independently the size and location of land to be transferred. Many villages do not have such plans, but some investors have been able to finance land-use planning and mapping of village land they were planning to acquire in Tanzania to meet this requirement (German et al, 2011).

**Women's Attitudes Towards their Neglect in LSLAs**

---

[14]Interview with the Interim General Manager of PAMOL in Ndian, December 18th, 2014

The reaction from women to LSLAs in Cameroon has been timid and mixed, particularly in the four administrative divisions surveyed. As discussed in the paragraphs that follow, women have been acquiescent, and when communities try to react, women rarely take the lead; they join existing campaigns, with mitigating results. There was no strong reaction from the women in places like Kupe Manenguba but for the fact that a few elderly women belonging to different sacred cults in Nguti marched to the chief threatening to carry out demonstrations if land was sold to the prospective investor.[15] In 2013 these women blocked the nursery belonging to one of the plantation companies in the area but their action produced very little results because of the division in the villages among those for and against LSLAs, and secondly because they lacked conviction as they were easily dispersed by a few bags of rice and other food stuffs donated to them by the company.[16] Scott (1985) believes that the rich (investors) can always use money to buy their way out of such situations and help to disintegrate the social ties among the poor in local communities.

The case of Nguti does not necessarily portray the general trend of women in Cameroon and Africa who have been known to fight committedly against injustices in the past and are still doing so today. Women sacred societies like in Mezam, North West Region of Cameroon fought successfully in 1958 and 1987 against the Fulanies and chiefs toying with their farmlands. Ahire et al, (2015) also noted the success story of women in Uganda who can defy government orders and intimidation to resist the process of LSLAs. As observed, elderly women in the Mubede and Amuru districts marched naked, lay across major streets blocking the government convoys in their areas in protest against their land being grabbed by investors.

With no land to farm and forest to harvest NTFPs that bring income to the homes, a good number of women, along with other community members, are migrating to urban centres in search of alternative sources of livelihoods. One female informant from Talangye (Kupe) said "... women have abandoned the villages

---

[15] Interview with the sub Divisional Delegate for Women' Empowerment and the Family (MINPROFF), Nguti December 18th 2014.

[16] Interview with the sub Divisional Delegate of Wildlife and Forestry, Nguti

because of poverty...since there are no farmlands to cultivate crops..."[17]

Overall, where women have done nothing in the face of losing their land, the general reason has been fear and lack of education and information. The women are afraid of traditional beliefs that keep them out of land matters or of being identified and stigmatized as rebellious by the chiefs and their accomplices. In most cases, women have not been educated on the different avenues to seek recourse when their prior and informed consent is not sought. Even the few who know what can be done do not have the means to do it. They are preoccupied with how to feed their homes. These were the general arguments advanced by women when asked why nothing was being done on their part to stop the phenomenon in their localities instead of fighting government or government-backed investors with predictable results.

These findings support those of previous studies that land-related investments promoted in the name of "rural development" will miss their mark unless the many stakeholders involved recognize and address the needs of women and men. A gender-inclusive agricultural investment that integrates women's and men's dimensions in the design, implementation, monitoring/evaluation of all agricultural policies and programs as Opio (2000) has also noted, ensures that women and men benefit equally. Although women may have secure plantation jobs, they are missing from senior management levels for various reasons. They are often over-represented among casual or gender-stereotyped workers who earn less than men and fewer succeed in climbing the career ladder.

A properly designed and well executed gender-inclusive agro-investment will provide opportunities for both women and men through the introduction of new employment, income generating activities/opportunities, and new technologies and services. It may also assist in the redistribution of local resources in a more equitable manner among men, women and the youth. Even investors are equally likely to benefit from social stability, security, cohesion and

---

[17] Interview with female member of Talagaye traditional council, May 25th 2015

higher labor productivity from both men and women, which according to Behrman et al, (2011) result in significant increase in companies' output, profit and expansion in the long run.

## Efforts at Engendering the Process of LSLAs in Cameroon (Gender-shared Opportunities)

Many investors have carried out important activities to involve women who are those worst affected by LSLAs. One of such efforts is through the creation of outgrower schemes for women. PAMOL Cameroon has prioritized women in the new outgrowers, targeting the population of most of the villages in Ndian where the company has taken land for its palm plantations. FAO (2013a) reports that the Kelaya Small Holder Company (KASCOL), Zambia offered access to land to 160 outgrowers with 43 being women and 117 men, with reasonably secure tenancy. These female outgrowers are performing well in diverse areas and usually producing marginally higher yields on average than men. Furthermore, PHP has empowered about 1500 women organized in groups of 30 with a representative per group in Mungo Division. They have been given about 2500 plots of cultivable land for crops and vegetables. This is because PHP recognizes the indispensable role women play in food security.

Women are happy and appreciative of this move as seen in the comments of the leader of one group that has benefited from this initiative. She says "PHP is really helping us because most of our members are widows and orphans without land or means of survival......we sell and are able to meet with our needs.... and it is a great motivation to others who see us grow..."[18] FAO (2013b) also recognizes the impact of the KASCOL outgrower scheme on food security especially for the families of outgrowers in Zambia. Food production has improved especially with the introduction of improved farm inputs, technology, and capacity.

Plantations have offered employment opportunities for women. Companies that have acquired land generally hold that they have no

---

[18] Interview with the President and vice of Societe Cooperative des Femme Dynamique in Mungo

employment policy that is biased against women. Men and women are given equal opportunities for all types of jobs and positions. In cases where men outweigh women, some companies explained that this happens only where more men than women applied for the position, and not because men were preferred over women. These examples corroborate some of the arguments raised: There are 94 women employed in CDC Matouke Estate and in Malende rubber estate, 40% of the 227 tappers are women; six out of the 13 supervisory staff are women, 60% of the 140 weeders are women and 4 of the 14 Foremen are women.[19] PHP has employed over 6000 personnel with equal opportunities given to men and women. In Kupe Manenguba and Ndian, some of the natives, including the community-based organizations acknowledged that the situation of some has positively changed since they were employed by SG-SOC.[20]

Employment of women is commonplace in plantation agriculture across Africa. Women employed by Chisumbanje plant in Zimbabwe have earned incomes that serve as an important source of livelihood (Mutopo, 2014). The Integrated Tamale Fruit Company (ITFC), Ghana, employs women almost in every sector of the company. According to FAO, (2013b), they work in the pack house, nursery, beekeeping, and in the management of the plantation outgrowers. Statistically, 40 out of ITFC 252 permanent workers are women and women numbered 155 out of 216 seasonal workers. However, critics of companies involved in plantation agriculture, including Fairhead et al, (2012), argue that if women continue to shoulder all household responsibilities, combining paid plantation employment with domestic work and other responsibilities only go to increase their burden. Most governments need broad and holistic gender policy frameworks that accommodate women's triple roles and special sectoral gender-inclusive policies in LSLAs.

Social infrastructures (schools, roads, and health centres, water, electricity) created by agro companies to boost production and productivity of their workers have also benefitted neighbouring communities and women. This has been observed with PAMOL,

[19] Interviews with CDC Malenda Estate Manager, November 16th, 2015
[20]Interview with the President of Women's Forum Ndian, May 22nd 2015

CDC, and PHP. Here, these amenities are shared by the communities, like what Mutopo, (2014) highlighted with the Chisumbanje plant in Zimbabwe. For example, PHP runs a private school (Les Tisserins) from Kindergarten through 12 grades for children of staff and those from surrounding communities, with an enrolment of close to 400 students in 2012. In this same year, the company allocated 101 million FCFA for the improvement of communal school infrastructures.

The employment of women in plantations has sometimes been criticized because of the poor working conditions (long hours, risky operations, strenuous tasks, low pay and position, slow mobility, etc.) which these women are subjected to. Some management, however, believe women are well treated in the companies. Women are reassigned from work stations considered as highly risky to mother and baby, handling of agrochemical products for example, when they become pregnant in PHP.[21] CDC even goes a step further to ensure that women working inside the plantation are reassigned to do few hours of light work around the offices during the last months of pregnancy. Women like all the other CDC workers and family members below 18 receive free medical care at all clinics of the company and receive additional two days paid leave for each child below the age of six. Other free amenities provided to their workers include houses, water and electricity[22] although the houses are too small to accommodate large families. Nevertheless, these amenities and employment considerations provide a huge relief for women in the discharge of their triple role. In so doing, women productivity is high because of high moral and job satisfaction that also easily enables them to be involved in other tasks that could be empowering.

**Some Challenges to Mainstreaming Gender into the Process**

According to OECD (2012), a woman's economic independence is one of the greatest assets to her empowerment. It is fundamental in strengthening women's rights, enabling them to have control over

---

[21] Interview with the General Manager of PHP, December 4th 2014
[22] Interview with the Estate Manager of Pendamboko, November 3rd 2015

their lives and exert influence in society. It is also a source of stability that enhances the woman's productivity and output in the plantations. Providing employment, social amenities and farmlands to women in their plantations by investors in Cameroon means they can use their facilities and remunerations to sustain their families and other needs without having to depend on their husbands. The extent to which investors can assist women through inclusion in LSLAs depends not only on their good will but on the cultural, socio-legal and political contexts which can either be a liability or an asset. This implies for example, that the degree to which investors are successful in mainstreaming gender in LSLAs may only be as good as the laws in place. Investors are still likely to continue exploiting both men and women if local laws remain without gender-inclusive clauses on how both genders are to be treated.

Cultural norms that remain static in an evolving socio-economic context as recorded in most localities are a major handicap to women and even to investors who may want to treat women fairly. For example, women's access to better jobs and pay in plantations depends on their level of education. But most women in these rural areas are uneducated and so can only be employed as labourers, leaving the white-collar opportunities to men and migrants. A holistic policy must promote the education of the girl child in affected regions. This means going against social and cultural discrimination in education so that more girls can acquire capacities that will increase their opportunities for better jobs and working conditions without which they will continue to be marginalized and exploited in the plantations in addition to losing their farmland.

National laws and local policies governing LSLAs should be revised. The process of revision should be participatory to enable the voices/interests of the affected communities and rural women who depend on the land to be reflected in the policy statement. This should be followed by educational and literacy programs carried out by NGOs, government institutions and women groups to raise women's awareness on land issues and to improve their negotiating skills and capacity. It is only through this and other measures that the process of LSLAs can be envisaged to result in a win-win, else women will forever remain the victims of the process.

Women have been very critical of the process of compensation associated with LSLAs in Cameroon. Although they are those whose farms are destroyed, compensation is often paid to the men and only for the crops on the land, using unfair government tariffs which are usually old and lower than existing market prices. This is similar to the situation in Tanzanian farms where compensation to some households was paid for tree crops such as mangoes, coconuts and cashew nuts but excluded annual crops (German et al, 2011 and Cleaver et al, 2010). In Mungo Division, women can receive semester allowances paid by PHP to natives of the area only when they become widows. Generally, compensation in most sub-Saharan African nations is always highly controversial. German et al, (2011), in the case of Tanzania, for example, note that it is mired in allegations of unfairness and characterized by a lack of disclosure of the valuation techniques and rationale used to generate compensation data and schedules. In other cases, compensation was paid for loss of access to communally used land, while in still other cases loss of access to communal land remained uncompensated and, indeed, the land itself excluded from valuation (German et al, 2011).

As already discussed above, women are generally more vulnerable to the effects of land deals than men, mainly because they primarily depend on land for their livelihoods. Moreover, women lack voice and agency with respect to land-related decision-making as they are ignored and bypassed by land deal negotiations, making the implication of land deals different for men and women. Given the differential impact of land deals on different members of the community, adopting gender mainstreaming by identifying men's and women's concerns, challenges and difficulties arising from LSLAs could translate into actions that reduce their negative consequences on women and strengthen women's roles in ensuring household survival. To mainstream gender, all planned actions of large-scale land deals should be assessed based on the implications for women and men in order to perpetuate equality.

Gender mainstreaming will involve a range of activities to reduce vulnerability and build resilience. For example, the community has to accept and view women's role as significant and full of potentials that can make contributions to ensure the survival of larger communities.

This may lessen the impact of LSLAs and hence reduce long term consequences on communities and ensure that both men and women displaced are able to benefit equally from compensations resulting from land deals.

A gender analysis is recommended for investors on the profile of women and all other vulnerable members of affected communities. To ensure that gender is mainstreamed, policies should recognize the socially determined roles, responsibilities and concerns and challenges of men and women. To achieve this, conscious efforts or practical modalities should be made to consult with men and women during discussions and meetings concerning the process of acquisition. Consultations with and the participation of women in land deals must be ensured and the role of women's groups and networks strengthened to engage grassroots women and men.

## Conclusion

The present context in which LSLAs operate do not benefit women because it is not gendered, making women to suffer disproportionate effects of losing land compared to men in the process. The process in Cameroon is male-centred, leaving women's voices and views on LSLAs to be suppressed in a predominantly patriarchal environment where women are likely to be silent or simply support views expressed by their male colleagues (Kaven, 2004; United Nations, 2013). Such exclusion will in the mid and long term not prove beneficial even to investors. In other to overcome some of the challenges, it is important to follow clear measures which guide land acquisition for investment in the country as is the case in Uganda where the state determines sectors open to foreign direct investment and carries out cost-benefit analysis on public facilities before pulling them down to allocate the land to private investors (Ahikire 2011). This requires government departments related to land, women, or the economy to first of all recognize women's invisible work on land in order to adopt frameworks for auditing agricultural investment proposals to ensure that they are aligned with the national objectives that protect the rights of vulnerable rural communities, land users and women. Such frameworks are alone not enough and gender policies adopted at higher levels for implementation at lower levels dominated by men might not necessarily work. Men therefore have to be educated to see to see women as useful equal partners in local development and to also share power. This will foster the acceptability of women and their views in village land committees that negotiate the terms of land deals with investors. Government thus needs to commit both human and financial resources in this direction. Gaynor and Jennings (2004) believe that gender equality policies can only be successful if they are explicitly backed by requisite resources that translate them into programs that are consistently monitored to ensure that women's voices are heard in group works and negotiations.

African governments cannot achieve a gender inclusive culture in LSLAs alone without considerable support from NGOs and the media who in some instances, have been fighting against some of the unorthodox land deals in the continent. Both NGOs and the media landscape needs to be engendered in reporting both positive cases and cases that fail to live up to commitments or have a negative impact on local communities and women. NGOs, the media, and the state must therefore see themselves as partners rather than rivals in the process. Above all, women' effective participation in LSLAs has to begin with the securization of customary land tenure, and customary land that have been devalued and often defined wrongly as "waste or unused land by governments/investors. This also means strengthening women agency, overcoming cultural restrictions against women's land rights which are likely to place them in a weaker negotiating or bargaining position with authorities and investors on potential land deals.


**References**

Agarwal, B. (2005). Gender and land rights revisited: exploring new prospects via the state, family and market. *Journal of Agrarian Change* 3(1&2): 184-224.

Anseeuw, W. Alden Wily, L. Cotula, L and Taylor, M. (2012). Land Rights and the Rush for Land: Findings of the Global

Commercial Pressures on Land Research Project. Available onlineat:http://www.landcoalition.org/sites/default/files/publi cation/1205/ILC%20GSR%20report_ENG.pdf

Behrman, J., Meinzen-Dick, R. and Quisumbing, A. (2011). *The gender implications of large scale land deals. Sustainable solutions for ending hunger and poverty.* International Food Policy Research Institute. IFPRI. Available online at: www.iss.nl/fileadmin/ASSETS/iss/Documents/conference_pa pers/LDPI/56-behrman-Meinzen_Dick-Quisumbing.pdf

Bigombe L., Patrice & Elise-Henrietta Bikie. (2003). *Women and land in Cameroon: Questioning women's land status and claims for change.* A paper prepared for Emory University's Women and Land Studies series. Emory University, Atlanta. http://www.law.emory.edu/wandl/WAl-studies/Cameroon.htm

Cleaver, J., Schram, R. and Wanga, G. (2010). *Bioenergy in Tanzania: the country context. In: Bioenergy and food security in Tanzania.* Food and Agricultural Organization, Rome. Available online at: http://www.fao.org/docrep/012/il544e/il544e.pdf

Cotula, L. and Vermeulen, S. (2010). Over the heads of local people: Consultation, consent and recompense in large scale deals for biofuel projects in Africa. *Journal for Peasant Studies.* 37(4),899-916.

Cotula, L. (2011). *Land deals in Africa: what is in the contracts?* IIED

Cotula, L., S. Vermeulen, R. Leonard, and J. Keeley. (2009). *Land grab or development opportunity? Agricultural investment and international land deals in Africa.* <http://fr.allafrica.com/sustainable/resources/view/00011918. pdf>.

Daley, E. (2010). *Commercial pressures on land gender study.* Final Report for the International Land Coalition's Global Study of Commercial Pressures on Land. Headington, U.K.: Mokoro.

De Schutter, O. (2009). *Report of the Special Rapporteur on the Right to Food – Addendum, 'Large-Scale Land Acquisitions and Leases: A Set of Minimum Principles and Measures to Address the Human Rights Challenge.* 28 December 2009. UN Doc. A/HRC/13/33/Add.2.

Doss, C., Summerfield, G., &Tsikata, D. (2014). Land, gender, and food security. *Feminist Economics,* 20(1), 1–23.

238

Fairhead, J., Leach, M. and Scoories, I. (2012). Green grabbing: A new appropriation of nature. *Journal of Peasant studies*. Vol. 39(2).

FAO. (2011). *The state of food and agriculture: Women in agriculture— Closing the gender gap for development*. Rome: Food and Agriculture Organization of the United Nations (FAO).

FAO. (2012). *Voluntary Guidelines for the Responsible Governance of Tenure of Land, Fisheries and Forests in the Context of National Food Security*. Rome: FAO

FAO. (2013a). *The gender and equity implications of land-related investments on land access, labour and income-generating opportunities. A case study of selected agricultural investments in Zambia*. FAO, Rome.

FAO. (2013b). *The gender and equity implications of land-related investments on land access, labour and income-generating opportunities in Northern Ghana. The case study of Integrated Tamale Fruit Company*. FAO.Rome. Available online at: www.fao.org/uploads/media/gender.pdf

Fofack, H. (2012). A Model of Gender Production in Colonial Africa and Implications for the Post-Colonial Period, Forthcoming World Bank Policy Research Working Paper, the World Bank.

Fombe, L., Sama-Lang, I., Fonjong, L., & Mbah-Fongkimeh, A. (2013). Securing tenure for sustainable livelihoods: A case of women land ownership in Anglophone Cameroon. *Éthiqueetéconomique/Ethics and Economics*, 10 (2), 72-86. Accessed, March 31, 2015 at: *http://ethiqueeconomique.net/*

Fonjong, L. (2010). *Customary Law and its Implications for Women's Rights and Access to Land in Africa: The Case of Anglophone Cameroon*. Paper presented at IDRC symposium on Gendered Terrain: Women's Rights and Access to Land in Africa.14-16 September. Nairobi.

Fonjong, L., Sama-lang, I., and Fombe, L. (2012). *The Impact of land tenure Practices on Women's Rights to Land in Anglophone Cameroon and Implications on Sustainable Development*. International Development Research Centre. Technical Report Available at http://idlbnc.idrc.ca/dspace/bitstream/10625/48424/1/IDL-48424.pdf.

Fonjong, L., Sama-Lang, I. and Fombe, L. (2015). *Disenchanting voices from within: Interrogating women's resistance to large scale agro-investments in Cameroon*. Paper presented at the 2015 World Bank conference on Land and Poverty. The World Bank. Washington DC, March 23-27, 2015.

German, L., Schoneveld, G. and Mwangi, E. (2011). *Contemporary processes of large-scale land acquisition by investors. Case studies from sub-Saharan Africa.* CIFOR, Borgor Barat.

Harrington, A. & Chopra, T. (2010). Arguing traditions: reviewing Kenya's women access to land rights. Justice for the poor. Research Report, No. 2

Kevane, M. (2004). *Women and development in Africa: How gender works.* Boulder, Colo., USA and London: Lynne Rienner

Kimani, M. (2008). Women struggle to secure land rights: Hard fight for access and decision-making power.' *Africa Renewal,* 22 (1): 10.

King, R. and Bugri, J. (2013). *The gender and equity implications of land related investments on land access, labour and income generating opportunities in Northern Ghana. The case study of integrated tamale Fruit Company.* FAO, Rome.

Nadasen, N. (2012). Rural women's access to land in sub-Saharan Africa and implications for meeting the Millennium Development Goals Agenda. *Empowering Women for Gender Equity,* 26: 1, 41 – 53.

Mope S. (2009) "Challenges to Chieftaincy Today: Governance Issues and *how Fons* strategise to overcome obstacles of overarching structures in the Western Grassfields of Cameroon. In Tamajong, E. (ed.). *Les mutations en Afrique.* Yaoundé: Presses d'UCCAC. Pp. 159-193.

Mutopo, P. (2014). *Women, Mobility and Rural Livelihoods in Zimbabwe: Experiences of Fast Track Land Reform*; BRILL: Leiden, The Netherlands.

Oakland Institute. (2012*). Understanding Land Investment Deals In Africa. SOCFIN land investment in Sierra Leone.* Land Deal Brief, Oakland Institute, Oakland.

OECD. (2012). *Women's economic empowerment.* Promoting pro-poor growth: the role of empowerment

Opio, F. (2003). Gender mainstreaming in agriculture with special reference to Uganda: Challenges and prospects. *African Crop Science Society,* 6:699-703.

Peters, P. (2004). Inequality and Social Conflict over Land in Africa. *Journal of Agrarian Change* 4(3):269-314

Scott, C. (1985). *Weapons of the Weak: Everyday Forms of Peasant Resistance.* New Haven: Yale University Press.

UN System Task Team. (2012). UN System Task Team to support the preparation of the Post-2015 UN Development Agenda Draft Concept Note.

Yanou, M. & Sone, P. (2012). Women and land registration in Anglophone Cameroon: lessons from South Africa. In Fonjong, L. *Issues in women's land rights in Cameroon.* Bamenda, Langaa Research and Publishing.

# Natural Resource, Development Challenges and Policy Options

# Chapter 10

# Biodiversity Conservation and Survival of Food Crop Producers around the Mount Cameroon National Park

*Lotsmart Fonjong and Ayemeley Betrand Ayuk*

**Abstract**

The Mount Cameroon National Park (MCNP) was created in 2009 to preserve the rich biodiversity of the Mount Cameroon Region. Biodiversity conservation comes with the displacement of farmers from their farmlands as they are denied access into the protected areas. This chapter assesses the survival strategies for food crop producers around the MCNP as a result of the creation of the park and eventual displacement of the farmers. It is based on data collected from 252 food producers in four sampled communities around the MCNP and the main stakeholders of the park. Simple descriptive and inferential statistical analysis were carried out on field data to complement data obtained from context analysis of existing reports collected from stakeholders. Findings reveal that the creation of the MCNP led to loss of close to 8000 hectares of farm land and the displacement of 65% of sampled farmers around the park. Over 70% of farmers who lost their farmlands after the park were forced to change from extensive mixed cropping to intensive mixed cropping to keep up with demand for food. Most of the farmers affected also must learn or adapt new farming skills such as the use of improved seeds and modern farming in their search for alternative effective production techniques. These and other efforts from the displaced farmers led to increase in output and incomes although this was not felt by every farmer. The fact that all farmers were not positively affected by measures created by the park undoubtedly explains the recurrent problem of encroachments in the protected area which the authorities of the park are called to deal with.

**Keywords**: Cameroon, Biodiversity Conservation, food crop production, coping strategies.

245

# Introduction

Tropical rainforests account for more than half of the plant and animal species on earth with some estimates ranging up to 90%, although they only cover about 7% of global land area (Wilson, 2002). Globally, rapid population growth, poverty and unregulated access to tropical forest resources threaten critical tropical forest biomes that were until recent times protected by their inaccessibility. Wilson (2002) believes that worldwide coverage of tropical rainforests has declined rapidly in recent years to roughly 20 million km² at the start of the 21st Century. World Wide Fund for Nature, WWF (2006) notes that the forests of the Congo Basin account for about a sixth of the world's remaining tropical forest cover and are among the most bio-diverse places on earth. The same forests provide food, materials and shelter to some 40 million people. Unfortunately, close to 0.5 million hectares of these forests are being lost annually, due mainly to illegal logging activities that is reinforced by widespread corruption and weak governance in the sub-region. Urgent steps are necessary to safeguard the remaining world forests, located mostly in the Amazon Basin, Central Africa, Canada, Southeast Asia, and Russia (WWF, 2006). The tropical forest under threat extends to Cameroon where deforestations estimated at about 0.6 % per year between 1990 and 1995, is attributed mostly to population growth and shifting cultivation (Neil et al., 2001), and in recent years to indiscriminate exploitation by the logging companies.

In the face of forest loss and the resulting decline in wildlife population (Nomsa, 1992), most African countries have opted for the creation of protected areas and national parks as management approach for biodiversity conservation (Kimengsi et al, 2016). The management of protected areas has come under scrutiny with many advocating for local participation and community development as part of a comprehensive strategy for biodiversity conservation (Kimengsi et al, 2016). Such community involvement should be driven by context-specific income generating and economically friendly economic opportunities based on the socio-economic and cultural realities of the affected communities (Lambi et al, 2012).

Cameroon has witnessed some efforts in wildlife conservation. More than 20 protected reserves comprising national parks, zoos, forest reserves and sanctuaries have been established. The protected areas were first created in the Northern Region under the colonial powers in 1932. The first two reserves were the Mozogo Gokoro reserve and the Benoue reserve followed by the Waza reserve in 1934. The protected areas cover 28,104 square kilometres with prominent parks such as the Bouba Bek National Park, Campo Ma'an National Park, Kurop National Park, and Mount Cameroon National Park amongst others (Dowsett et al, 2000).

The ability of world agriculture to provide food for the ever-growing human population can be regarded as one of the great success stories of human civilization (Nakhauka, 2009). Agriculture in general and food crop production account for one-third of global Gross Domestic Product (GDP) and contributes immensely to the economy of many countries, particularly in Africa (Cincotta et al, 2000). Yet, Cincotta et al. (2000) hold that 80% of the food-deprived human population lives in developing countries, where demographic pressure and biodiversity are highest. Agriculture in Cameroon remains the backbone of her economy, accounting directly or indirectly for about 70% of its workforce, 42% of its Gross Domestic Product and 30% of its export revenue (Fouda, 2008). Cameroon has a favourable climate and fertile land for agriculture and by 2007, the total land reserved for agriculture was estimated at 91,600 km2 (NBSAP 2012). The recent growth in large-scale corporate agri-business in Cameroon has intensified the tensions over land between commercial interests, local communities and conservation priorities. The tension between agricultural expansion and biodiversity conservation is a global problem which is not common only to Cameroon. The Millennium Ecosystem Assessment (MA) of Nambu (2003) documented the dominant effects of biodiversity conservation on food crop production. Yet, global demand for associated agricultural products is projected to rise by at least 50% over the next two decades (UN Millennium Project, 2005). The need to reconcile agricultural production and biodiversity conservation has prompted widespread innovation to coordinate landscape and policy action and various coping strategies for food crop producers around national parks (Scherr, 2003; Sayer, 2004).

## The research problem

Cameroon is one of the most biologically rich countries on the continent including South Africa (Bond and Frost, 2008). The country encompasses an intricate mosaic of diverse habitats with moist tropical forest predominating in the South and South East, Montane forest and alpine savannah in the highlands and Sub Sahelian savanna in the Far North (Usongo, 1996). The diverse habitat harbours over 9000 species of plants, 320 species of mammals, 920 species of birds, 542 species of fresh water fish (Nambu, 2001). Most of these species are concentrated around the Mount Cameroon Area (WCMC, 1994), making it very rich in biodiversity. Nonetheless, Cameroon also contains a high percentage of threatened or endangered species including 18 mammals, 16 birds and 5 reptiles (Birdlife International, 2000). The Mount Cameroon Area is a replica of the national picture just painted above. It has over 400,000 inhabitants, two-thirds of whom live in urban and peri-urban areas and the rest in villages (MINFOF, 2014) which put enormous pressure on its biodiversity resources. Agriculture is the most important source of livelihood in the Mount Cameroon area accounting for about 80% of household income in most villages (Tanjong, 2014). This simply means agriculture remains pivotal in the socioeconomic progress of the area and many families see no life outside agriculture. They depend on it to feed their families and then market the excesses in order to acquire incomes and other basic needs. But food production and biodiversity conservation are not compatible development objectives in the area.

Nkembi et al. (2002), Nchanji and Plumptre (2000) and Pretty (1997) have observed that biodiversity conservation has negative impacts on food crop production. These authors hold that biodiversity conservation leads to loss of arable land, fall in food crop production and complete change in farming systems. The Divisional Delegation of Agriculture and Rural Development for Ndian (2004), corroborates this observation by stating that the creation of the

248

Korup National Park has prompted a fall in food crop production. It is against this backdrop of competing objectives for biodiversity conservation and food crop production that this study examines the situation of food crop production and strategies of farming communities in the Mount Cameroon National Park.

## Methodology

The Mount Cameroon National Park is a biodiversity hotspot created by Prime ministerial decree No. 2009/2272/PM of 18th December 2009 with technical and financial support of PSMNR-SWR. The MCNP covers the Fako and Meme Divisions of the South West Region of Cameroon approximately between Latitude 4.055° - 4.378° N and Longitude 9.031°- 9.294° E (Cheek et al., 1994). The park covers an area of 58,178 ha and shares external boundaries of 128.73 km in length with five sub-divisions: Buea sub-Division (46.79 km), Limbe 2 sub-Division, Muyuka sub-Division (19.82 km), Idenau sub-Division (24 km) and Mbonge sub-Division (38 km). The southern boundary is about 2 km from the sea. Four protected areas are in closest proximity to the park: the Mokoko Forest Reserve (FMU 11-008B), the remnant of Bomboko Forest Reserve, the Southern Bakundu Forest Reserve (including FMU 11-008A) and Meme River Forest Reserve (MRFR). Furthermore, three community forests also share direct boundaries with the park: Etinde (4,976 ha), Bakingili (905 ha) and Woteva (1,865 ha) (Cheek et al., 1994).

The park is bordered by forty-one (41) villages whose activities directly or indirectly affect its management. Also, the MCNP shares boundaries with large scale oil palm and rubber plantations belonging to the Cameroon Development Cooperation (CDC), as well as privately owned plantations, some of which are up to 50 ha. The establishment of oil palm plantations is a major contribution to forest clearance in the area.

**Figure 1: Location map of Mount Cameroon National Park**

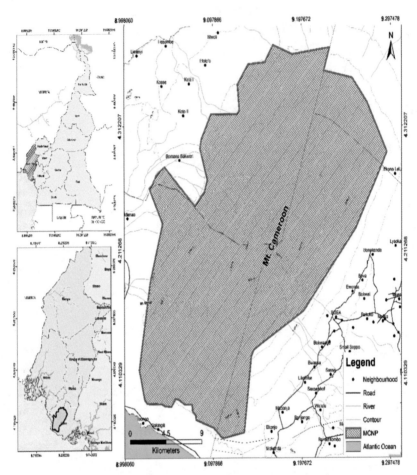

Source: Extracted from US Geological Survey Aster DEM by Anold, 2018

## Data Collection and Analysis

Primary data was collected from a self-administered questionnaire with some 252 respondents (Male and female head of households) within four communities (Bomana, Bonakanda, Etome and Ekona Lelu) around the four corners of the Mount Cameroon National Park. This was done using the stratified random sampling technique. The communities were selected based on their involvement in food crops and not cash crops. A further selection was based on those who carried out food crops within the present park boundary and were displaced after the park was created. Such communities felt the impacts of park more and its food crop producers had to adjust their agricultural activities. A designed questionnaire was drafted to capture the various effects of the creation of the MCNP on food crop production and to identify some hypothesized coping measures for food crop producers after the park and possible outcomes of those strategies.

The data generated from the questionnaire were entered through a designed template in EpiData Version 3.1 database. This software program was preferred for the data entry because of its in-built consistency and validation checks. Before the actual data analysis, the demographic information and test items on the respective objectives were all coded with assigned numbers which were then used to enter the data into the software. This process of codification eased the data entry process and avoided infelicities. Furthermore, consistency, data range and validation checks were also performed in SPSS version 21.0 (IBM Inc., 2012) to identify invalid codes, before proceeding to data analysis. In SPSS version 21, the data were then reported as descriptive and inferential statistics in the form of frequency and proportions and percentages. Finally, findings were presented using frequency distribution and charts, all inferential statistics were presented at 95% confidence interval with alpha set at 0.05 levels accepting only 5% margin of errors. By implication, any statistical result with a P value of <0.05 was therefore significant while those >0.05 were not significant because they exceeded the 5% margin of error. Thematic analysis was applied on the secondary data obtained

**Effects of park creation on food crop production**

Almost all the respondents (89%) are affected by the creation of the Park. The most remarkable effect is the loss of farmlands and displacement of farmers from their farms. Close to 50.4% of respondents lost their farmlands to conservation activities while 30% of respondents changed their farming systems. Both scenarios affected their agricultural activities and output. For example, after the creation of MCNP, farmers were restricted from their farmlands inside the new boundary created by the park as seen in figure 2.

**Fig 2: Surface area covered by farmland prior to and after park creation**

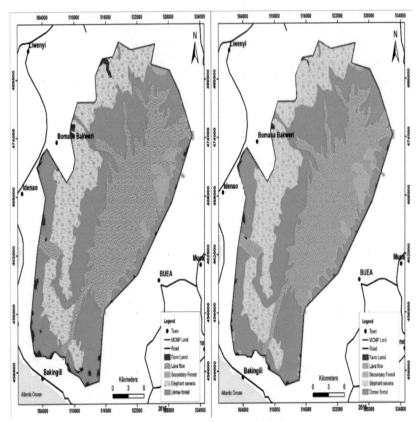

Source: Adopted from MCNP Maps by Anold, 2018

It is noted that prior to the creation of the park, farmlands occupied a total of 9,696 hectares within the park boundary, but after it creation, only 1,616 hectares of land is available for farming, representing 83% decline in total farmland area. Table 1 shows that 65% of respondents have lost their farms to conservation activities in the MCNP. Interestingly, the trend is almost the same across the four communities even though a slightly higher number of farmers in Bomana than anywhere else were affected. This was explained by the existence of a very high number of patrols by Eco-guards which help to reduce the number of encroachments by farmers.

**Table.1: Proportion of farmers displaced after park creation**

| Cluster | Total no of sampled farmers | Displaced farmers relative to total sampled | Percentage of farmers displaced |
|---|---|---|---|
| Bonakanda | 92 | 57 | 61.9 |
| Etome | 72 | 48 | 66.6 |
| Bomana | 55 | 39 | 70.9 |
| EkonaLelu | 76 | 49 | 64.4 |
| **Total** | **295** | **193** | **65.4** |

**Fieldwork, 2018**

As Samdong (2009) observes, conservation leads to "de-agrarianization" and the loss of farmlands. This is also the case of MCNP. Nzouango (2000), Nkembi et al. (2002) and Pretty (1997) all hold that biodiversity conservation lead to loss of arable land. Balmford et al. (2003), explaining what prevails in Chobe, Botswana, remarks that although farmers are not physically dispossessed from their farmlands, wildlife conservation has negatively impacted the agrarian sector and in some cases, eliminated the ability to farm. Their findings are similar with those from MCNP as its creation negatively affected farming. The only difference in both cases is that farmers in Chobe were not physically dispossessed from their farm lands. The World Conservation Monitoring Centre (1992) pointed out that the problems between food crop producers and conservation stakeholders stem from the fact that farmers living next to parks do not have inputs into the establishment of the parks. The same observations is true with MCNP where farmers have been displaced and denied access into the park.

### Coping Strategies by Food Crop Producers

The loss of land with the creation of MCNP forced farmers to rethink other innovative effective food production farming systems around the park. Over 38% of farmers adopted the improved seeds and 34% opted for intensive agriculture to maintain and even improve food crop production. To a lesser extent, farmers sought new education in farming while others received incentives to relocate and acquire new farms out of the park area. Byerlee et al. (2000), Afolayanet al (2009) and Baofoet al (2004) have all explained coping strategies put in place by various stakeholders around parks in

Botswana, South Africa and Kenya respectively. Their works highlight the importance of strategies such as intensification, use of improved seeds, education and training which are the same as what currently prevail among communities around the MCNP.

### Intensification of agriculture

More than 70% of sampled farmers in the MCNP have changed their farming systems from extensive mixed cropping to intensive mixed cropping system. This is the case with the system of cultivation for dominant crops (cocoyam, yam, plantain and cassava) cultivated in the area prior to and after the creation of the park.

**Table 2: Farming system practiced prior to and after the creation of the park for dominant food crops**

| Main food crops | Total farmers involved | System practiced prior to the park | | System practiced after the park | |
|---|---|---|---|---|---|
| | | Extensive mixed cropping (%) | Intensive mixed cropping (%) | Extensive mixed cropping (%) | Intensive mixed cropping (%) |
| Cocoyam | 203 | 89.6 | 10.4 | 23.0 | 77.0 |
| Yam | 170 | 64.7 | 35.3 | 36.4 | 63.6 |
| Plantain | 210 | 91 | 9 | 27.1 | 72.9 |
| Cassava | 215 | 89.3 | 10.7 | 43.2 | 56.8 |

**Field work, 2018**

Prior to the creation of the park, 89.6% of farmers sampled cultivated cocoyam through extensive mixed cropping system while just 10.4% carried out the intensive mixed cropping system. The situation changed after the establishment of the park. Seventy-seven percent of farmers sampled in the same locality now practice intensive mixed cropping system for cocoyam. The same trend is witnessed with plantains where 91% of sampled farmers who before the park practiced extensive mixed cropping system (for plantains) have drop to 27%, with 72% now opting for intensive mixed cropping. Similar shifts also apply to cassava production. The number of farmers practicing intensive mixed cropping has moved up from 11% to 57% following the creation of the park. Intensive agriculture thus provides part of the solution to the scarcity of land resulting from the creation of the Mount Cameroon National Project. Tataw el al (2001) and Etiendem et al (2011) note that the creation of the Bayang-Mbo wildlife sanctuary and Bechati Cross River gorilla sanctuary respectively produced similar effects on farmers as these farmers moved away from large scale extensive farming to small scale intensive farming.

Baofoet al (2004) explains that conservation experts in Kenya in collaboration with the government subsidized farming in many adjacent communities of conserved areas. This was the case with the Masonge community since farmers complained that changing farming methods from extensive to intensive agriculture (so as to maintain agricultural output) was quite expensive. Conservation stakeholders have been subsidizing farmer's inputs financially and materially for a change in their farming system.

### The use of improved seeds

MCNP has worked with affected communities through the village forest management committees (VFMC) to distribute improved seedlings to small farmers outside the park. MCNP donated plantain propagators and improved cassava seeds to these farmers in order to boast production. Many respondents (74.5%) who received these improved seeds from MCNP and worked in close collaboration with the local Delegation of Agriculture and Rural Development admitted their effectiveness. Improved seeds mature faster and thus produce more food.

**Table 3: Farmers' participation in the application of improved seedlings in sampled villages**

| Communities | Total numbers of sampled farmers | Farmers applying improved seeds | Percentage of farmers using improved seeds |
|---|---|---|---|
| Bonakanda | 92 | 80 | 86.9 |
| Etome | 72 | 51 | 70.8 |
| Bomana | 55 | 37 | 67.3 |
| EkonaLelu | 76 | 52 | 68.4 |
| Total | 295 | 220 | 74.5 |

**Fieldwork, 2018**

Bonakanda has the highest number (86.9%) of farmers using improved seeds because of its relatively high population and its proximity to the town of Buea where there is a large market and pressure for food. Farmers' use of improved seedlings around nature protected areas is not new but a common phenomenon reported by many authors in the literature. Afolayanet and Jimoh (2009) for example, describe the situation of communities adjacent to protected areas in South Africa. Here, the government created two categories of support programs for farmers affected by conservation activities: the Citizen Entrepreneurial Development Agency (CEDA); a national level program that gives loans to farmers to assist in production, and the Integrated Support Program for Arable Agriculture Development (ISPAAD) that distributes improved seedlings, fertilizers, and other farming implements to affected farmers. The ISPAAD also helps to reduce the demand for household farm labour during the ploughing season by providing farmers with tractors and government paid tractor drivers. These measures have the capacity to maintain and even boast food production from around the protected areas.

Other measures including farmers' education, relocation of new farmers and techniques of mechanization have also been applied by farmers to contribute to the growth of food production after the park. Agricultural experts were brought in by conservation experts to train farmers on the best methods of farming and how to use the improved seeds distributed to them. This was done through seminars and field work demonstrations. Over 183 farmers trained by these seminars produce high multiplier effect on food production. More than 90% of farmers who participated in these seminars expressed satisfaction in the training on the use of improved seeds and modern methods of farming. These seminars were followed by field demonstrations to help farmers on how to use improved seeds distributed to them by authorities of Ministry of Forestry and Wildlife (MINFOF). The different programs are very useful particularly to farmers unfamiliar with new techniques and seedlings, thus reducing the rates of non-participation in these communities. Lenne and Woods (2011) report similar educational/sensitization for farmers around the Calaba primate sanctuary, Nigeria and the Wildlife

Conservation Society (2008) around the Ebo Forest in Littoral, Cameroon. However, in both cases farmers were not trained on modern farming systems and the use of improved seeds but were rather educated on the need to conserve the forests and find alternative sources of livelihood.

The culmination of these farming innovations discussed above produced unprecedented resulted compensating for the loss of farm land after the creation of the MCNP. Table 4 gives an idea of the trends witness in production after these measures based on the experiences of over 90% of farmers who adhere to them.

As seen in Table 4, cassava production rose from 3,279 bags before the park to 4,856 bags after the creation of the park indicating a 19.4% increase in its output. The same positive trends are also noticed with cocoyam, plantain, yams, which are the dominant food crops in the area. From all the dominant crops considered, yam had the highest change (24.2% increase) while plantain had the lowest change with 13.9% increase. Generally, all the dominant food crops in the area as noted in Table 4, witnessed increases in production. These trends are a mark contrast to what prevails in other protected areas. Nzouango (2000), Nkembi et al. (2002) and Pretty (1997) all hold that there is a fall in agricultural outputs after the creation of protected areas. According to these authors, biodiversity conservation and food crop production are mutually exclusive. The Divisional Delegate of Agriculture for Ndian (2004) corroborates these findings observing that the Kurop National Park has led to a fall in agricultural output in the area. The differences in the trends of output after park creation between the MCNP and other parks as seen above can be attributed to proper training of farmers on best farming methods. We realized that in other parks like Ebo forest and Calaba primate sanctuary, sensitizations are done on the need to protect the forest and emphases are laid more on alternative means of livelihood than alternative farming systems notably intensification out of the park.

## Table.4: Food output before and after the creation of MCNP

| Food crops Cultivated | Yields before park creation | Yields after Park Creation | Change | |
|---|---|---|---|---|
| | | | Change | % |
| Cassava (in Bags) | 3279 | 4856 | 1577 | 19.4 |
| Cocoyam (in Bags) | 3112 | 4172 | 1060 | 14.5 |
| Tomatoes (in Baskets) | 805 | 994 | 189 | 10.5 |
| Pepper (in Baskets) | 62 | 62 | 0 | 0 |
| Groundnut (in Basins) | 62 | 52 | -10 | -8.7 |
| Maize (in tins) | 196 | 259.25 | 63.25 | 24.7 |
| Plantain (in Bunches) | 12460.5 | 17220 | 4759.5 | 13.9 |
| Banana (in Bunches) | 2333.5 | 3737.5 | 1404 | 23.1 |
| Vegetables (in Bundles) | 4259 | 19680 | 15421 | 64.7 |
| Yams (in Tubers) | 12009 | 19680 | 7671 | 24.2 |

**Field work, 2018**

### Increase in farmers' incomes

The resulting changes in production from the application of mechanization and improved seeds measures by farmers assisted by conservation stakeholders have significant effects on their incomes. Field work reveals that prior to the park, majority of farmers cultivating cocoyam, yams, plantains, cassava, generated less than 100,000 FCFA annually from sale and very few of them generated more than this amount. In concrete term, those who made above 100,000FCFA were just 14% for cocoyam farmers, 27% for those dealing with yams, and 12.5% for plantain farmers.

As indicated on Table 5, the creation of the park came with increase in incomes. The income of the majority of farmers sampled was more than a hundred thousand CFA/annum with yam producers registering the highest figure of 82%. This increase in incomes emphasizes the importance of improving farming technics and inputs in poor countries to raise production, livelihoods and improve living standards.

## Table 5: Famer's incomes from the sale of main food crops around the MCNP

| Main crops | Prior to park creation (in FCFA) | | After park creation (in FCFA) | |
|---|---|---|---|---|
| | % of farmers making <100,000 FCFA | % of farmers making >100,000 | % of farmers making <100,000 | % of farmers making >100,000 |
| Cocoyam | 86 | 14 | 15.9 | 84.1 |
| Yam | 73 | 27 | 17.4 | 82.6 |
| Plantain | 87.5 | 12.5 | 50.5 | 49.5 |
| Cassava | 82.3 | 17.3 | 24.2 | 75.8 |

**Exchange rates: 500CFA=1US$ at the time.**
**Field work, 2018**

The positive trends in incomes after the creation of Mount Cameroon National Park are not very common with farmers around many protected areas around the world. Buck el al (2007) studied agricultural activities around protected areas in the Democratic Republic of Congo especially around Garamba National Park and Maiko National Park and noted that despite putting in place several coping strategies, farmer's incomes dropped due to falling output since they have been denied accesses into the protected areas. Their assessment is corroborated by the World Bank. The World Bank (2011) reported that one of the challenges faced by farmers in Africa has been the creation of national parks which often cause a drop in the incomes of farmers, especially for those farming around these protected areas. We however, note that unlike with the MCNP where conservation stakeholders implemented and supervised coping measures for farmers, the case of many protected areas around Africa (D.R Congo for example), is different. Whenever conservation stakeholders attribute resources to the agriculture stakeholders after creating parks without proper follow-up and supervision, a good proportion of these resources (money and farm inputs) often than not, do not get to the farmers. The misappriopriation of these resources is what account for the poor results (in outputs and incomes of farmers) around many protected areas in Africa rather than the failure of the measures implemented.

Copping measures implemented by MCNP were in synergy with directly compensation to mitigate the immediate impact of the park on faccted population. However, some farmers around the MCNP are still complaining that compensation was not commensurate to the loss they suffered. These complains were sometimes found to be legitimate because of the lack of faireness in the framework for compensating farmers. In some case, farmers were compensated at the same rates even though they were not affected to the same degree. It was also observed that some farmers still benefit relatively little from the conservation credit put in place by the project since money went to the entire community and shared equally. Farmers who lose more farmlands should be compensated more. In that way, big and small farmers would have been fairly treated and protected.

**Conclusion**

In the creation of the MCNP, the survival measures that followed and the results that so far obtained highlight opportunities for coexistence between conservation and local development in Cameroon. The decision to create the park was initially contested by inhabitants of adjacent communities because of its perceived potential to increase poverty. However, collaboration between stakeholders (experts, management and inhabitants) leading to the putting in place of acceptable measures have produced positive results that have challenged previous local perceptions. The measures instituted after the park have been successful as proven by increase in food production and farmers' incomes. Thus, the dictum of Buck el al (2007), Nkembi et al (2002), Nchanji (2000), and Pretty (1997) insinuating that conservation and food crop production are mutually exclusive is not completely true for the MCNP. In other words, conservation and food crop production are not usually mutually exclusive. The MCNP has so far achieved the goals of wildlife conservation and improved food production in the area. Nevertheless, for conservation activities to succeed, an integrated or collaborative approach is necessary. This calls for a community-based wildlife management whereby both parties (conservation stakeholders and food crop producers) are satisfied and respect each other's activities. These efforts must continue without ceasing if these projects exist to maintain the sustainable management of natural resources and feed the ever-growing population.

While it is important to provide compensation to those displaced from protected areas, compensation alone is not enough since it is usually not sustainable and cannot replace for example, the fruit trees that would been harvested and sold for generations. The MCNP authorities should create specific funding programs for farmers. This fund wills also subsidize farming inputs since many farmers complained that the change in farming system brought about extra farm expenditures. Creating a special funding program for farmers in communities around MCNP will address emerging problems of farmers that will keep current production stable, poverty low and linit further encroachments into the conservation area. This measure in fact, require a comprehensive approach that will also put an end to occasional destruction of crops by wildlife from the park which breed frequent conflicts between farmers and MCNP. What this entails is that for conservation projects to be successful and sustainable, they must be concived as long-term endeavors that integrate measures capable of of adapting and accommodating change and emmerging local challenges and even externalities.

# References

Afolayan, A.J. and Jimoh, F.O (2009): 'Nutritional quality of some wild leafy vegetables in South Africa', International Journal of Food Sciences and Nutrition, vol 60, pp.424–431.

AfriMab, M (2013): Biosphere reserves in Sub-Saharan Africa. UNESCO MAB programme. http://unesdoc.unesco.org/images/0022/002269/226919E.pdf Accessed May 13, 2016

Agrawal, A. (2002): Common Resources and Institutional Sustainability: In Ostrom et al (2002), (eds) The Drama of the Commons, National Academy Press, Washington DC

Balmford, A., Gaston, K.J., Blyth, S., James, A. & V. Kapos (2003): Global variation in terrestrial conservation costs, conservation benefits, and unmet conservation needs. Proceedings of the National Academy of Science 100: 1046-1050

Buck, L. E., Gavin, T. A., Uphoff, N. T. & Lee, D. R. (2007): Scientific assessment of ecoagriculture systems. In Farming with nature: the science and practice of eco-agriculture (eds S. J. Scherr & J. A. McNeely). Washington, DC:

Byerlee, D and Murgai.R (2000): Sense and sustainability revisited: The limits of total factor productivity measures of system sustainability. Agricultural Economics

Cincotta, P.R, Wisnewski J, Engelman R (2000): Human population in the biodiversity hotspots. Nature 404:990–992

Cohen, J. E. (2003): Human population: the next half century Science 302, 1172–1175. (doi:10.1126/science.1088665)

Dowsett, F. & R.J. Dowsett (2000): Further biological surveys of Manenguba and Central Bakossi in March 2000, and an evaluation of the conservation importance of Manenguba, Bakossi, Kupeand, Nlonako Mts, with special reference to birds. Final report by Tauracoa.s.b.l.for WWF-Cameroon. 45 pp

Etiendem, D.N., Hens, L. & Z. Pereboom (2011): Traditional knowledge systems and the conservation of Cross River gorillas: a case study of Bechati, Fossimondi, Besali, Cameroon. Ecology and Society 16: 22. http://dx.doi.org/10.5751/ES-04182-160322

Fouda, C.E (2008): A demographic survey around the Banyang-Mbo Wildlife Sanctuary. Final report prepared for the Wildlife Conservation Society's Cameroon Biodiversity Programme. 34pp.

Global Forest Report (2008): Corridor Conservation – West Africa. Final Report April 2005.

Kimengsi JN, Azibo BR and Ngong JT (2016): Improving Cocoa Processing and Marketing for Conservation in the Mount Cameroon National Park Communities: Challenges and Way Forward. Greener Journal of Social Sciences, 6(1):001-010, http://doi.org/10.15580/GJSS.2016.1.051815073

Lambi, C. M., Kimengsi, J.N., Kometa, C.G. and Tata E.S. (2012): The Management of Protected Areas and the Sustenance of Local Livelihoods in Cameroon. Environment and Natural

Resources Research (ENRR), Volume 2 Number. 3, October 2012, pp 10-18 Published by the Canadian Centre of Science and Education (CCSE), Canada.

Lenné, J.M. and Wood, D. (2011): Agricultural biodiversity Management for Food Security: A critical review, CAB International, Wallingford

Nakhauka, E.B. (2009): 'Agricultural biodiversity for food and nutrient security: The Kenyan perspective', International Journal of Biodiversity and Conservation, vol 1, pp.208– 214.

Nambu, M.D (2001): Botanical inventory of the Banyang-Mbo Wildlife Sanctuary, South West Province, Cameroon. Final report prepared for the Wildlife Conservation Society's Cameroon Biodiversity Programme. 62pp

Neil et al (2001): Protected Areas, Biodiversity Management, and the Stakeholder Analysis Approach. Draft working paper.

Nkembi, L. C. Tataw& M. Achuo (2002): The non-timber forest products from the Banyang-Mbo Wildlife Sanctuary, South West Cameroon: a survey of household use, existing value addition practices and economic viability. Final report prepared for the Wildlife Conservation Society's Cameroon Biodiversity Programme. 48pp.

Nomsa, D. D. (1992): Protecting the African Environment: Reconciling North-South Perspectives. Critical Issues, 3 (1992).

Nzouango, D. & A. Willcox (2000): Bushmeat extraction survey within the Banyangi and Mbo tribes in the South West Province of Cameroon. Final report prepared for the Wildlife Conservation Society's Cameroon Biodiversity Programme. 53pp.

Pretty, J. (2011): 'Editorial: Sustainable intensification in Africa', International Journal of Agricultural Sustainability, vol 9, no 1, pp.3–4.

Pretty, J. N (1997): Sustainable Agriculture, People and the Resource Base. Impacts on Food Production. Forum for development studies No.1.

Sayer, J.A (2004): The Science of Sustainable Development. Local Livelihoods and the Global Environment. Cambridge University Press, Cambridge, UK.

Scherr, A.D. & R.M. Bia. (2003): Ornithological surveys of Nkwende Hills, Bakossi Mt, Ejagham, Mawne and Rumpi Hills Forest Reserves, UFA (11-001 and 11-002) for biodiversity conservation and priority setting in the Cameroon-Nigeria transboundary region. Report prepared for the Wildlife Conservation Society (WCS), Cameroon. 67pp.

Tanjong. E. (2014): Socio-economic survey of the villages of Mount Cameroon National Park (MCNP). Program for Sustainable Management of Natural Resources Cameroon – South-West Region, Buea, Cameroon.

Tataw, C.E., D. Nzouango, L. Nkembi, A. Willcox& D. Ngwesse (2001): Socio-economic overview of the Banyang-Mbo Wildlife Sanctuary Villages. Final report prepared for the Wildlife Conservation Society's Cameroon Biodiversity Programme. 33.

UN Millennium Project, Task Force on Hunger (2005): Halving hunger: it can be done. London, UK: Earthscan

Usongo, L. (1996): Ethnozoological inventory of Ejagham Forest Reserve, South West Province. A report to the CEU Korup Project. 38pp.

Wilson. E. (2002): The Future of Life. New York Alfred A Knopf 256 pp

World Bank, (2011): *Africa Development Forum: Challenges for African Agriculture*, (ed) Deveze, J, Washington D.C, Pp 1-267

World Conservation Monitoring Centre (1992): Global Biodiversity: Status of the Earth's Living Resources. Chapman and Hall, London A report compiled by The World Conservation Monitoring Centre.

WWF and IUCN, (2006): Centres of Plant Diversity: A Guide and Strategy for their Conservation. Volume 1. Europe, Africa, South West Asia and the Middle East. WWF/IUCN, IUCN Publications Unit, Cambridge, United Kingdom

# Chapter 11

# Old Age Security and Indigenous Mutual Support System in Marginal Pastoralist Enclaves

*Charles C. Fonchingong*

**Abstract**

Pastoralists' kin system sustained on reciprocity and solidarity (pulaaku) is a prevalent social safety net in marginal Fulani pastoralists' communes of North West Cameroon. This ethnographic case study points to communal support networks that are increasingly fragmented, eroded by ecological insecurity, farmer-herder conflicts and social change, triggered by alterations in livelihoods in rural landscapes, urbanisation and migration. Frequent skirmishes with local farmers over land, accentuated by narrowing of grazing areas are jeopardizing livelihoods. Embedding social security in rural herder societies requires a co-partnership approach with institutional authorities. Pastoralists' kin resilience are susceptible to unpredictable rural ecosystem, climate variability and dislocation in herding practices. Rural development policy should encapsulate symbiotically flourishing aspects of pastoralists' social capital and traditions, often missed by government, development agencies and other donor organizations

**Keywords**: Kin reciprocity; Old age; Pastoralists; Social capital; Social security; Marginal populations

## Introduction

Global development discourse on ensuring the most marginal populations (pastoralist groups in this case) have access to social security, particularly in old age, remains a topic of interest in rural development. Formal and informal social protection programs in the Horn of Africa, and Sahel are mostly deficient, fragmented, and largely donor-driven (Catley, Lind, & Scoones 2013, Fonchingong,

2014, World Bank 2015, del Ninno, Coll-Black, & Fallavier, 2016). Focusing on Fulani enclaves of North West Cameroon, this paper uncovers the vulnerability and resilience of indigenous mutual support systems as a social safety net. This ethnographic case study engages with kin protection and old age security, as the wider implications on rural development policy remain unclear. Exacerbated by sporadic welfare provision, safeguarding social protection for vulnerable groups such as indigenous and tribal people, who often live in remote areas, are problematic (Midgley 2014). Development policy is yet to articulate concerns in old age security in marginal communities -a key component of poverty reduction strategies (World Bank 2015, del Ninno et al. 2016). The central question guiding this study is how well The Mbororo Social, Cultural and Development Association (MBOSCUDA) – an organization created to implement policies that underpin indigenous safety net for pastoralists is coping?

Development interventions constantly fail to achieve their asserted objectives of enhancing pastoral resilience (Liao & Fei, 2016). Escalating drylands in sub Saharan Africa (SSA) render pastoralists vulnerable with more impediments to their way of life than ever before. These factors are accentuated by Climate variability, demographic pressures, protracted farmer-herder conflicts, reduced access to grazing land (African Union (AU) 2010; Moritz, 2010; IIED, 2010, ISS Africa 2012; Upton 2012; Catley et al. 2013; Little & McPeak 2014, World Bank 2015, del Ninno et al. 2016, Fonchingong, & Ufon 2016).

As pastoralists are largely uncovered in formal social security, (mostly state pensions and other forms of social insurance), they rely on indigenous mutual support systems to cope with land conflicts, not helped by elevated levels of deprivation and shortfall in infrastructure in most rural areas of Cameroon (Fonchingong, 2014).

Adverse events and weather are triggering livelihood shocks and decline in household welfare among pastoralists in sub Saharan Africa. With roughly 23.4 million pastoralists in the Horn of Africa; 14.8 percent of the region's population rely on pastoralism; thus, social protection programs will be required to mitigate chronic poverty and reduce vulnerability of those unable to meet their basic needs (AU 2010, World Bank 2015, Fonchingong, 2014; del Ninno et al. 2016).

Fulani pastoralists constitute about 12% of Cameroon's population, over 24 million and it is estimated elderly Fulani stand at 200,000 (about 25%). With over 1.5 million inhabitants, Cameroon's North-West Region is home to approximately 100,000 Fulani pastoralists (MBOSCUDA, 2014). Pastoralists inhabit large rural segments where subsistence agriculture is predominant, thereby putting their activities at risk as they navigate grazing sites. Historical accounts link the Lamidat of Sabga (established in 1905), a precursor to herder settlement in the region (Aliou, 2004; Davis 1995). According to the Ministry of Livestock, Fisheries and Animal Industries (MINEPIA, 2013), there are approximately six million cattle in Cameroon, mainly distributed over the mountainous North-West region, the Adamawa plateau and Northern regions of Cameroon. Fulani pastoralists are susceptible to recurrent skirmishes with neighbouring farming communities due to dispersed settlement patterns. Similarly, old age security is further jeopardised by factional politics of belonging, and a history of social and political marginalisation (Hickey, 2011). Colonial policies developed to control and sedentarise nomadic pastoralists (Davis, 2010); exacerbates cattle insecurity for mobile pastoralists (Moritz & Scholte, 2011). These factors restrict pastoralists' traditional strategies for coping with perennial disturbances such as drought (Catley et al. 2013, World Bank 2015). However, there is less rigorous articulation of a useful theoretical framework for old age security and rural development policy calibrated around indigenous mutual support system for marginal pastoralists.

**Conceptual Proposition: Social security, social capital and Kin reciprocity**

In sub Saharan Africa (SSA), social security provisions premised on formal, state-organised systems, covering small segments of citizens warrant further scrutiny. Expanding coverage is problematic (Nino-Zarazua et al., 2011, Midgley 2014, del Ninno, Coll-Black, & Fallavier, 2016). Social security (social protection) aim to provide certain minimum income security, ensure affordable access to health care, and other support related to old age, sickness, disability, death and maternity, with the major aim of alleviating existing poverty and exclusion (ILO, 2008:11, World Bank 2012). Extending these programs are now widely recognized as an effective policy framework, to address extreme deprivation and vulnerability in marginal communities (AU, 2010). Indigenous safety nets and informal mechanisms of social security, often instrumental in mitigating the negative impacts of shocks in pastoralist enclaves, are becoming overstretched (del Ninno et al. 2016). Given the limited coverage, the role of social protection as a social development strategy is now widely recognised (Midgley 2014). Similarly, familial care provision for older adults are fragmenting, require a rethink of the role of social capital (Bernier and Meinzen-Dick 2014) and firming up of institutional policy (Fonchingong, 2014).

In guaranteeing old age security, pastoralists rely on social and family networks (nuclear and extended), kinship-based systems, and other agencies, based on the principles of solidarity and reciprocity (Fonchingong, 2013, Midgley 2014). However, development policy is yet to respond sufficiently. A major problem, impeding the effectiveness of social protection has been the importation of 'western styled' social protection programmes, without considering its relevance to local demographic, social, cultural and economic needs (Midgley 2014).

In pastoral societies, herders are mobile with livestock, targeting patchy availability of grazing areas, while other household members remain sedentary for parts of the year (Moritz & Scholte, 2011). Pastoralists deploy myriad livelihood security strategies within their social and ecological contexts, to cope with risks and vulnerabilities. Socio-economic factors such as changes in land tenure, agriculture, and sedentarization lead to fragmentation of pastoral systems (Galvin, 2009). The challenge is to ensure policies improve household livelihoods (Little & McPeak, 2014), with livelihood diversification crucial to smooth household income (Liao & Fei, 2016). This study's theoretical proposition is in alignment with the epistemological standpoint that whilst indigenous mutual support systems are vital, social changes trigger dislocation and vulnerability.

Such changes are conflictual with pastoralists' lifestyle, geriatric protection, livelihoods and relations with institutional authorities. These informal social safety nets are fragmenting (Fonchingong 2014). Opportunities to integrate these indigenous mutual systems with statutory, formal provisions have been missed by governments in the global South (Midgley 2014:180), which creates a spiral of disadvantage for pastoralists.

**Methods and context**

An ethnographic approach (Atkinson and Hamersley 2007) informs the methodological design of this paper, based on empirical evidence gleaned from semi-structured interviews, involving 67 Fulani pastoralists, mostly elderly aged over 55 years. Data grounded on a purposive sample, reflects pastoralist community layers of power, and kin dynamics. Other interviewees included MBOSCUDA officials, and 15 women inhabiting pastoralist enclaves. Female interviewees were enlisted with the assistance of Ardo (group chief), owing to the regulated kin regime in place. Participants, drawn from rural pastoralists' enclaves of Sabga, Jakiri, Wum and Nkambe – constitute major arteries and cattle grazing areas of the region. Semi-structured interviews are recognised within ethnographic research; it enables data to be collected in a rigorous and methodical manner whilst allowing the interviewer to modify the sequence or wording of questions where necessary (Becker et al., 2012).

A purposive sample were employed to cover designated enclaves and open-ended questions were used to explore the social dynamics, potential of informal social security and viability of kin arrangements, largely driven by pastoralists. Given the variations in living patterns among Fulani pastoralists, purposive sampling was considered a suitable approach of capturing different voices in dispersed pastoralist settlements. Focusing on a target population and specific group enables the researcher to generalise results that can be replicated, informed by desired information sought (Neuman 2011). Purposive sampling enables the "selection of participants or sources of data to be used in a study, based on their anticipated richness and relevance of information in relation to the study's research

269

questions" (Yin 2011:311). The sampling strategy was contextually appropriate, covering the spatial administrative units and rural grazing site. The ethnographic approach ties up with the rigours of small case studies, anchored on a case study logic, a technique which might yield more reliable data applied to in-depth, interview-based studies (Yin, 2002). Small (2009:5) avers that case studies do not only generate theory, but also somehow speak to empirical conditions in other cases not observed. The challenge is to make such cases contextually relevant, allowing the respondents to freely air out their experiences, captured in direct quotations. In a case study, sampling applies to selecting cases and selecting data sources "that best help us understand the case" (Stake, 1995: 56). The case is made that ethnographic researchers facing today's cross-methods discourse and critiques should pursue alternative epistemological assumptions, better suited to their unique questions, rather than retreat toward models designed for statistical research (Small 2009). Given the diversity of pastoral systems, questions were framed to explore the sustainability of mutual support arrangements permeating the communes, how pastoralists are coping and adapting to social changes.

To ensure the veracity of interviews conducted, data generated were triangulated with community elders, and other participants from the chosen settlement sites. MBOSCUDA officials interviewed provided an insight into existing partnerships with pastoralists. The MBOSCUDA served as a focal point for initial engagement of research participants and pathways into the community. There were no conflicts of interest as the research process was explained, consent agreed, confidentiality assured with selected interviewees. To shed light on 'invisible aspects' in pastoralist communities, a translator was hired to help with semi-structured interviews and other observed events. Questions discussed centred around forms of support, gender and livelihoods, geriatric protection and care arrangements for older pastoralists. In addition, women's role in enhancing old age security, threats to kin resilience, ecological factors affecting pastoralism, and relations with institutional authorities are explored. Other unexpected social changes and the role of younger pastoralists in kin protection are considered. Transitional arrangements occasioned by 'modernization drive' and other risk factors making kin protection system less viable. The probability of imprecise information lost in translation services was a difficulty; however, these biases were minimised through triangulation with key informants. Transcripts from the interviews represented thematically featuring location, age and gender of participants.

## Findings and Discussion

### Kin obligations and reciprocity

Findings point to the fragility of kin protection system, resulting from rural-urban migration, conflicts with neighbouring farming communities. Livelihood diversification strategies for pastoralists are impeded by lethargic institutional support, coupled with inadequate social assistance and essential veterinary services, in short supply.

Kin reciprocity hinges on the *pulaaku* – a cultural code and moral template for regulating social relations. The code sanctions good animal husbandry, communal obligations and a 'social care contract' for elders. The *pulaaku* has four tenets: *munyal* (fortitude in adversity and ability to accept misfortune), *hakkilo* (sound common sense and manners), *semteende* (reserve and modesty in personal relations) and *neddaaku* (dignity). For pastoralists, *pulaaku* conveys a uniqueness and difference; it dictates kin norms regarding dignity, social resilience, humility, endurance, secrecy and respect for elders. The *pulaaku* helps maintain an ethnic boundary around the Fulani category (Hickey, 2011). Identity consciousness remains an ideology of racial and cultural distinctiveness, and superiority that uniquely ranks pastoralists from other ethnic groups (Burnham, 1996). Fulani herders equate their pastoral way of life to ethnicity and heritage, which implicitly enforces lineage bonds. The erstwhile coordinator of MBOSCUDA stated:

> *There is a continued tendency to marry within pastoralists groups, often with 'close relatives', as a means of preserving pulaaku and herds.*

Preserving the *pulaaku* is primordial in kin arrangements; however, ethnic tensions are often a trigger for conflicts with neighbouring farming communities. The coordinator disclosed '*The natives see Mbororo as uneducated, primitive 'aku' people. In rural areas, Fulani look down on the natives as haabe, meaning people who are poor*'.

Prevalent perceptions about pastoralists centre on minority status and a tendency to minimise their traditions as archaic and outmoded (IIED, 2010), reinforcing notions of contested citizenship (Hickey 2011). Regulated through the political economy, mutual support systems follow an indigenous structure with elders at the helm, and in-charge of kin governance institutions. The Lamidat of Sabga holds the most senior level of political authority in the region. *Ardos* within the *Ardorate* provide guided leadership in micro enclaves, located between households and wider power structures of the Lamido (head-chief in charge of tax collection and relations with the state). Ardos are custodians of kinship, and pillars in community building and fostering geriatric arrangements. Usually, the Ardorate comprises a group of grazing families from the same lineage. The Ardo's authority relates to cattle, rather than territory. In line with kin support, the major duties of Ardos (mostly elders) include the protection of subjects' interest, negotiating with local power holders for access to land and collecting of cattle tax *(jangali)* from herders within the Ardorate. Akin to the *Ardorate* are Council of elders of grazing associations in Kenya *(jaarsa mata dedha)*, saddled with political, social and decision-making functions, in synergy with the government (Oba, 2012). Similarly, amongst the Afar herders of Ethiopia, they cope with the severity of drought, through customary and clan elders who meet, whenever necessary, and communicate policies; evaluate and decide when to allow access to preserved grazing areas (Davies and Bennet, 2007). Caring for livestock are central to obligations of kin protection. The Ardo (chief) affirmed: '*Mbororos are proud of their tradition and cattle is everything to us. The lineage earns a livelihood from cattle. For men, cattle confer respect while women look after the herds*'. Herds are integral to pastoralists and a major means of livelihood security (Alary et al., 2011).

### Social capital and household welfare

Kin obligations follow a structured pattern with elders managing herding practices, legitimating marriages, family cohesion, child upbringing, deaths and funeral rites. Since cattle is a "lifeblood" in livelihoods, elders inculcate "good herding practices", taught in Fulani schools and passed on through epic stories, folktales and songs. Kinfolks look after elders, and core kin arrangements, often gendered, with task descriptors for boys/men and girls/women shown in Table 1.

**Table 1: Social capital, Kin arrangements, and tasks descriptors**

| Boys/Men | Girls/Women |
|---|---|
| -Herding practices (escort cattle to new pasture, setting up enclosures, manage herds, buy and sell cattle) | -Milking calves, restraining calves from their mothers for milking, sorting out fodder and forage |
| -Knowledge of herbs, treatment of cattle diseases/ailments and charms to protect cattle theft | -Preparation of cheese, butter, milk and other dairy products |
| -Shepherding cattle, rope making and horse-riding skills | -Upkeep and home maintenance (cooking, laundry, cleaning) |
| -Fetch firewood | -Fetch water |
| -Protect cattle and provide lineage security | -Process grain and other dairy products |
| -Serve Fulani elders with food and tea | -Household provisioning in rural markets and food preparation |
| -Act as emissary in farmer herder conflicts | -Child rearing and cater for well-being of lineage |
| -Listen to folktales and epic stories on herding practices and grazing | -Listen to folktales and songs on safeguarding the lineage |
| -Learn Fulani herbal remedies and fortune telling | -Learn herbal remedies to cater for child health and care |
| -Handle commercial, marketing activities and veterinary care of cattle | -Petty trading and marketing of finished dairy products |

Critically, the task descriptors appear blurred depending on settlement patterns. Apart from child rearing and guaranteeing food security, women play key roles in sustaining the lineage. An interviewee recounted:

*'culturally, before a woman's first delivery, she left her home to reside with her parents and stayed over for at least one to two years after delivery. These women learned how to use herbs. During the naming ceremony, the baby's head was shaved after being soaked in a bowl of milk and a sheep was slaughtered'.*

These intrinsic birthing practices point to prescribed gender roles and kin social obligations for women (Lesorogrol et al. 2013). Practically, in all African pastoral communities, women play the traditional role of livestock rearing, processing milk, selling dairy products and maintaining households. Yet, they do not own valuable property, are the least educated, are excluded from decision-making processes, resource management and allocation (AU, 2010, World Bank 2015).

However, both male and female elders are instrumental:

*Elders pass on core knowledge in livestock practices. Younger herders, aged seven to twelve years of age, are trained on cattle grazing and other skills such as rope making, horse riding and care of cattle.*

Pastoral communities rely on systems of indigenous knowledge of rangeland management to make decisions that influence livelihoods (Oba, 2012). Women gain skills in preparation of dairy products such as milk, cheese, butter, snacks. An elderly woman stated:

*We build girls' skills on how to milk cows; restrain calves when extracting milk. We also demonstrate domestic tasks such as cooking; cleaning and fetching water to ensure elders have food.*

Amongst the Samburu of Kenya, a patrilineal society, livestock inheritance primarily entails the transfer of livestock from fathers to sons, thus ensuring that property remains in the lineage. At numerous points during the life course, livestock are bartered: at birth, initiation to warrior hood, prior to marriage, and finally, upon the father's death. Women are caretakers for the livestock that their sons ultimately inherit (Lesorogrol et al, 2013).

Additionally, herders' historical knowledge of landscape suitability are disseminated through folklores, fostering interactions between their livestock and the environment. Incantations and songs of bravery, survival and resilience deemed a form of social insurance are bequeath to lineage. The cattle folklore describes livestock watering, grazing movements and coping with environmental stress (Oba, 2012). Livestock is a fundamental form of pastoral capital and wealth with implications on sustainability and resilience (Moritz, 2010; Catley et al., 2013, Little & McPeak, 2014).

Household welfare and familial arrangements are central in kin obligations. At household levels, the male family head oversee cattle ownership. Household roles within 'compounds' (larger households) are distributed per gender and age. Elderly men are responsible for all aspects of decision-making and activities regarding movement, health and sale of cattle. Spouses of the family head have 'milking rights' and not the authority to sell cattle. Respect for elders is entrenched in kin reciprocity, which resonates with prevalent forms of informal social security. Apart from the Ardos, other community leaders (*Nyako)* are highly revered. An interviewee stated:

> *The younger generation huge respect to a Nyako. They are required to assist with basic needs like fetching water, washing, dispatching messages and looking after herds of cattle.*

Besides the Nyako (most senior), the Ndotijo (family head) are esteemed for the duty of care to the lineage. According to Oba (2012), such a status is noticeable amongst *the Matheniko's* indigenous institutions of Ethiopia, where decision-making is the prerogative of elders-senior age set (*kathiko).* The senior elders meet and discuss the migration of livestock; protection of the community from raids, and stresses induced by droughts. In beefing-up support for pastoralists, the MBOSCUDA leader explained:

> *If the elderly has children in school, they benefit from sponsorship programs. In communities where projects are undertaken, women benefit from literacy programs and micro credit schemes.*

On social security, he stated:

*Providing old age protection is a problem. Frail herders are unable to walk for long distances in search of green pasture, so their livelihood is threatened. In addition, diseases affect our cattle and we do not have access to veterinary services.*

Demographic pressures on land and perennial farmer-herder problems are forcing young herders out of settlements. Formal security schemes serves the needs of workers in regular employment, but ignores those eking out a living in informal and subsistence agricultural sectors (Midgley, 2014:186). Ever-shrinking pasture and water resources lead to farmer-herder skirmishes, which threaten traditional livelihoods due to growing pressures on land and recurrent droughts, exacerbated by climate variability, have forced pastoralists to relocate from traditional grazing lands (ISS Africa, 2012, Moritz, 2010). Due to declining green pasture, some cattle owners move beyond pastoralist settlements to seek for pasture. As access to land remain contentious, pastoralists with larger herds are engaging in food production that put them on a collision course with local farming communities (Fonchingong and Ufon 2016).

Elderly pastoralists see MBOSCUDA as a platform for social insurance in old age. As a minority group, pastoralists consider kinship as a 'life line' in preserving their sense of identity and belonging. The coordinator of MBOSCUDA stated:

*MBOSCUDA fights against discrimination, marginalization, exploitation, and oppression of pastoralists, particularly land seizures and evictions.*

Ethnicity remains a key marker of marginalization for pastoralists (Hickey, 2011), as they endure with spatial isolation, and political marginalization in many African countries (AU, 2010). Realising the human rights of mobile pastoralists requires political will and good intentions, translated into obligations through national legal institutions, regional and international legal regimes (ISS Africa, 2012). Targeted in social safety net programs, addressing social changes and other factors creating vulnerability are required to mitigate long-term shocks.

**Fragmentation of kin protection**

The resilience of indigenous safety nets is impacted by social change, institutional context and dynamics of kin arrangements. A female pastoralist stated how women feel the knock-on effects of social change:

> *We depend on men for livelihoods, if men are affected by a drop-in cattle activity, then these uncertainties transfer unto women; we feel the pain too as we rely on sales of milk, cheese, butter and other dairy products to add to household cash.*

Whilst kin arrangements conjure a sense of common ancestry, its traditional resilience is tested. Addressing vulnerability to droughts and other shocks to promote capacity are major concerns for pastoral settlements in the dry lands of SSA (Galvin, 2009, del Ninno et al. 2016). Other concerns include the difficulties of accessing basic social services. Health care facilities are largely out of reach for a clear majority in sedentary settlements, though semi ambulant pastoralists live in enclaves with limited access to electricity and running water. An elder put this worry:

> *We live in fear of being chased away from our land. Though we pay cattle tax (jangali), we have no electricity and water. When we talk of care for the elderly, we think about cattle; it is our only way of survival. We look up to cattle as insurance in old age (MF elder, Sabga).*

Pastoralists feel disenfranchised from existing welfare packages, available in neighbouring farming communities. Land contestations between pastoralists and crop farmers continue to engender tensions between these space partners. The protracted dissonance, delaying tactics deployed by administrative authorities, through fruitless commissions of inquiry have not helped in redressing farmer herder conflicts (Fonchingong, C & Ufon, 2016).

Another interviewee said:

> *'Our biggest problem stems from neighbouring farmers due to tensions about cattle trespass and destruction of food crops. We struggle to find grazing areas. This insecurity weakens our chances of securing income' (MF elder, Sabga).*

Pastoralists are susceptible to fractious inter-community relations. As conceptualised by Chambers (2006), vulnerability has two sides: an external side of risks, shocks, and stress to which an individual or household is subject; and an internal side, which is defencelessness, meaning a lack of means to cope with damaging loss. Livelihood changes occur among pastoralists, but the most prevalent are diversification into agriculture and intensification of livestock production. The loss of key resources, especially of dry-season grazing areas, and watering points, poses a huge challenge to pastoralism (Homewood, 2010; Behnke & Kerven, 2011, Liao & Fei, 2016).

Another said:

*We have no land rights as we are classed as intruders. It is even worse as administrative authorities through inspection fees' dupe us.*

Yet, another stated:

*We have limited government support in old age. Most of our children do not have public service jobs. Though we pay taxes, we do not have access to water, health centres, electricity and veterinary services.*

Another view expressed:

*Local people accuse us of offering bribes to administrative officials. We feel exploited as we give money and get empty promises in return.*

Still, an interviewee intimated:

*Even when we go to Court to present our case, we do not get justice as we are always seen as occupiers (MF elder, Nkambe).*

Participants concerns echoed above resonate with Midgley (2014), who contends that though governments are still the primary sponsors of social protection in the global South, yet, there are limited rates of social insurance coverage, inadequate funding, and administrative challenges, impeded by a shortfall in social investments.

Similarly, other interrelated factors undermine pastoralists' kin bonds. Another interviewer said:

*Our cattle remain our history, identity, social security, culture and mode of subsistence, yet, we do not get much support from the state (MF elder, Sabga).*

Again, the lack of veterinary services poses a threat to social resilience visible in pastoralist enclaves.

Further, another interviewee noted:

*We walk a long way to find pasture. We must arrange for veterinary care and the forward and backward movements create conflicts with crop farmers.*

From the quotations, it is surmised that pressures on grazing land affects pastoral social networks, reciprocal rights and obligations (Galvin, 2009). Additionally, the shoddy delivery of key services, not helped by tenuous access to land, exacerbates tensions and strains with pastoralists' kin arrangements. Incidents of crop damage by pastoral animals are escalating into violent conflicts between herders and farmers (IIED, 2010). In most cases, pastoralists pay veterinary professionals with little or no support from government due to false perceptions of pastoralists' as wealthy citizens.

An elder noted: *we are wrongly seen as wealthy people, so we are cut off from any social assistance schemes.*

These interconnected factors and social perceptions, compounds the fragility within pastoralists enclaves, exacerbated by protracted farmer-herder conflicts. These factors threaten the viability of kin arrangements. The recurrent conflicts take a heavy toll on pastoralism in Horn of Africa engendering the volatility of social security (World Bank 2015, del Ninno et al. 2016). Such conflicts have resulted in deaths, destruction of cattle and food crops, heightening the dislocation of the rural economy. A herder noted:

*The lingering court sessions impact on our kin support as the lineage are taken off normal herding practices to show up in tribunals as witnesses.*

The MBOSCUDA president proffered:

*Old age is a headache for the elderly; our eggs are in one basket as we rely on cattle. If things go wrong, the whole basket is gone and the herder becomes weak.*

A worsening sense of vulnerability is evident:

*Grazing lands are constantly under threat putting off the Fulani from expanding. There are many cattle diseases and we need frequent intervention of veterinary technicians. Worst still, we still hold strongly to age old practices of looking after livestock.*

In bolstering kin arrangements as a guarantor of social protection, a MBOSCUDA official noted:

*Though our interaction with other neighbouring farming communities are not ideal, we can borrow off the model of Njangi (rotating credit and saving associations), a notable activity of treasury and pooling finances to improve credit allocation within pastoralist settlements.*

As outlined above, in reducing shocks to pastoral livelihoods, expanding income opportunities are crucial. Del Ninno et al. (2016) argue other types of social protection programs, which enable chronically poor households to build their productive assets, and expand their income earning opportunities, should supplement social safety net programs.

Other concerns raised by participants square with five key challenges threatening the resilience of pastoral systems: loss of land due mainly to encroachment of neighbouring agriculturalists and farming by herders themselves. Also, endemic conflicts that disrupt markets and increase vulnerability during droughts, increased population and settlement; resilience for whom and level of wealth differentiation that affects how different households (poor, middle, or better-off) respond to market opportunities and their capacity to recover after droughts; and finally, climate variability and change is a challenge to resilience in pastoralist areas (Little & McPeak, 2014:76-77).

Another informant was worried with declining income from dairy farming:

*Our cattle trade is plunging due to frequent conflicts with crop farmers. Though cattle are our lifeline, young pastoralists are finding alternative employment; relocating to urban areas for education and business ventures.*

Pastoralists are susceptible to ecological threats and unexpected changes as they seek out alternative livelihoods. A respondent held:

*Though MBOSCUDA is the perceived mouthpiece of marginalised Fulani, it has become an elite association, hijacked by some Mbororo elite who exploit it for personal political gains.*

Some Ardos feel relegated from mainstream activities of MBOSCUDA, considering their significant role in grassroots mobilization. These tensions undermine kin support and resilience. Most elders feel a sense of isolation and marginalization from projects undertaken by MBOSCUDA as echoed by an elderly Fulani:

*Most MBOSCUDA projects focus more on youth development than elderly welfare schemes.*

MBOSCUDA counteracted this by stating that projects indirectly benefit the elderly pastoralists. In this light, literacy programmes and other micro-credit schemes should empower and build on the capacity of young herders to care for the elderly. Donor organizations like DFID UK, Village AID UK should look at possibilities of baseline research aligning development aid in line with material needs identified by herders. External interventions from government and other institutions strongly affect ethnic pastoralists' herding practices and choices of livelihood strategies (Liao & Fei, 2016), warranting a rethink of rural development policy options.

## Policy rethink and revitalizing rural development

As noted previously, pastoralist grapple with several contending issues. Kin solidarity that has existed for generations, are integral to livelihoods for old people within pastoralist communities. Yet, such traditional safety nets and informal mechanisms are increasingly fragmented. Providing tailored welfare packages from government towards pastoralist raises many issues. Pastoralists pay cattle tax (*jangali*), yet do not benefit evenly from welfare facilities. They feel disenfranchised from government and deem their relationship with institutional authorities as distant. Human development and food security indicators remain low, and the provision of public services in pastoral zones is still weak, and generally far lower than in other areas of a given country (AU, 2010). External induced processes are unsettling for social security arrangements in old age, resulting from diminished herding and the transfer of livestock to younger generation as a buffer for old age security. As del Ninno et al. (2016) aver social protection policies, and programs have a key role in promoting resilience of marginal populations, living in dryland regions.

Another issue centres on the *pulaaku* and the need for adaptation. Thriving aspects of pastoralists' traditions should be co-produced, and implemented in collaboration with pastoralists, without crowding-out pre-existing indigenous safety nets. Core assessments on aspects of vulnerability, can be undertaken by social workers, and welfare assistants, to inform a rethink of rural development policies. The documentation, demarcation and monitoring of farming plots, designated grazing areas and watering points for cattle is important to minimize farmer herder conflicts. Although pastoral systems are clearly under numerous constraints and risks have intensified, pastoralists are adapting and trying to remain flexible (Galvin, 2009). Inevitably, these forms of support risk being diluted further, due to pressures on land and social changes that are unsettling.

A related issue are pastoralists' perceptions of cattle, as a marker of identity and social security. Elders hand down herds of cattle to younger pastoralists, as insurance in old age. Targeting young pastoralists with social assistance, deployment of social workers to

282

work with them in needs identification and problem solving; building on their inner strengths and resources are policy options.

Equally, greater access to veterinary services, basic education and literacy training, youth vocational programmes (as paravets), provision of essential services and infrastructure development such as roads, drinkable water, power supply, schools, and health clinics especially for semi sedentarized Fulani are crucial. Service delivery models have incorporated education; these include distance learning and alternative basic education approaches; in health, community case management and community health worker programs have been effective in augmenting basic veterinary care (AU, 2010). The availability of veterinary services and public health infrastructure will stem the tide of out migration by younger generation, seeking such amenities away from neglected settlements.

Efforts to secure land rights, central to kin arrangements, can foster stability and address shocks. A secured access to land and other ways of securing livelihoods would guarantee better social protection for the elderly. Whilst grazing permits obtained from the Ministry of Livestock is salutary, land demarcation for pastoralists, in consultation with neighbouring communities is important. The creation of cooperative societies, a treasury and credit union would provide financial stability. Policies to embed innovation, information transfer, and adaptation of livestock and herding practices in synergy with pastoralists, MBOSCUDA, NGOs and Government Departments (Health, Agriculture and Rural development, Livestock and Veterinary, Education, Social Affairs) would enhance livelihoods. Government interventions should focus on revitalizing the conditions for resilient pastoral systems, such as restocking, safeguarding their rights for mobility, both within nations and across borders. People are constantly adapting, often incrementally to new opportunities and constraints on their livelihoods (Galvin, 2009, Upton 2012). Participatory policymaking and implementation in a way that ensures the right for self-determination is mandatory (Hickey 2011).

A useful way of guaranteeing social security requires joint-up investments in rural services and infrastructure (roads, water, power supply, rural employment) to retain the younger generation.

Increasing levels of poverty, out-migration and urbanization are forcing poor pastoralists out of their enclaves, and, in the process, diminishing the potential pool of available labour, for bolstering kin support. Since cattle is at the heart of kin arrangements, the introduction of more resistant breeds; training in improving milk quality and production levels, would boost yields, permitting households to generate additional income. The ILO (2011) 'social security floor' initiative (recommendation 202), that establishes a minimum level of social protection for all citizens, are crucial. These efforts cater for large numbers of poor families, usually based on social assistance principles (Midgley 2014:187).

More so, to improve geriatric care for ambulant pastoralists, governments and other development partners can coordinate assistance packages based on needs identification, documentation of pastoralists and farmers to be captured for interventions where available. Mobile veterinary, educational and health care services should be provided to improve rural infrastructure in sedentary communities. Pastoral systems are under numerous constraints, and risks have intensified, yet pastoralists are adapting, and trying to remain flexible (Galvin, 2009).

It is noteworthy that mobility is the backbone of pastoralism, yet, policy makers, donors, international and local agencies design, implement or fund 'projects,' that do not take into consideration the importance of mobility in pastoral livelihoods (IIED, 2010). Consulting the tiered structure of leadership within pastoralist communities are important for external interventions to be successful. Therefore, the need to formulate social protection policies that are adapted to meet specific needs and circumstances (Midgley 2014).

In addition, rural development projects aligned to the protection of human rights for indigenous populations, advocated by the United Nations Declaration on the Rights of Indigenous Peoples, requires the protection of marginal pastoralist groups, and their unique ethnic, cultural and linguistic identity within the territories in which they live. While 'development' is important in pastoral areas, it should not undermine pastoral livelihoods; rather external interventions should be co-created and implemented (IIED, 2010; Liao & Fei, 2016), with a mix of long term and periodic short-term support (del Ninno et al. 2016).

## Conclusions

This paper has explored the thorny discussions on how to ensure the most marginal populations can access old age security. Locating the discourse of social security and kin protection within a rethink of rural development policy, some inferences are drawn:

a) Embedding social security in pastoralist societies requires a co-partnership approach with institutional authorities, recognising pastoralists' lifestyles that have proved socially resilient. A substantive discussion anchored on old age security within rural pastoralist enclaves, and rural development policy require a revamp.

b) Pastoralists' kin system, so far sustained on kin reciprocity and solidarity fostered through the *pulaaku,* are becoming fragmented. However, the risks associated with kin protection, anchored on the *pulaaku* have been relatively successful and anchored on indigenous safety nets for generations.

c) Pastoralists are battling with unpredictable and harsh rural environment, climate variability and dislocation in the ecosystem, exacerbated by new, and accelerating political, economic, and environmental challenges that undermine kin resilience.

d) Frequent skirmishes with local farmers over land, accentuated by narrowing of grazing areas are threatening livelihoods. Such obstacles, driven by both internal and external pressures require a rethink of rural development policy.

e) Social safety nets require co-production and implementation, alongside a kin protection system, in synergy with pastoralists. Such opportunities for joint-up projects often missed by government, development agencies and other donor organizations create an atmosphere of mistrust.

Embedding social protection through a mix of formal and informal social protection measures (pensions, infrastructure, health care, education, veterinary services) to build on kin traditions, whilst securing land rights, supplementing income and enhancing livelihoods for both pastoralists and smallholder farmers, are crucial in rural development policy. Power relations and improving transhumance, demarcating grazing areas and the enclosure of rural farming plots may bolster the capacity of pastoralists to cope with shocks in the medium and long term. Further, ethnographic research and rigorous case studies, investigating land tenure rights and use, livelihood strategies, measuring the impact of climate change and implications on livestock-small holder relations warrant a rural policy rethink in marginal pastoralists' communities.

Training and deployment of social workers is vitally important; these practitioners would undertake robust core assessments, evidence-based analysis, and engage in joint-up working and interventions with government departments and development agencies. A re-calibration of government approach to pastoralism and rural development are mandatory to enhance livelihoods for elderly pastoralists. These strategies would enable pastoralists to overcome shocks, and inherent vulnerabilities of kin protection.

## References

African Union (2010). Policy framework for pastoralism in Africa: securing, protecting and improving the lives, livelihoods and rights of pastoralist communities. Department of Rural Economy and Agriculture, African Union, Addis Ababa, Ethiopia.

Alary, V. Corniaux, C. & Gautier, D. (2011). Livestock's contribution to poverty alleviation: how to measure it? *World Development* 39: 1638–1648.

Aliou, S. (2004). Socio-economic assessment of traditional grazing amongst pastoralist groups: Case study of the Mbororo-Fulani in the North West Province of Cameroon, Dissertation Submitted to the Department of Agricultural Economics and Rural Sociology, University of Dschang, Cameroon.

Atkinson, P. and Hamersley, M. (2007) Ethnography: Principles in Practice. New Yok: Taylor and Francis. Google Scholar

Babbie, E. (2011) The practice of social research, 7th ed, Belmont: Wadsworth

Becker, S., Bryman, A. & Ferguson, H. (2012) Understanding Research for Social Policy and Social Work: Themes, Methods and Approaches, 2nd edn, Bristol, Policy Press.

Bernier, Q. and Meinzen-Dick, R. (2014). Networks for Resilience: The Role of Social Capital. Washington, DC: International Food Policy Institute. Google Scholar.

Burnham, P. (1996). The politics of cultural difference in Northern Cameroon. Edinburgh: Edinburgh University Press.

Catley, A, Lind J, & Scoones I, (eds). (2013). Pastoralism and Development in Africa: Dynamic Change at the Margins. London: Routledge and Earthscan p.295-296

Chambers, R. (2006). Vulnerability Coping and Policy (Editorial introduction), IDS Bulletin.

Davis, D. (1995). Opening Political Space in Cameroon: The ambiguous Response of the Mbororo. *Review of African Political Economy*, 22(64): 213-228.

Davis, D. (2010). Environmentalism as social control? An exploration of the transformation of pastoral nomadic societies in French colonial North Africa, *The Arab World Geographer*, 3, 182–198.

Davies, J. & R. Bennet (2007). Livelihood adaptation to risk: constraints and opportunities for pastoral development in Ethiopia's Afar Region. doi: 10.1080/00220380701204422.

Del Ninno, C; Coll-Black, S & Fallavier, P. (2016) Social Protection Programs for Africa's Drylands. World Bank Studies: Washington, DC: World Bank

Fonchingong, (2013). On the fringe of poverty: care arrangements for older people in rural Cameroon. In: Pranitha Maharaj, (ed) (2013), Aging and Health in Africa, International Perspectives on Aging 4, New York: Springer, p.157-170.

Fonchingong, (2014). Firming up institutional policy for deprived elderly in Cameroon, *Politics and Policy*, Vol 42 (6): 948-980.

Fonchingong, & Ufon, B. (2016). Space partners or mortal enemies: Contentious lands, farmer-grazier conflicts and women's militancy in Cameroon, In Tukumbi Lumumba-Kasongo (Ed.),

Land reforms and Natural resource conflicts in Africa, New development paradigms in the era of global liberalization (pp. 55-74), Routledge African Studies, New York: Routledge.

Galvin K. A. (2009). Transitions: pastoralists living with change. *The Annual Review of Anthropology*, 38:185–98, doi: 10.1146/annurev-anthro-091908-164442.

Hickey, S. (2011). Toward a progressive politics of belonging? insights from a pastoralist "hometown" Association, *Africa Today*, Vol. 57, No. 4 (Summer 2011), pp. 29-47.

Homewood, K. (2010). *Ecology of African pastoralist societies.* Oxford, UK: James Currey; Athens, OH, US: Ohio University Press.

IIED (2010). Modern and mobile the future of livestock production in Africa's drylands, available at: http://pubs.iied.org/pdfs/12565IIED.pdf, Retrieved 21/08/2015.

Institute for Security Studies (ISS) Africa (2012). Situation report, Kenya's neglected IDPS internal displacement and vulnerability of pastoralist communities in Northern Kenya, available at: https://www.issafrica.org/uploads/SitRep2012 8Oct.pdf accessed 08/09/2015.

International Labour Organization (ILO), (2008). Can low-Income countries afford basic social security? *Social Security Policy Briefings Paper* No 3. Geneva. http://www.ilo.org/public/libdoc/ilo/2008/108B09 73 engl.pf

ILO, (2012). Social security for all: building social protection floors and comprehensive social security systems. Geneva: ILO. http://www.ilo.org/wcmsp5/groups/public/---ed emp/---emp ent/---multi/documents/publication/wcms 213761.pdf

Lesorogrol, C., Chowa, G. & Ansong, D. (2013). The roles of livestock inheritance and formal education in intergenerational wealth transmission among pastoralists in Samburu District, Kenya, *Journal of Developing Societies*, 29 (2): 213-232.

Liao Chuan & Fei Ding (2016). Resilience of what to what? Evidence from pastoral contexts in East Africa and Central Asia, *Resilience*, 4:1, 14-29, http://dx.doi.org/10.1080/21693293.2015.1094167

Little, P. & McPeak, J. (2014). Resilience and pastoralism in Africa south of the Sahara, In: Pastoralism and resilience South of the Sahara, 2020 Conference Brief (Washington, DC: International Food Policy Research Institute, 2014).

Midgley, J. (2014). Social development: theory and practice, London: Sage Publications Ltd

Moritz, M. (2006). Changing contexts and dynamics of farmer-herder conflicts across West Africa, *Canadian Journal of African Studies* 40 (1): 1-40.

Moritz, M. (2010). "Crop-livestock interactions in agricultural and pastoral systems in West Africa", *Agriculture and Human Values* 27: 119–128.

Moritz, M. & Scholte, Paul. (2011). Ethical predicaments, advocating security for mobile pastoralists in weak states, *Anthropology Today* 27(3): 12-17

Neuman, W. (2011) 7th edn, Social research methods: qualitative and quantitative approach, Boston: Allyn and Bacon

Nino-Zarazua, M. Armando Barrientos A, Hickey, S. & Hulme, D. (2012). Social protection in sub-Saharan Africa: Getting the politics right, *World Development*, 40 (1): 163-176, doi:10.1016/j.worlddev.2011.04.004

Oba, G. (2012). Harnessing pastoralists' indigenous knowledge for rangeland management: Three African Case Studies, *Pastoralism: Research, Policy and Practice* (2)1: 1-25.

Schilling J, Opiyo F., & Scheffran, J. (2012). Raiding pastoral livelihoods: motives and effects of violent conflict in North-Western Kenya, *Pastoralism: Research, Policy and Practice*, 2:25 (1-16).

Scott, J. C. (1998). Seeing like a state: how certain schemes to improve the human condition have failed. Yale Agrarian Studies. New Haven (CT): Yale University Press.

Small, M. L. (2009). 'How many cases do I need?' On science and the logic of case selection in field-based research, *Ethnography*, 10, 5–38. doi: 10.1177/1466138108099586.

Stake, R. E. (1995). *The art of case study research*. Thousand Oaks, CA: Sage.

Upton, C. (2012). Adaptive capacity and institutional evolution in contemporary pastoral societies. *Applied Geography, 33*, 135–141.

World Bank (2015) Opportunities for social protection to address poverty and vulnerability in a crisis context. Mali social protection policy note. Africa Social Protection, Washington DC: World Bank

Yin, R. K. (2002). Case study research. Thousand Oaks, CA: SAGE.

Yin, R. K. (2011). Qualitative research from start to finish. New York, NY: Guilford Press.

# Chapter 12

# Pollution of Water Resources and Challenges for Efficient Water Development in the Republic of Cameroon
*Celestin Defo*

**Abstract**

Since the industrial revolution of the 19th century, water pollution has been one of the subjects of several research works around the world and more specifically in Cameroon. These studies showed among many constraints, that weaknesses in institutions and legal frameworks constitute the roots of poor management of water resources which is structurally overdrawn. This chapter primarily describes the availability and quality of water resources and sources in the Republic of Cameroon. It is based on surveys and the research works conducted by the previous authors on the categorization of the pollution of water sources. Like previous research, the study reveals various types of water pollution, their sources, their effects on human health and environment, and possible solutions for the protection of water resources. It indicates that many types of pollution are found in groundwater and surface water resources across Cameroon, resulting in dire consequences on the availability of potable water to the population, the proliferation of water borne diseases and serious threats to public health.

**Keywords:** Water borne diseases, Sanitation, Contamination, and Policies

## Introduction

Water resource is very important for human wellbeing and dignity all over the world. In fact, its uses are related to all aspects of human development including health, agriculture, education, economics, and even peace and stability (Pradeep, 2016). Many authors have examined the situation of water resources in Africa and stated that

African countries suffer from economic water scarcity, while physical water scarcity could be controlled through good water management practices (Pradeep, 2016, Defo et al., 2016). Dunmade (2015) points out that a huge amount of billions of dollars has been invested over the years towards the provision of potable water in Sub-Saharan Africa. However, despite the huge investment in water infrastructure, only about 50% of the populace has access to potable water in the continent. Moreover, this situation has become alarming in different sub Saharan Africa countries due to poor sanitation systems that lead to water pollution and severe threats to public health (Danmade, 2015, Defo et al., 2017; Pradeep, 2016). Danmade (2015) observes that many people must hike far and spend hours to fetch water. A significant percentage of sub Saharan African population is suffering from waterborne diseases such as cholera due to consumption of unsafe water from unwholesome sources like rivers, lakes and shallow aquifers generally vulnerable to surface pollution. These observations align with the water management situation in Cameroon. The country is a well-watered, with irregular distribution of rainfall from one part of the country to another (Defo et al., 2016). The country boasts of important surface water and groundwater resources spread over the main water-bearing areas (Fantong et al. 2005; Keleko et al. 2013). But, the proportion of Cameroon's population with access to safe water was estimated at 57.8 % in 2005 against 65 % today in rural area while 77 % of urban population have access to safe drinking water (Folifac et al. 2009, Defo et al., 2016, Defo and Yerima, 2005) although this water is not regularly available. Keeping these observations in view, the resource is polluted and contaminated due to anthropogenic sources in different water basins in the country. Pollutions originate from agriculture, administrations, factories and households (Nganti, 2012, Nguendo, 2010; Mpakam, 2008; Defo and Yerima, 2005). However, perusing through literature discloses the need for a consolidated review of the range of the contaminants that have been found in water resources, their assets/limitations, and future considerations for improving water resources protection in Cameroon.

There is lack of a comprehensive review of the water pollution status highlighting and putting together the limited and disseminated data about this subject in different areas. This is a major problem and shows ambiguity on how pollutions, climate change should affect water resources. It therefore makes difficult the development, protection and adoption of real structural planning, mitigation and adaptation strategies necessary to improve water resources management in the country (Wirmvem et al. 2014; Tchaptchet, 2012; Defo and Yerima, 2015). This study focuses on the state of Cameroon's water resources profile, issues of water use and supply, indicators of water pollution and the types of pollutions found in surface water and groundwater in Cameroon. It further investigates sustainable ways address the identified water resources protection issues.

## Geographical realities and water supply

Cameroon is a country situated between West and Central Africa at the north-eastern end of the Gulf of Guinea. It is bordered by Chad to the north-east, the Central African Republic to the east, the Congo, Gabon and Equatorial Guinea to the south, and Nigeria to the west. It has about 400 km of Atlantic coastline in the southwest, and shares Lake Chad with Chad in the north (Figure 1).

The country's total surface area is about 475 650 km$^2$, and the estimated population is 18 million (INS, 2015), with more than half under age 25. The urban and rural populations are about the same size, although urbanization is increasing at 4.7% per year on average. The country's 1200 km length, proximity to the sea and topography give it a varied climate with wide differences in rainfall and vegetation (Molua and Lambi, 2002).

# Figure 1. Map of Republic of Cameroon showing different hydrological basin

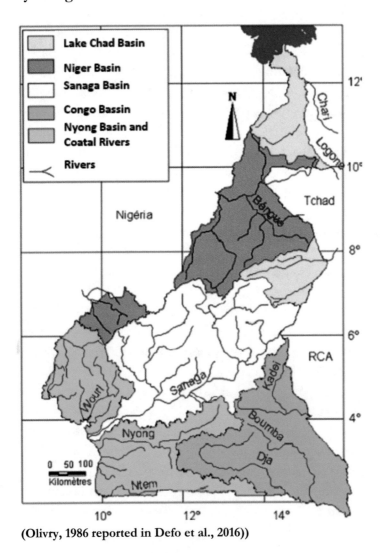

(Olivry, 1986 reported in Defo et al., 2016))

## Land cover and vegetation

As reported in Defo et al. (2016), the land use and land cover conditions of the Republic of Cameroon is a mix stand of forest vegetation, scrub land and agricultural lands. The central highlands are void of much vegetation while the northern and southern slopes have a moderate to good vegetative cover. Cameroon's coastal plain extends from 20 to 80 kilometres inland from the Gulf of Guinea (part of the Atlantic Ocean). The mass of Mount Cameroon reaches almost to the sea. The plain is densely forested including areas of Central African mangroves especially around Douala and in the estuary of the Cross River on the border with Nigeria. The low South Cameroon Plateau, rising from the coastal plain and dominated by tropical rain forest, has an average elevation of 500 to 600 metres. It is less humid than the coast. In western Cameroon is an irregular chain of trees and water bodies that extend from Mount Cameroon almost to Lake Chad at the southern tip of the country. The terrain of the Republic of Cameroon is largely flat, interspersed with lofty mountain systems aligned along the Cameroon Volcanic Line (CVL) where the highest elevation is found at Mount Cameroon (4100 m). The coastal area is largely a plain with lower elevations, most of it is slightly different from the undulating plains in the southern plateau.

**Climate variability and change**

Average rainfall in Cameroon has been declining since the 1950s. In the last three decades it has decreased by about 5% (Aquastat, 2007). Reduced flow rates have been more pronounced in areas with a Sahelian climate, where reductions ranging from 15% to 25% have been recorded. These changes have led to increased desertification in the north and a falling water table due to reduced recharge. In addition, previously permanent wells are drying up late in the dry season. Equally, uncontrolled deforestation in the southern region during the last decades have significantly affected season variation and rainfall (Aquastat, 2007). The maximum rainfall of 10.000 mm occurs in the equatorial climate zone in the south, and the minimum of 500 mm in the extreme north on the edge of the Sahara. The average annual rainfall is about 1684 mm. The average annual temperature is $24^0$C in Yaoundé, in the equatorial climate and $28^0$C in Maroua, in the sahelian climate for north and the extreme north regions (Molua and Lambi, 2002).

Che (2013) reports that the ten regions in Cameroon encompass 27 soil groups that belong to 8 out of 12 soil orders. Among them are differentiated Alfisols, Andisols, Aridisol, Inceptisols, Oxisols, Ultisols, and Vertisols. According to Che (2013) and Yerima and Ranst (2005), climate and parent materials stand out as the most important soil forming factors. Rainfall and temperature are the two most significant components of climate, while humidity and evapotranspiration have a rather indirect influence on vegetation.

## Cameroon water resources profile

Cameroon has a dense network of streams which take their rise from the Central Adamawa Plateau and flow north or south and constitute abundant water resources in relation to current demand. The six main basins are Sanaga, Sanaga West, Sanaga South, Benoue, Congo and Lake Chad. The Sanaga basin, located in the centre of the country, is the largest, covering about 29% of the territory. The Atlantic basin is drained by River Sanaga and River Wouri in the south and west directions respectively. Cameroon's total annual renewable water resources amount to some 283.5 billion $m^3$ or about 17000 $m^3$ per capita, according to the 2006 population (20 million inhabitants) estimates (GWP/AC, 2010). The groundwater resources is estimated at 100 billion to 120 billion $m^3$. In Cameroon, the amount of surface water volume is about 267.88 $km^3$, 32.52 $km^3$ for the Lake Chad basin; 43.91 $km^3$ for the Niger basin; 63.18 $km^3$ for the Sanaga basin 33.45 $km^3$ for the Congo and 94.82 $km^3$ for the coastal rivers while groundwater distribution in different river basin is estimated in Table 1 as function of the geological context of each region.

**Table 1. Estimation of groundwater amount in $km^3$ in major saturated watershed in Cameroon**

| Aquifers | Water Volume) | Percentage olume with report to total volume |
|---|---|---|
| Lake Chad Sedimentary Basin | 3.2 | 5.72 |
| Benue Sedimentary Basin | 15.75 | 28.14 |
| Douala Sedimentary Basin | 21.6 | 38.64 |
| Bedrock areas | 15.40 | 27.51 |
| Total | 55.98 | 100 |

**Source: GWP/AC (2010) reported in Defo et al., (2016)**

Due to the lack of comprehensive monitoring of water resources, exact consumption patterns are not known. However, it is estimated that about 1 billion $m^3$ of the total renewable water resources is withdrawn annually. From this, roughly 2.96 % is used in domestic activities, 0.88 % for livestock, 7.25% for irrigation and less than 1% for industries and mines, while 88.74% is used for hydropower (GWP/AC, 2010).

**State of water availability and withdrawal**

Findings reveal that of the sampled water demand by different economic sectors of the country, majority (88.74%) of the water is harnessed for Hydro-Electric Power (HEP) development with a total of 9769 $10^{-3}$km water use. This is justified by the country's potentials to develop the industrial sector and improve on economic growth. The agricultural sector needs to be improved upon bearing in mind the changing climatic conditions and the advancement of drought that tend to affect productivity. Improvement especially in the Sahel region where mean rainfall is only 250mm suggest revitalisation of the sector through irrigation practices accounting about for 7.25%.

**Table 2 presents different water utilisation in different river basins**

| Water use | Lake Chad | Niger | Sanaga | Congo | Other coastal rivers | Total Cameroun ($10^{-3}$ km³) | % |
|---|---|---|---|---|---|---|---|
| Domestic | 55.07 | 65.9 | 101.6 | 14.9 | 88.8 | 326.27 | 2.96 |
| Livestock | 84.01 | 13.4 | / | / | | 97.41 | 0.88 |
| Irrigation | 328.95 | 377.08 | / | / | 91.79 | 797.82 | 7.25 |
| Hydro-power | / | 7600 | 2169 | / | | 9769 | 88.74 |
| Industries | / | 0.33 | 8.16 | 0.06 | 6.62 | 15.17 | 0.138 |
| Mines | / | / | / | 2.9 | | 2.9 | 0.026 |
| Total ($10^{-3}$km³) | 468.03 | 8056.71 | 2278.76 | 17.86 | 187.21 | 11008.57 | 100 |

**GWP/AC (2010) reported in Defo et al., (2016)**

Agriculture is the backbone of Cameroon's economy, accounting for about 41% of GDP and 55% of the workforce (UNESCO, 2011). With about 69.750 $km^2$ arable land representing 15% of the overall

297

surface area, 29% of the arable land is cultivated, mostly in the west and south-west. The portion of the population working in agriculture has been decreasing since the 1970s. Although as productivity may have increased over the same period, food security has not been directly affected. Irrigation has contributed substantially to agricultural productivity, making cultivation possible during the dry season and in the Sahel regions of the country. In the year 2000, irrigated area was about 224.5 km$^2$ (UNESCO, 2011).

Table 3 shows that in 2002, the amount of renewable freshwater was 285.5 109 m$^3$/year while the freshwater withdrawal as a percentage of total is 0.3%. This indicates that the country is enriched with a huge quantity of water resources in contrast to the present water paucity widespread in urban and rural areas.

**Table 3. Freshwater availability and withdrawal in Cameroon.**

| Water Availability | | Withdrawals % | |
|---|---|---|---|
| Average precipitation in depth (mm/yr) | 1604 | Total freshwater withdrawal (surface 2000 water + groundwater) (10$^9$ m$^3$/yr) | 0.9 |
| Total renewable water (actual) (10$^9$ m$^3$/yr) | 285.5 | Total water withdrawal per capita 2002 59.6(m$^3$/inhab/yr) | 59.6 |
| Total renewable per capita (actual)(m$^3$/inhab/yr) | 14 957 | | |
| Surface water: total renewable (actual) (10$^9$ m$^3$/yr) | 280.5 | Freshwater withdrawal as % of total 2002 Renewable water resources (actual) (%) | **0.3** |

Source: UNEP (2002)

## Data collection and analysis

Primary data was collected during field work. Water samples were collected from a river called 'Ngoua' in Ndokoti-Douala, representing surface water pollution by contaminants from anthropogenic sources. Besides this, groundwater samples from boreholes were collected from different sites in Cameroon and were also analysed. All the samples were collected according to standard procedures (Rodier et al., 2006) and were transported to the

298

laboratory for analysis. For surface water samples the parameters analysed were: Physicochemicals (pH, temperature, electrical conductivity, phosphorus, Nitrogen, Chloride, iron (Fe), Biochemical Oxygen Demand for 5 days [DBO$_5$], Chemical Oxygen Demand [DCO], total dissolved solids [TDS]) and microbiological parameters (faecal and total coliforms). All these parameters were analysed in the laboratory following standard procedures described by Apha (1998). Equally, samples of groundwater from boreholes were collected and analysed following the standard procedures (Alpha, 1998) for the following parameters: colour, temperature, turbidity, electrical conductivity, total dissolved solids, hydrocarbonates, chloride, calcium, magnesium, sulfates, nitrates, nitrites, iron, manganese, phosphate, silicium, phenol and suspended matters. Overall, these parameters help to assess exposure to water borne diseases, groundwater pollution and the danger of eutrophication of water bodies.

## Results and Discussions

### Water resources pollution

Many cases of water-borne diseases such as typhoid cholera and amoebic dysentery are recurrent in most of the urban cities in Cameroon (Nguendo, 2010). Hydric diseases (intestinal helminthiases) affected more than 10 million Cameroonians between 2003 and 2006. These diseases are associated to water and sanitation systems. Between 1984-1993 for example, 8000 cases of cholera, 11500 cases of typhoid, 46400 of dysentery were recorded. Over 70% of the household expenditures on health between the period 2003 and 2006 were spent on water-related diseases. Moreover, the application of pesticides has an implication on water pollution in Cameroon. Some indications are stated as follows:

- Increasing number of dams to solve acute energy shortages may increase mosquitoes and black flies.
- The current method used by the Electricity Development Corporation like larviciding in the rivers upstream to the dams. If approximately $2 million is pumped into the project in the next three

years, tons of insecticides will be poured into Cameroonian waters before the runoff from agricultural activities. This will be an unnecessary evil and serious environmental problem if not checked (Tarla et al. 2014)

- Besides, the country is moving to the second-generation agriculture revolution in which large surface area will be cultivated using tractors and fertilizers. Therefore, pesticides worth 31 million FCFA (about $ 64 000) was given to farming associations (Bambe, 2010). Plantations such as PHP Banana plantation, Djombe Penja Banana plantation, Group Delmonthe etc., that producing high quality cocoa and coffee occupy 300,000 and 100,000 hectares respectively and use approximately 100,000 litre/ha of pesticides.

According to several studies, any chemical, biological and physical change in water quality that has a harmful effect on living organisms or makes it unusable for agriculture is water pollution. This is because of the massive quantity of pollutants produced by more than 6 billion humans, their machines, plants, animals when compared to the limited supply of fresh liquid water into which most water-destined pollutants are discharged into. It is also due to the growing number of 'technological pollutants' released into the environment, i.e. manufactured synthetic materials.

In Cameroon, available information on the amount of pollution reaching surface and groundwater resources or on the severity of the problem are relatively insufficient. Some studies have indicated that most industries discharge waste into the environment with little or no treatment (in different cities such as Doaula-Bonaberi, Limbe, Kribi, Bafoussam, Garoua, Ngaoundere, etc.). Others have demonstrated that urban waste such as faecal sludge and waste water from households, hospitals and municipalities are sources of water pollution. Equally, wastewaters from agriculture have been mentioned by some studies as sources of water pollution.

### Sources of pollution

In Cameroon, there are several sources of water pollution including point sources (e.g., factories, sewage treatment plants, mines, oil wells, oil tankers), non-point sources (e.g., acid deposition, substances picked up in runoff, seepage into groundwater) and agriculture as seen in figure 2.

**Figure 2. View of point-source and Non-point source of water pollution (Mannoj, 2013)**

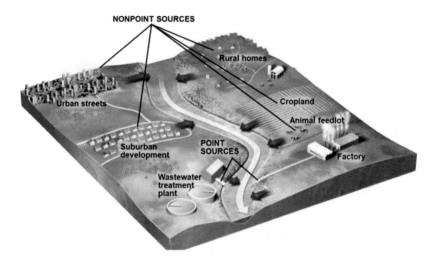

The point referred as source pollution is a specific source of pollution that can be identified (pipe gushing colored water into a river), while a widely spread source of pollution that cannot be tied to a specific point of origin is called nonpoint source pollution (runoff from a farm field, a street, or a construction site). In Cameroon, there are many sources which could be associated to water pollution: (i) wastewaters from laboratories of the two main hospitals (Gyneco-opcetrical and General Hospitals) of the Yaoundé city are discharged into the environment without treatment for many years (Figure 2); (ii) management of urban rainwater is difficult in the Yaoundé due to the urbanistic problems: massive population growth, anarchic housing, lack of sewer and urbanistic equipment which are the cause of the accumulation of pollutants in the city; (iii) washing of urban surfaces by the runoff (roof and public road network) (Figure 3), transport of waste from garages and other repair shops (old batteries and old air conditioners) by the rainwater, proliferation of the solid wastes dumpsites, air pollution (incineration of urban wastes) and motor exhaustion; (iv)industrial wastewater, V) improper

301

solid waste dumpsites, etc. (Bemmo et al., 1998, Mpakam, 2008, KouamKenmogne et al., 2013, Defo et al., 2015).

Effluents generated by hospitable activities are a potential danger for human beings and the environment considering the nature of specific substances which they contain (medicinal residues, chemicals, antiseptic, detergent, fixative sprays used in radiography).

## Types of water pollution in Cameroon

Three main types of water polluting substances are inorganic, organic and biologic pollutants. These pollutants are released into natural or artificial water reservoirs, leading to the pollution of streams, lakes, ocean, groundwater, and potable water sources. Several research works have been focused on water pollution in Cameroon. We reviewed the pollution status of surface water and groundwater.

### Surface water pollution in Cameroon

Baok (2007), Jessie et al (2014), Kouam Kenmogne et al (2013), Djuikom et al. (2009), Ajeagah (2013) and Sieliechi et al. (2013) have researched on the pollution of different rivers in Cameroon by organic pollutants and nutrients from anthropogenic sources. Table 4 presents the quality of water collected from some rivers in Cameroon. It indicates that the physico-chemical parameters are greater than the MPL (Maximum Permissible Limits). There are also three classes of compounds (pesticides and herbicides, materials for common household, and materials for industrial use). Many agro-industrial companies and cooperative farming groups use chemicals (pesticides and herbicides) to produce banana plantain, rubber, the, coffee, cocoa, etc. It is obvious that, with the lack of monitoring in the environmental framework, water resources could be polluted by the uncontrolled rate of application of the chemicals in the farms and this affects streams and other water sources in the environment.

**Table 4. Water quality of some rivers in Cameroon. Overview of some physic chemical parameters**

| Rivers | TDS (mg/l) | BOD$_5$ (mg/l) | COD (mg/l) | EC (µS/cm) | NH$_3$ (mg/l) | NH$_4^+$ (mg/l) | NO$_3$ (mg/l) | PO$_3^4$ (mg/l) | pH | Source |
|---|---|---|---|---|---|---|---|---|---|---|
| Ngoua | 587.8 | 187 | 421 | 420 | 9.33 | 10.22 | 14.35 | 0.74 | 7.8 | Baok, 2007 |
| | 15EPA-PAHs-Polycyclic Aromatic Hydrocarbons (PAHs): 4 to 5 rings (140.42 µg/g to 229.47 µg/g) | | | | | | | | | Jessie et al (2014) |
| Abiergue | / | 360 | 601 | / | / | 37.2 | 70.4 | / | 7.2 | Kouam et al 2013 |
| Olezoa | 270 | 308 | 406 | 1292 | / | / | / | / | 7.2 | |
| Mfoundi | | 297.5 | 500.25 | / | / | / | / | / | 7.8 | Djuikom et al. (2009) |
| Monatele | 70.3 | 110.0 | 205.0 | 303 | / | / | / | / | 7.04 | Ajeagah (2013) |
| Obala | 151.9 | 106.5 | 200.0 | 140 | / | / | / | / | 7.28 | Ajeagah (2013) |
| Dang | / | / | / | 517.83 | / | 1.54 | 4.4 | 2.02 | / | Sieliechi et al. (2013) |
| MPL | 2100 | 30 | 250 | / | / | / | 10 | / | 9.0 | |

MPL=Maximum Permissible Limits; TDS=Total Dissolved Solids; BOD=Biochemical Oxygen Demand; COD=Chemical Oxygen Demand; EC=Electrical Conductivity

Fonkou et al., (2005) have analysed the concentrations of cadmium (Cd), copper (Cu), zinc (Zn) and lead (Pb) in water, sediments, fish organs and plants from two ponds of the Olezoa wetland complex. Plants investigated were *Cyperus papyrus*, *Enydrafluctuans*, *Ipomoeaaquatica* and *Echinocloapyramidalis* while the fish species studied was the walking catfish *Clariaslazera*. Heavy metal concentrations were found in the digestive tract, gills, flesh and liver of the fish. Average concentrations in water were $6 \times 10^{-2}$ ppm for

303

Cd, 14.53 ppm for Cu, 2.88 ppm for Zn and 17.69 ppm for Pb. These values were low compared to those recorded in the sediments, plants and fish organs. Results revealed an increase of heavy metal concentrations from water to plants and fish organs, with magnification factors ranging from 580 to 5700 and from 577 to 8173, respectively. In the sediments and the floating mat of the eutrophic fish ponds, these factors ranged from 491 to 1065 and 624 to 758, respectively. The four plants studied appeared to be good candidates for phytoremediation of water metal pollution. The quantity of heavy metals in this wetland complex is considerable and will constitute a potential hazard for biota.

Studies involving faecal pollutants are most common in Cameroon, especially in urban areas where water supply and sanitation constitute major difficulties of the municipalities. Many studies have reported the pollution of surface water, groundwater and lakes by these contaminants. Njine et al., (2002) investigated the deteriorating bacteriological water quality of the Yaoundé Municipal Lake and the degree of pollution of the Mingoa Stream. The main tributary of the lake was evaluated for total coliforms, thermotolerant coliforms, and fecal streptococci. Concentrations of these bacterial indicators in Mingoa Stream were higher than those allowed by international norms for the bacteriological quality of recreational water. They concluded that this stream contributes to the high levels of bacteria in the water column of the Municipal Lake. All the investigations cited above agree with the study of Bemmo et al. (1998) on the impact of bacteria and viral pollution of surface and ground water in urban equatorial area on potable water supply systems in Cameroon (Table 5).

**Table 5. Distribution of drinking-water sources in Yaoundé according to microbiological assessment**

| Quality | Sources of drinking-water | | | | | | | | | |
|---|---|---|---|---|---|---|---|---|---|---|
| | Boreholes | | Springs | | Households (sored waters) | | Community standpipes | | Wells | |
| | F | % | F | % | F | % | F | % | F | % |
| Safe | 0 | 0.0 | 0.0 | 0 | 10 | 3.3 | 15 | 55.6 | 25 | 4.9 |
| Contaminated | 154 | 100 | 25 | 100 | 292 | 96.7 | 12 | 44.4 | 483 | 95.1 |
| Total | 154 | 100 | 25 | 100 | 302 | 100 | 27 | 100 | 508 | 100 |

**F= Frequency**
**Source: Nguendo (2010)**

These water sources in Table 5 have different degrees of exposure and pollution in the different parts of the city of Yaounde.

In the north of Cameroon, Maïworé et al (2013) have evaluated the bacteriological and physicochemical characteristics (temperature, pH, salinity, conductivity, turbidity, suspended matter, organic matter, phosphates, sulphates, nitrates, chloride, calcium, magnesium, iron and nitrogen) of water and sediment collected in four fisheries. The results showed that all the analysed parameters were the highest, except for chlorides. The study further assessed Total mesophile, salmonella, *Staphylococcus, Clostridia, Pseudomonas,* Faecal *Streptococcus and Vibrio* in different rivers and lakes in the North and their results indicated that, total mesophile aerobic flora varied between $1.4 \pm 0.50 \times 105$ in Tibati and $5.57 \pm 0.50 \times 106$ CFU/mL in Lagdo. *Salmonella* concentration was between $66.66 \pm 1.62$ in Tibati and $274 \pm 3.16$ CFU/mL in Yagoua. There was about $10 \pm 0.50$ CFU/mL *Vibrio* in Lagdo and $342.27 \pm 5.53$ CFU/mL in Maga. *Staphylococcus* concentration was between $1.4 \pm 0.55 \times 103$ CFU/mL in Tibati and $4.44 \pm 0.9 \times 104$ in Maga. *Clostridia* was between $0.33 \pm 0.00$ in Tibati and $226.66 \pm 4.29$ CFU/mL in Maga while *Pseudomonas* concentration was between $16.26 \pm 0.70$ in Tibati and $326.66 \pm 6.00$ CFU/mL in Lagdo. Faecal *Streptococcus* varied between $0.33 \pm 0.00$ in

305

Tibati and 238.66±8.15 CFU/mL in Yagoua. The total mesophile aerobic flora was significantly high (P<0,005) in Lagdo while *Clostridium,* faecal *streptococcus*, and *Streptococcus* concentration were significantly high in Maga, Yagoua and Lagdo. Lake sediments in Maga were the most infected.

The different analysis revealed that the fisheries were relatively polluted. Some of the bacteria counted like *Pseudomonas* and *Vibrio* might be pathogenic for fishes. Studies from different parts of the country indicate that many water resources used for household consumption are polluted to varying degrees because waste disposal infrastructure is insufficient in urban areas, and the capacity to enforce existing laws is very weak. Most affected are areas where latrines and septic tanks, for example, are located near springs and shallow wells used without treatment for household water supply (Figure 3).

**Figure 3. Distribution of diarrhea associated from wells and spring water in Yaounde Cameroun (Nguendo, 2010)**

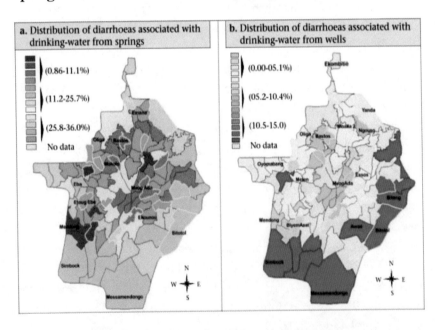

There is little information on the amount of pollution reaching surface and groundwater resources, or on the severity of the problem. Some studies have indicated that most industrial facilities discharge waste into the environment with little or no treatment. The companies know they are polluting, but because monitoring and enforcement are inadequate, they lack any incentive to invest in wastewater treatment. Water-related diseases are quite common in Cameroon and particularly affect children (OMS, 2004). The main causes of death in children under 5 are diarrhoea, malaria and measles. Among children under 4 years old, diarrhea accounts for about 10% of all deaths while malaria affects about 46% of the population. Health expenditure in Cameroon for 2001/2002 amounted to around US$110 million, which corresponded to 4.5% of the national budget and about 1% of GDP (GWP/AC, 2010).

Table 6 presents the amount of faecal coliform and total coliforms found in some rivers in Cameroon.

| Rivers | FC (FCU/100ml) | FS (FCU/100ml) | TC (FCU/100ml) | Authors |
|---|---|---|---|---|
| Ngoua | 30 | 90 | / | Baok (2007) |
| Abiergue · | 18200 | 8800 | / | Kouam (2013) |
| Mingoa | $3.1 \times 10^7$ | $2.3 \times 10^7$ | $2.7 \times 10^{10}$ | Jugnia and Simé-Ngando (2001) |
| M. Lake Yde | 6160 | 387 | / | Demanou and Brummet (2003) |
| Melen Lake | 11000 | 3300 | / | Demanou and Brummet (2003) |
| Mfoundi | Mean ± SD=$6.8 \times 10^5$ ± $2.4 \times 10^3$ CFU/100 ml | Mean ± SD=$7.3 \times 10^5$ ± $2.1 \times 10^3$ CFU/100 ml | (Mean ± SD=$5.6 \times 10^8$ ± $2.5 \times 10^6$ CFU/100 ml) | Djuikom et al.(2006), Kuitcha et al., (2008) |
| Douala Lagoon | $2.4 \times 10^2$ | $2.3 \times 10^2$ | $2.4 \times 10^2$ | Ajeagah (2013) |
| Monatele | 684 | 52.75 | 67.3 | Ajeagah (2013) |
| MPL (WHO) | 2000 | | 10000 | |

FC=Faecal Coliform; FS =Faecal Streptoccoci; TC=Total Coliform; CFU=Colony Forming Units

The pollution of different rivers shown on Table 6 is mainly due to faecal contamination, which is above the acceptable limits. According to Defo et al. (2015), the effect of faecal sludge on the health of populations is deplorable because the embankment of River Noun is covered by faecal waste collected in the city of Bafoussam. These investigations show that these diseases are caused by contact with the fecal contamination (diarrhea, amebiasis, infectious hepatitis) and water contamination (cholera, typhoid).

**Ground water pollution in Cameroon**

Water from the polluted wetlands is still used by the riverside populations for urban agriculture and domestic purposes (Figure 4), and the contaminated fish is regularly caught for consumption. Such activities should be reconsidered by public authorities and banned in this area.

Water containing high concentrations of nitrate is unsafe for human consumption and if discharged into freshwater or marine habitats, can contribute to algal blooms and eutrophication. The level of nitrate contamination in groundwater of two densely populated, agro industrial areas of the Cameroon Volcanic Line (CVL) consisting of the Banana Plain and Mount Cameroon area was evaluated by Ako et al. (2011). A total of 100 samples from boreholes, open wells and springs (67 from the Banana Plain, 33 from springs only, in the Mount Cameroon area) were collected and analyzed for chemical constituents, including nitrates. The average groundwater nitrate concentrations for the studied areas are: 17.28 mg/l for the Banana Plain and 2.90 mg/l for the Mount Cameroon area. Overall, groundwaters were relatively free from excessive nitrate contamination, with nitrate concentrations in only 6 % of groundwater resources in the Banana Plain exceeding the maximum admissible concentration for drinking water (50 mg/l). Sources of $NO_3^-$ in groundwater in this region was attributed to the anthropogenic variables (N-fertilizers, sewerage, animal waste, organic manure, pit latrines, etc.). Multivariate statistical analyses of the hydrochemical data revealed that three factors were responsible for the groundwater chemistry (especially, degree of nitrate contamination): (1) a geogenic factor; (2) nitrate contamination factor; (3) ionic enrichment factor. The impact of anthropogenic activities, especially groundwater nitrate contamination, was more accentuated in the Banana Plain than in the Mount Cameroon area.

Various authors have studied the issue of nitrate contamination of groundwater resources, especially in the North (Njitchoua and Ngounou, 1997; Ngounou and Ndjoret, 2010), which is the main agro-pastoral zone of Cameroon. Ako et al. (2011) also reported about nitrate contamination of groundwater and surface water resources in the Banana Plain. Their study of water sources around Mount Cameroon of weathered volcanic and sedimentary rocks like the Banana Plain showed that these waters did contain trace elements and a dominance of $Na^+$ and $K^+$ as major cations closely associated with nitrates.

Currently, there is lack of information and understanding of $NO_3^-$ input and its effect on the quality of groundwater resources and ecosystem health within these densely populated, agro-industrial areas of the Cameroon Volcanic Line. Therefore, it is essential to conduct detailed assessments of the degree of nitrate contamination of their groundwater resources. As an objective, this paper focus on the application of hydrochemistry and principal component/factor analysis for the identification of factors responsible for nitrate contamination of groundwater in the Banana Plain and Mount Cameroon area, two important areas of the Cameroon Volcanic Line.

Other studies have revealed the pollution of water resources by heavy metals such as Pb, Cd, Cr and Ni in the urban city of Yaoundé Cameroon, in the Ntem watershed (Defo et al. 2015). The source of this inorganic pollution was associated to a point source as wastewaters from hospitals, repair shops and hostel which are discharged in the environment without treatment, exhaustion from petrol combustion of vehicles, washing of urban areas, run off and incineration of solid waste in the town.

Nguendo (2010) analysed the water quality from wells and population susceptibility to cholera outbreaks with respect to income levels in some neighbourhoods of the city of Douala, Cameroon. His results showed that, the presence of bacterial agents like *vibrio cholerea*, *sucrosefermenting* and *non-sucrose fermenting* organisms in water from wells poses great health threats in the study area.

Equally, Djuikom et al. (2009) analysed total coliform (TC), fecal coliform (FC) and fecal streptococci (FS), the microbiological water quality of the Mfoundi River and four of its representative tributaries in Yaoundé, Cameroon. There results revealed that water sources were not safe for human use or primary contact according to the standards for water quality established by the Word Health Organization (WHO). Indeed, these waters exhibited high concentrations of TC (Mean ± SD = 5.6 × 108 ± 2.5 × 106 CFU/100 ml), FC (Mean ± SD = 6.8 × 105 ± 2.4 × 103 CFU/100ml) and FS (Mean ± SD = 7.3 × 105 ± 2.1 × 103 CFU/100 ml) that varied with the sampling sites and points. FC/FS ratio suggested that this contamination was more from warm-blooded animals than humans and correlation analysis points to the role of rainfall as a contributing factor enhancing the bacterial numbers detected. They concluded that there is a great potential risk of infection for users. The results of the pollution status of the small river in Dokoti-Douala are presented in Table 7.

## Table 7. Pollution of River 'Ngoua'at Ndokoti-Douala

| Parameter investigated | Mean value and SD | Norms WHO |
|---|---|---|
| Temperature (°C) | 23,87 ± 5,22 | 25 |
| pH | 6.50 ± 1.83 | 6.5-8 |
| Electrical Conductivity (EC) 25°C (µs/cm) | 1734.86 ± 409.35 | <0.2 |
| TDS (ppm) | 805 ± 205.90 | 405 |
| Fe (mg/l) | 1.76 ± 2.19 | 0.1 |
| Phosphorus Total (mg/l) | 60.09 ± 14.42 | 2 |
| Cl (mg/l) | 0.06 ± 0.03 | <1 |
| Total N (mg/l) | 57.16 ± 2.63 | <5 |
| DBO$_5$ (mg/l O$_2$) | 466.43 ± 62.36 | 50 |
| DCO (mg/l O$_2$) | 1082 ± 52.91 | 250 |
| MS (mg/l) | 204.71 ± 35.15 | 50 |
| Total Coliforms (x $10^4$ CFU /100 ml) 37°C | 677.40 ± 579.81 | 40 |
| Faecal Coliforms (x $10^4$ CFU/100 ml) 44°C | 99.40 ± 59.45 | 40 |

Table 7 indicates that the river studied is polluted. This is shown by the values of parameters found above the WHO norms: Suspended Matter (MS), DBO₅, DCO, N, Fe, total dissolved solids (TDS), EC except pH, Cl and temperature. Total and Faecal Coliforms are widely above the acceptable limits of WHO indicating that this river is polluted by faecal contaminations thus, exposing the populations to diverse water borne diseases.

Table 8 presents the different kinds of pollutants found in shallow and deep aquifers in several sites in Cameroon.

**Table 8. Overview of different pollutants found in groundwater in Cameroon**

| Aquifer | Region | Type of pollutant/Range | Source | Authors |
|---|---|---|---|---|
| Shallow Deep | South west (Ekondo'Titi) (CVL) | As (III): 0.2 mg/l 2mg/l NO₃: 2.9-17.28 <50 mg/l (WHO) | Agriculture (Pamol plantation). Lobe Sediments N-fertilizers (Banana Plantation). Animal waste. | Mbotake (2006) Ako et al., (2012) |
| Shallow | North West (Ndop) | TC: 1.100 CFU/100ml pH: 5.89; | Cattle grazing. pit latrines | Mengnjo et al., (2013) |
| Shallow | North (Garoua) | TC: 8.19*E9 CFU/100ml FC: 3*8 E3 CFU/100ml E.Coli: 5.8E1 CFU/100ml FS: 3.8E1 CFU/100ml | Pit latrines. open rubbish dumps. open drains | Moussa et al., (2013) |
| Well | Littoral | Heterotrphic bacteria: 2.5 E3 CFU/100ml; TC: 1.4E3-44E3 CFU/100ml FC: 6.03E3-29E5 CFU/100ml | High population density; pit latrines. sceptic tanks. poor drainage system | Akoachere et al., (2013) Djuikom et al., (2009, 2011) |
| Shallow | Centre (Yaoundé) | Pb: 0.33    Cd: 0.08 Cr:1.31    Ni:0.61   in mg/l CF: 270-37E4 CFU/100ml; FC: 5 -35 E2 CFU/100ml; FS: 5-9.6E3 CFU/100ml NH4 : 11.02 mg/l> 0.5 ppm (WHO) | Auto exhaust runoff. wastes dumpsites. Urban agriculture. Pit latrines. Open drains. sceptic tanks | Defo et al., (2015) Bemmo et al., (1998). Nganti (2012). KouamKemogne et al., (2011) |
| Well | West (Bafoussam) | NO3: 220.9 mg/l; NH4: 0.7mg/l FC: 30-5000 CFU/100ml TC: 10 000 CFU/100ml | Poor sanitation system. Agriculture | Mpakam (2008) |

Table 8 also reveal that different shawallow aquifers of Cameroon are polluted by diverse contaminants from human activities. Table 9 on the other hand, presents the water quality of boreholes constructed in deep aquifers in certain regions of Cameroon.

**Table 9. Water quality of some boreholes in Cameroon**

| Aquifer/work | Area/Region | Water quality | Remarks |
|---|---|---|---|
| Deep/borehole | Diel/Adamaoua | Good | All the physico-chemical analysed were less than WHO norms |
| Deep/borehole | Ouro Ade/Adamaoua | Good | |
| Deep/borehole | Kette/Extrem North | Good | |
| Deep/borehole | Nabemo/Adamaoua | Good | |
| Deep/borehole | Dir/Adamaoua | Good | |
| Deep/borehole | Ganha/Adamaoua | Good | |

Table 9 indicates that the water quality of boreholes is good, without danger for human consumption. The parameters investigated were: colour, temperature, turbidity, electrical conductivity, total dissolved solids, hydrocarbonates, chloride, calcium, magnesium, sulfates, nitrates, nitrites, iron, manganese, phosphate, silicium, phenol and suspended matters. All the concentrations obtained were below the threshold fixed by WHO norms, regardless the water quality parameter analysed. These results do not indicate that deep aquifers of groundwater resources are not polluted. Another borehole constructed at Bali (Douala) for the AES-SONEL company (present ENEO) contained unsafe water for human consumption due to the excess amount of Fe (2.230 mg/l), that was greater than WHO norms (0.2 mg/l).

**Policy framework and decision-making**

Water is considered a public good in Cameroon, and thus water protection and management are government responsibilities. Several institutions are involved in water management. Under the 1998 Water Law, the National Water Committee coordinates their actions.

312

The committee is also responsible for: (i) proposing actions to the government, (ii) ensuring conservation, (iii) ensuring protection and sustainable use of water resources; (iv) providing advice on water-related problems and making recommendations on rational water management, particularly concerning the development and implementation of sustainable water and sanitation projects. Chaired by the minister in charge of water resources, the National Water Committee includes high-level representatives of major stakeholders involved in water management in Cameroon, including the ministries in charge of finance, public health, environment, land management, urban development and housing, agriculture, livestock and fisheries, commerce and industry, territorial administration and meteorology, as well as associations of mayors and concessionaires of public water and energy services. The National Water Committee was formed by decree in 1985 as a consultative body to coordinate activities in the water sector. It has met infrequently but never fulfilled its intended role. Some signed enabling decrees under the 1998 Water Law, however, could give the committee new impetus and allow it to function more effectively (GWP/AC, 2010). Integrated water resources management (IWRM) is accepted in Cameroon as the starting point for policies that can enhance sustainable water resources management and development and ensure water security. However, conditions for effective use of the IWRM approach are not yet in place. Not only does Cameroon lack comprehensive information on water resources, but the distribution of the water management authority is highly fragmented, and sectoral management approaches predominate. Moreover, the political will and commitment to enforce existing laws and regulations is inadequate, as are human and institutional capacities, and investment for assessment and monitoring.

Nevertheless, some measures to improve water security have been carried out or are under way, including: public-private partnerships for electricity and urban water supply; an IWRM plan, expected by the end of 2019; and transfer of some water management responsibilities to local levels following implementation of a law on decentralization (GWP/AC, 2010).

## Main constraints and challenges

Major constraints are pointed for influencing the known difficulties recorded in water development projects in Cameroon. Some of these include: (i) poor management and development of resources coupled with inadequate political will and commitment for the long term. (ii) the patchiness of information available on the quality and quantity of water resources is a major constraint for successful water resources management and a handicap for poverty alleviation efforts. (iii) the enabling environment for application of the IWRM approach (Integrated Water Resources Management) is weak (Policy Development, planning new undertaking, Budgeting), as are legal and institutional frameworks (UNESCO/WHO/JMP, 2010). (iv) the capacity of the government of Cameroon to developing (expenditure of funds; equity in the use of funds; service output) and sustaining the service (facility of maintenance; expansion of infrastructures; use of the services) is very low in comparison with many other countries (UNESCO/WHO/JMP, 2010).

## Poor water services, rural-urban disparities

While Cameroon is not yet on track to meet the targets of the Millennium Development Goals (MDGs) for water and sanitation, it has made notable progress since 1990. In 2006, 70% of the population had access to safe drinking water. The coverage in urban centres is 88%, significantly better than the 47% in rural areas (GWP/AC, 2010). Of Cameroon's 300 urban centres with 5,000 inhabitants or more, however, only 98 have water supply networks. Moreover, rapid urbanization in smaller towns has often rendered existing infrastructure inadequate, with frequent service interruptions. Many peri-urban dwellers also lack access to safe drinking water. Another problem is the amount of water unaccounted for: the average rate of loss rose from 25% in 1990 to 40% in 2000, clearly indicating an aging network and poor maintenance. Hence the reality is that supply situation is worse than the figures imply. The figures do not reflect the true picture of the masses without steady supply of clean water be it in the rural; or urban areas. Sanitation coverage is also poor. In urban areas only 58% of the population has access to improved sanitation facilities, while

314

the rate in rural areas is 42% (Aquastat, 2007; UNESCO/WHO/JMP, 2010).

### Decreasing biodiversity, wetland degradation

Cameroon has a wide variety of natural resources, including its forests, which occupy about 50% of the country's surface area. With its climatic and ecological variety, Cameroon is rich in terms of biodiversity. However, an inadequate legal and institutional framework, combined with lack of political will and commitment to the enforcement of regulations, has led to decreased biodiversity. Wetlands are also at risk because of various pressures, including overgrazing and pollution of water resources. Other activities that have resulted in degraded wetlands include drainage for agriculture and construction in urban and periurban areas. Today, however, environmental impact assessment is required for all major development projects in Cameroon to prevent further water resources pollution.

### Conclusion

The biggest problem in Cameroon is not the availability of water but the poor management and development of the resources, coupled with inadequate political will and commitment. The patchiness of available information on the quality and quantity of water resources is a major constraint to their successful management and a handicap for poverty alleviation efforts. Although some progress has been made in water supply and sanitation coverage, much more needs to be done to improve the situation, especially in rural areas. In this situation, Cameroon is lagging in meeting the Millennium Development Goals (MDG) targets. Improving water information systems, as well as completing and implementing the IWRM plan would go a long way towards improving water security and reducing water pollution in Cameroon, in addition to contributing to poverty alleviation.

Based on the analysis and our understanding of the system we recommend the implementation of the following six-point strategies by the government in order to enhance the availability and parity in water use by the rich and poor alike, and ensure efficient water management in Cameroon:

1.  A comprehensive water inventory in Cameroon is needed. This will help to sufficiently address various important issues including the extent of water use by the various sectors (domestic, agriculture-irrigation and livestock, and industry), the spatial and social patterns in water use, the background of households using the resource, and comparative cost analysis of using groundwater and surface water for community water supply, irrigation and livestock watering.

2.  The government of Cameroon should initiate a country wide program of educating the masses, empowering institutions and local population to take care of water resources by cleaning polluted rivers, protecting unpolluted ones (mitigating groundwater contamination) around the country and maintaining water infrastructures (boreholes, wells, mini water conveyances and sanitation systems).

3.  The Government should apply the law related to environmental protection to restrict the production of wastes and pollutants and avoid improper waste dumpsites.

4.  Wastewater recycling (at low cost through constructed wetlands technology) as strategy to mitigate environmental pollution should be encouraged in industries, municipalities and in agriculture.

5.  Application and monitoring of integrated water management approaches in different basins: Combining public (government and councils) and private actors, inter sector activities (water supply, sanitation, industries and agriculture),

6.  Improvement of the groundwater governance through enabling actions (putting services in place such as policy improvement, planning new actions and budgeting), developing (expenditure of funds, equity in funds use), and sustaining (Facility of maintenance, expansion of infrastructures) services.

# References

Ako, A., Jun, S., Takahiro H.H., Kimpei I. Elambo N. Gloria E., Takem E. and Ntankouo N. (2010). Hydrogeochemical and isotopic characteristics of groundwater in Mbanga, Njombe and Penja (Banana Plain) Cameroon. *J Afr Earth Sci.*, 75, 25–36.

Ako, A. A., Jun S, Takahiro, H., Kimpei, I., Nkeng, G. E., Fantong, W. Y., Eyong, G. E. T., Ntankouo, N. R. (2011). Evaluation of groundwater quality and its suitability for drinking, domestic, and agricultural uses in the Banana Plain (Mbanga, Njombe, Penja) of the Cameroon Volcanic. *Environ Geochem Health* 33:559–575.

Bemmo, N., Njine, T., Nola, M. & Ngamga G. (1998). *Impact des différents dispositifs d'évacuation des eaux de vidange, des eaux usées, des excrétas humains et des déchets solides sur les ressources en eau, la santé et l'environnement: cas des quartiers denses à habitats spontanés et des zones périurbaines de Yaoundé-Cameroun. Proposition de systèmesappropriés tenant compte des contraintes locales.* Rapport de recherche, 160p.

Che, C. (2013). Adaptation of regional representative soil project and soil judging for Cameroon. Retrieved from https://tigerprints.clemson.edu/all_dissertations/286

Defo, C., Yerima, K., Kengne, M., & Bemmo, N. (2015). Assessment of heavy metals in soils and groundwater in an urban watershed in Yaounde (Cameroon-West Africa). *Environmental Monitoring Assessment,* 187, 1-17. Retrieved from DOI 10.1007/s10661-015-4292-1.

Defo, C., and Yerima K. (2015). *Pollution de l'Eau souterraine dans les Pays en voie de développement.* Editions Universitaires Européennes., pp.84.

Defo, C., Mishra, K., Yerima, K., Ako A., Mabou, B. & Fonkou, T. (2016). Current conditions of groundwater resources development and related problems in the Republic of Cameroon, West Africa. *European Water,* 54 (2016), 43-68.

Djuikom, E., Temgoua, E., Jugnia, B., Nola, M. & Baane, M. (2009). Pollution bactériologique des puits d'eau utilisés par les populations dans la Communauté Urbaine de Douala, Cameroun. *International Journal of Biological and Chemical Sciences,* 3(5), 967-978.

317

Dunmade, I. (2015). Finding appropriate solution to Sub-Saharan water problem: A case for lifecycle sustainability design and management of water infrastructure. *International Journal of Development and Sustainability*, 4 (3), pp 242-257.

Epule, T., Changhui, M., Wase, M. & Ndiva, M. (2011).Well water quality and public health implications: The case of four neighbourhoods of the city of Douala Cameroon. Global Journal of Health Science *Canadian Centre of Science and Education 75*(3), 81-91.

Fantong, W.Y., Satake, H., Aka, F.T., Ayonghe, S.N., Asai, K., Mandal, A.K., Ako, A.A. (2010). Hydrochemical and isotopic evidence of recharge, apparent age, and flow direction of groundwater in Mayo Tsanaga river basin, Cameroon: bearings on contamination. *Environ Earth Sci* 60: 107–120.

Folifac, F., Lifongo, L., Nkeng, G., Gaskin, S. (2009). Municipal drinking water source protection in low income countries: case of Buea municipality—Cameroon. *J Ecolo Nat Env* 1(4): 073–084.

Fonkou, T., Agendia P., Kengne I. Amougou A., Focho D., Nya J. & Dongmo F. (2005). Heavy Metal Concentrations in some Biotic and Abiotic Components of the Olezoa Wetland Complex (Yaoundé–Cameroon, West Africa). *Water Qual. Res. J. Canada*, 40 (4), 457–461.

GWP/AC. (2010). Global water partnership Central Africa, Cameroon Report. 210 p.

Keleko, T., Tadjou , J., Kamguia, J., Tabod, T., Feumoe, A., Kenfack, J. (2013). Groundwater Investigation Using Geoelectrical Method: A Case Study of the Western Region of Cameroon, *Journal of Water Resource and Protection* 5 (6): 633-641.

Kouam K., R.G., Rosillon, F., Mpakam G.H., Nono, A. (2010). Enjeux sanitaires, socio-économiques et environnementaux liés à la réutilisation des eaux usées dans le maraîchage urbain cas du bassin versant de l'Abiergué (Yaoundé-Cameroun). *VertigO*. 10. 10.4000/vertigo.10323.

Kuitcha, D., Kamgang, K. B. V., Sigha, N., Lienou, G., Ekodeck, G. E. (2008). Water supply, sanitation and health risks in Yaounde, Cameroon. *African Journal of Environmental Science and Technology* 2 (11): 379-386.

Mannoj, S. (2013). Water pollution. Post Graduate School course. Environmental Science Division, IARI, India.

Mengnjo, J. W., Fantong, W.Y., Engome, R. W., Takeshi, O., Ndonwi, A. S. (2013). Sources of bacteriological contamination of shallow groundwater and health effects in Ndop plain, Northwest Cameroon. *Journal of Environmental Science and Water Resources*, 2(4): 127-132.

Mpakam, G. (2008). *Etude de la vulnérabilité à la pollution des ressources en eau dans la ville de Bafoussam (Ouest Cameroun) et indices socio-économiques et sanitaires: modalités d'assainissement.* (Thèse de Doctorat/PhD). Sciences de l'ingénieur, option hydrochimie et assainissement. Université de Yaoundé 1.

Molua, E. and Lambi, C. (2002). *Climate, hydrology and water resources in Cameroon.* Retrieved from http://www.ceepa.co.za/docs/CDPN°33.pdf.

Nganti, N. Y. (2012). Etude diagnostique de l'état de pollution des eaux souterraines de l'îlot de Nkolbikok-Yaoundé, Cameroun. Mémoire de fin d'etude 2Ie Ouagadougou, pp 70

Nguendo, Y.B. (2010). Suffering for Water, Suffering from Water: Access to Drinking-water and Associated Health Risks in Cameroon. *Journal of health, population, and nutrition.* 28. 424-35. 10.3329/jhpn.v28i5.6150.

Ngounou B, Djoret D. (2010). Nitrate pollution in groundwater in two selected areas from Cameroon and Chad in the Lake Chad basin. *Water Policy*, 12(5), 722–733.

Njine, T., Kemka N., ZebazeTogouet S.H., Niyitegeka D., Nola M., Ayissi T., Monkiedje A. & FotoMenbohan, S. (2002). *Yaounde municipal lake supply by untreated domestic waste water, and effect on assimilation capacity of the ecosystem. Proceedings of international symposium and workshop on environmental pollution control and waste management.* 7-10 January 2002, Tunis (epcowm'2002), pp.15-17.

Njitchoua, R. and Ngounou Ngatcha, B. (1997). Hydrogeochemistry and environmental isotope investigations of the North Diamare Plain, northern Cameroon. *J Afr Earth Sci*, 25(2), 307–316

OMS. (2004). Directives de qualité pour de l'eau de boisson. (3è Ed.). Recommandations. Genève: OMS. Retrieved from http://www.who.int/watersanitationhealth/dwq/gdwq3rev/fr/index.html.

Pradeep, N. (2016). Water crisis in Africa: myth or reality? *International Journal of Water Resources Development.* 10.1080/07900627.2016.1188266.

Tatsadjieu, L., Montet, D., & Mbofung, M. (2013). Research of some physicochemical and biological pollution indicators in four fisheries of the Northern part of Cameroon. *International Research Journal of Microbiology,* 4(6), 147-155.

Tchaptchet, D. T. (2012). Geology of the Kekem Area (Cameroun Central Domain): Metamorphic Petrology, P-T-t Path, EMP, LAICPMS Dating and Implications for the Geodynamic Evolution of the Pan-African North Equatorial Folt Belt," Ph.D. These de Doctorat, Université de Yaoundé 1.

UNESCO, (2011). http://webworld.unesco.org/water/wwap/wwdr/wwdr3/case_studies/pdf/Case_Studies_Africa.pdf.

Yerima, B.P.K. & Van Ranst, E. (2005). Introduction to Soil Science: Soils of the Tropics. Trafford Publishing, Victoria BC Canada.

Printed in the United States
By Bookmasters